An admirable statement of the aims of the Library of Philosophy was provided by the first editor, the late Professor J. H. Muirhead, in his description of the original programme printed in Erdmann's *History of Philosophy* under the date 1890. This was slightly modified in subsequent volumes to take the form of the following statement:

'The Muirhead Library of Philosophy was designed as a contribution to the History of Modern Philosophy under the heads: first of Different Schools of Thought—Sensationalist, Realist, Idealist, Intuitivist; secondly of different Subjects—Psychology, Ethics, Aesthetics, Political Philosophy, Theology. While much had been done in England in tracing the course of evolution in nature, history, economics, morals and religion, little had been done in tracing the development of thought on these subjects. Yet "the evolution of opinion is part of the whole evolution".

'By the co-operation of different writers in carrying out this plan it was hoped that a thoroughness and completeness of treatment, otherwise unattainable, might be secured. It was believed also that from writers mainly British and American fuller consideration of English Philosophy than it had hitherto received might be looked for. In the earlier series of books containing, among others, Bosanquet's *History of Aesthetic*, Pfleiderer's *Rational Theology since Kant*, Albee's *History of English Utilitarianism*, Bonar's *Philosophy and Political Economy*, Brett's *History of Psychology*, Ritchie's *Natural Rights*, these objects were to a large extent effected.

'In the meantime original work of a high order was being produced both in England and America by such writers as Bradley, Stout, Bertrand Russell, Baldwin, Urban, Montague, and others, and a new interest in foreign works, German, French and Italian, which had either become classical or were attracting public attention, had developed. The scope of the Library thus became extended into something more international, and it is entering on the fifth decade of its existence in the hope that it may contribute to that mutual understanding between countries which is so pressing a need of the present time.'

The need which Professor Muirhead stressed is no less pressing today, and few will deny that philosophy has much to do with enabling us to meet it, although no one, least of all Muirhead himself, would regard that as the sole, or even the main, object of philosophy. As Professor Muirhead continues to lend the distinction of his name to the Library of Philosophy it seemed not inappropriate to allow him to recall us to these aims in his own words. The emphasis on the history of thought also seemed to me very timely: and the number of important works promised for the Library in the very near future augur well for the continued fulfilment, in this and other ways, of the expectations of the original editor.

H. D. LEWIS

MUIRHEAD LIBRARY OF PHILOSOPHY

General Editor: H. D. Lewis

Professor of History and Philosophy of Religion in the University of London

MENTAL IMAGES

In Defence of Free Will by C. A. CAMPBELL
Indian Philosophy by RADHAKRISHNAN 2 vols revised 2nd edition
Introduction to Mathematical Philosophy by BERTRAND RUSSELL 2nd edition
Kant's First Critique by H. W. CASSIRER
Kant's Metaphysic of Experience by H. J. PATON
Know Thyself by BERNADINO VARISCO translated by GUGLIELMO SALVADORI
Language and Reality by WILBUR MARSHALL URBAN
A Layman's Quest by SIR MALCOLM KNOX
Lectures on Philosophy by G. E. MOORE
Lectures on Philosophy by G. E. MOORE edited by C. LEWY
Matter and Memory by HENRI BERGSON translated by N. M. PAUL and W. S.
    PALMER
Meaning in the Arts by LOUIS ARNAUD REID
Memory by BRIAN SMITH
The Modern Predicament by H. J. PATON
Natural Rights by D. G. RITCHIE 3rd edition
Nature, Mind and Modern Science by E. HARRIS
The Nature of Thought by BRAND BLANSHARD
Non-Linguistic Philosophy by A. C. EWING
On Selfhood and Godhood by C. A. CAMPBELL
Our Experience of God by H. D. LEWIS
Our Knowledge of Right and Wrong by JONATHAN HARRISON
Perception by DON LOCKE
The Person God Is by PETER A. BERTOCCI
The Phenomenology of Mind by G. W. F. HEGEL translated by SIR JAMES
    BAILLIE revised 2nd edition
Philosophy in America by MAX BLACK
Philosophical Papers by G. E. MOORE
Philosophy and Illusion by MORRIS LAZEROWITZ
Philosophy and Political Economy by JAMES BONAR
Philosophy and Religion by AXEL HAGERSTROM
Philosophy of Space and Time by MICHAEL WHITEMAN
Philosophy of Whitehead by W. MAYS
The Platonic Tradition in Anglo-Saxon Philosophy by J. H. MUIRHEAD
The Principal Upanisads by RADHAKRISHNAN
The Problems of Perception by R. J. HIRST
Reason and Analysis by BRAND BLANSHARD
Reason and Goodness by BRAND BLANSHARD
Reason and Scepticism by MICHAEL A. SLOTE
The Science of Logic by G. W. F. HEGEL
Some Main Problems of Philosophy by G. E. MOORE
Studies in the Metaphysics of Bradley by SUSHIL KUMAR SAXENA
The Subject of Consciousness by C. O. EVANS
The Theological Frontier of Ethics by W. G. MACLAGAN
Time and Free Will by HENRI BERGSON translated by F. G. POGSON
The Transcendence of the Cave by J. N. FINDLAY
Values and Intentions by J. N. FINDLAY
The Ways of Knowing: or the Methods of Philosophy by W. P. MONTAGUE

MUIRHEAD LIBRARY OF PHILOSOPHY

EDITED BY H. D. LEWIS

MENTAL IMAGES
A DEFENCE

BF367
H3
1971

MENTAL IMAGES
A DEFENCE

BY

ALASTAIR HANNAY
University of Oslo

MAY 3 0 1973

LONDON: GEORGE ALLEN & UNWIN LTD
NEW YORK: HUMANITIES PRESS INC

175825

FIRST PUBLISHED IN 1971

This book is copyright under the Berne Convention. All rights are reserved. Apart from any fair dealing for the purpose of private study, research, criticism or review, as permitted under the Copyright Act, 1956, no part of this publication may be reproduced, stored in a retrieval system, or transmitted, in any form or by any means, electronic, electrical, chemical, mechanical, optical, photocopying, recording or otherwise, without the prior permission of the copyright owner. Enquiries should be addressed to the publishers.

© *George Allen & Unwin Ltd, 1971*

BRITISH ISBN 0 04 100030 7

U.S.A. SBN 391 00181 7

PRINTED IN GREAT BRITAIN
in 12 point Fournier type
BY UNWIN BROTHERS LIMITED
WOKING AND LONDON

To Joanne

ACKNOWLEDGMENTS

For kind permission to quote from their works and publications I am grateful: to Gilbert Ryle as author and to both the Hutchinson Publishing Group, Ltd. and Barnes and Noble, Inc. as publishers of *The Concept of Mind*; to the Wittgenstein Executors and Basil Blackwell, Publisher, as publishers of *Philosophical Investigations* and *Zettel*; to J. M. Shorter for permission to quote from 'Imagination', *Mind*, LXI (1952), No. 244; to the Editor of *Mind* for permission both to quote from that article and to use some passages from my 'To See a Mental Image', forthcoming in *Mind*; and to Mrs Elizabeth Wolgast for permission to quote from 'Wittgenstein and Criteria', *Inquiry*, Vol. 7 (1964), No. 4.

PREFACE

Some preliminary clarification of this essay's scope and procedure is called for. Its central topic is imaging, more specifically visual imaging, since visual images best illustrate the issues we shall be concerned with. These issues form another, as it were, embracing topic: the general question of the nature of mind—or, now that we have taken the linguistic turn, of the content and reference of mental-concept terms. The sense in which this wider topic embraces the narrower one is not that in which, all too obviously, to say something about imaging is *ipso facto* to say something about the mind; but one in which to say something philosophically about imaging inevitably, and directly or indirectly, *reflects* an embracing view of the mind (or of 'mind'). This is no doubt true of any mental concept, but perhaps because of the peculiar elusiveness, and also variety, of the phenomenon of imaging, accounts of it tend more than usually to be sounding boards for special theories; the image has been made to dance or disappear to the tune of many a preconception. So rather than add to them, I shall proceed by a detailed examination of some recent accounts in order to uncover *their* underlying assumptions about 'mind'. Philosophical descriptions may be said to have the form of arguments, and my aim is to uncover the premisses to be found in the recent highly exaggerated reports of the non-existence, or just plain dullness, of the mental image. Dull the image may be, and certainly less exciting than some now discredited theories of mind would have it, but the power of the lowly image to provide an *experimentum crucis* for what philosophers would like to say about the mind gives it some eminence in terms of our wider topic. And in the context of theories of mind we may yet find that the notion of a mental image is more exciting than many would have us believe.

For helpful criticism of an earlier draft of this essay I would especially like to thank Guttorm Flöistad, R. C. Holland, Benson Mates, J. W. N. Watkins, and Richard Wollheim, though without wishing to incriminate them in any of its surviving errors and infelicities. I am grateful to the Norwegian Research Council for Science and the Humanities for generous financial support.

A. H.

Hvitsten, 1971

15

CONTENTS

B

I

INTRODUCTION

I'm not superstitious myself but some
things that folk call superstitions are
as true as God's own gospel. *An old man.*[1]

It would be an exaggeration to say there was a conspiracy against mental images. But 'campaign' would not be too strong a word. The author of a recent account admits, with disarming candour, that to be able to dispose of mental images would be 'a clear case of good riddance'.[2] The same sentiment is conveyed, less openly but just as unequivocally, in most major recent philosophical writings on imagination. I refer principally to the work of Ryle, Shorter, and Sartre, but not only to them. 'Away with the image!' is a call that finds a welcoming response among many contemporary philosophers of mind, whether the thesis with which they give it substance is a plain denial of the existence of mental images, or some more qualified denial, for example that there are no such objects, or that when we see in the mind's eye it is not a mental image that we see.

To the lay-imager it might seem madness to canvass for conclusions so manifestly falsified in at least his own experience. But philosophers themselves, especially those attuned to recent rumblings in Anglo-American philosophy of mind, will know the kinds of pressure that lead to the promotion of such apparently unlikely candidates for truth. The local pressures I will come to shortly. Here I would like to suggest that the situation bears witness to an important though not now widely recognized feature of philosophical life in general. When a philosopher seems to

[1] The quotation, from Vance Randolph's *Ozark Superstitions* (New York, 1947), p. 8, is taken from Reidar Thoralf Christiansen, 'European Folklore in America', *Studia Norvegica*, No. 12 (Universitetsforlaget, Oslo, 1962), p. 110.

[2] D. C. Dennett, *Content and Consciousness* (Routledge & Kegan Paul, London, 1969), p. 141. See below, p. 174.

be describing or analysing something, his descriptions and analyses are seldom if ever to be construed as reports or results of impartial observation and reasoning. They are more realistically construed as attempts to justify a particular way of looking at the thing in question, in other words a philosophical idea, theory, or programme from which the form of description he advocates can be derived, though not of course uniquely. That is to say, in a philosopher's account of things, the choice of descriptions, and also of what aspects of things are included in the descriptions, is typically a manifestation of a vested interest in the capacity of those descriptions and aspects to confirm an underlying idea; and the exposition, argumentational in structure, is an attempt to justify acceptance of the preferred descriptions— not of course, in the first instance, by an argument that cites the underlying idea as a reason for accepting the description, but by one that shows, for example, that the descriptions are reasonable or at least not *un*acceptable on their own merits, and perhaps also that they lack certain demonstrable weaknesses or undesirable implications of rival descriptions. A philosopher's piecemeal analyses are usually part of a grand design.

Berkeley is an example we shall return to more than once. The very power of Berkeley's arguments in support of his account of the material world tends to make us forget that for him that account was intended as a justification of an underlying theology. If this may escape us in his account of matter, his passing remarks on *mind* are patently riddled with bias. Take the well-known passage where he writes:

'I find I can excite ideas in my mind at pleasure, and vary and shift the scene as oft as I think fit. It is no more than *willing*, and straightway this or that idea arises in my fancy; and by the same power it is obliterated and makes way for another.'[1]

In this Berkeley sees the characteristically 'active' aspect of

---

[1] *Principles of Human Understanding* in David M. Armstrong (ed.), *Berkeley's Philosophical Writings* (Collier-Macmillan, London, 1965), p. 72. All other references to Berkeley's works are to this edition. Italics are in the cited text unless otherwise stated.

mental life—'This making and unmaking of ideas doth very properly denominate the mind active'[1]—and contrasts it with our enforced passivity in the face of the ideas 'actually perceived by Sense'. But clearly not all imaging can denominate the mind active in the way Berkeley means, for we find—if his emphasis in the quotation above did not already make us suspect—that by 'being active' he means willing (and not even, we note, the much broader conception of doing *what* one has willed). Thus he writes elsewhere: 'We cannot possibly conceive any active power but the Will.'[2] And more tellingly: 'The Spirit, the Active thing, that which is Soul and God, is the Will alone.'[3] But this immediately excludes day-dream imaging, for example, from *activities*, even activities of the mind. So what *we* might include under imaging can, for Berkeley, be very far from denominating the mind active. What notion he can provide for non-active imagings to denominate is another question. The point I wish to make here is that Berkeley's philosophical interest in mental activity, as in all else, was in its ability to lend experiential support to a conception of mind. The selectiveness of his focus and the narrowness of his concept of mental activity are both direct consequences of that conception. Observe it at work again in his suggestion, apt enough in this context, that imaging—or 'framing ideas'—is not an activity simply, but a creative activity. He asks: 'Why may we not conceive it possible for God to create things out of Nothing—certainly we ourselves create in some wise whenever we imagine.'[4] The selectiveness is again remarkable. Not the meaning or content of the image, but the image itself is the creation—a pictorial object which its producer needs no materials, no tools, no skills, nothing in fact but his mere willing, to bring into and out of existence. It is evidently the peculiarly unencumbered nature of the performance of imaging that commends it to Berkeley's attention and makes it such a good example of the kind of activity he regards as characteristic of mind or spirit; it impresses him that as a picture-maker the imager travels so light.

[1] *Principles*, ibid., p. 72.
[2] *Philosophical Commentaries*, ibid., p. 362, Entry 155.
[3] Ibid., p. 369, Entry 712.   [4] Ibid., p. 365, Entry 830.

Similarly with those philosophers who would relieve him even of his image. In arguing that mental images do not exist, or that mental images are not seen in the mind's eye these writers have been trying to vindicate various conceptions of mind, trying to persuade us to drop the use of certain formulations that imply or convey basic views of mind which they consider to be untenable in favour of formulations that imply or convey a tenable view (though not in each case the same one).

It is important to grasp the uncompromising nature of their denials. If they were less uncompromising there would be much more—and admittedly there is already a good deal—to agree with in the arguments for them. For instance, one context which gives special plausibility to the denial that mental images are to be called 'objects' is the rejection (at least implicit in all the accounts examined) of Berkeley's way of distinguishing imaging from perceiving. Thus where Berkeley construes the difference as one in external properties of objects present in both, namely *ideas*, they construe it as one between a way of attending or referring to what is *absent* in one case though present in the other, namely some *material object*. The disagreement is not just terminological: it reflects a change in philosophical point of view, a change that gives a clear point to the denial that images are *objects*; for simply by granting the conditions necessary for material identity in time and space one creates—or perhaps no longer obliterates—a noteworthy distinction between *material* objects ('objects proper') and mental images.

The rejection of immaterialism, however, doesn't account for the full force of the denials in question; for these are expressed not as claims that mental images differ from material objects in this or other important respects, but as *denials that images are to be described as objects at all*, denials in fact which amount to saying that in order to be objects mental images would have to satisfy conditions analogous to those of material identity. And it is in their denying mental images the status of 'object' on the grounds that mental images fail to satisfy such conditions that philosophers, as I aim to show, have been defending certain fundamental viewpoints. Of the main accounts examined this is most explicit in

Ryle and Sartre. For Ryle the denial that mental images are objects is required in order to rebut a particular dualistic view of mind; to describe images as objects is to subscribe to the view that 'the mental' comprises a sphere of specifically 'inner' acts and episodes. For Sartre, on the other hand, and quite to the contrary, the denial is *based* on and intended to *support* a specific and radical dualism: namely one which precludes mental images having properties which would make it appropriate (for Sartre) to describe them as objects either in or for the mind. A third view, exemplified by Shorter's approach, but best explained in terms of Wittgenstein's arguments for denying that psychological terms designate inner objects and processes, pins the inappropriateness of the label 'object' for mental images less on the image itself than on certain non-arbitrary restrictions on the use of the label. I shall return to this in a moment.

My second principal aim, and the one which stamps this essay's general procedure, is to show that no good argument for getting rid of mental images is forthcoming. The defence of each of these viewpoints therefore fails. And that seems a good reason for urging the philosophers whose views call for the disposal of mental images to dispose of their views instead—failing better arguments, that is, or—and this is an important qualification—failing modification of the view in question in some way which will allow it to embrace mental images and yet still retain something of its own essential character and content.

My third aim is to make something—though I'm afraid not nearly enough—of a fundamental issue which the examination of the accounts of imaging brings to the surface: namely speculation and conjecture in philosophy, specifically speculation about the nature of mental images and imagination. The reader may have already suspected that in claiming that philosophers like Ryle and Shorter have been using their accounts of imagination to defend basic concepts of mind, I am suggesting, contrary both to their spirit and explicit intentions, that under the analytical disguise they are at core (if not at heart) old-style speculative philosophers. Well, in fact, that isn't so very far from what I am suggesting, but the difference between old-style and new-style speculating is too immense to let the matter go without some anticipatory clarification.

In a recent autobiographical note Ryle depicts an attitude current among conceptual analysts in the early days of their and his activities. Regarding their philosophical forefathers the analysts' attitude was:

'If we are careful to winnow off their vacuously speculative tares from their analytical wheat, we may find that some of them sometimes did quite promising work in our own line of business.'[1]

The conceptual analysts' business, of course, was and is language, in particular sense and nonsense. Essentially theirs is a service industry, applying tools to language in order to answer questions of interest to language-users, though it has a design and manufacturing side too, in so far as analysts develop and make their own tools. The principal service rendered by the analyst is to be able to tell his customers when they are talking non-sense, and also, if required, to explain why it is that their words are vacuous. The tools he perfects are criteria of meaning. The analyst is not, at least in any *ex officio* capacity, equipped to say what sentences express true statements, or even whether one form of words is a better description than another. But he can hope to show what sentences *cannot* express true sentences because they are meaningless, and this is of course in itself enough to give him a place in the traditional philosophical arena, though still suitably white-coated to mark him off from those who *use*, and perhaps want to *reform*, language. Thus if he can show that some of the sentences employed or proposed by the users are meaning-less, or if meaningful at least lacking in any sense that the users mean them to have, his service will have had the positive effect of weeding out some of the more disreputable tares.

But the discussions of analysts often suggest that they have now doffed their white coats and taken up a line of business that was once the *speculators'*; namely truth-claiming. True, they reject the old way of carrying on that business, for they regard

[1] Gilbert Ryle, 'Autobiographical', in Oscar P. Wood and George Pitcher (eds.), *Ryle* (Macmillan, London, 1970), p. 11.

the 'speculative tares' which they winnow off from the 'analytical wheat' to be vacuous just because they are speculative. But not content with that they seem to suggest that a true concept of mind will emerge from analytical wheat alone, perhaps suitably blended with the latest results of science, as if the criteria of sense and nonsense were at the same time criteria of nature. This idea— surely the most significant philosophical speculation of our time —is found in its most subtle and beguiling form in the work of Wittgenstein. The nature of a mental phenomenon, Wittgenstein suggests, will emerge as the result of an investigation of the 'grammar' of the corresponding mental-concept term. No one, I venture to suggest, could reasonably deny that grammatical investigations of the kind Wittgenstein means provide an invaluable source of enlightenment about what might be called our 'mental ascriptions'—about the subtleties of our actual use of mental-concept terms and also conditions of their having a use— or that the results of such investigations are philosophically significant. But there are, I shall suggest, contexts of inquiry and controversy, about imagination, and therefore about other things too, in which grammar, in Wittgenstein's sense, cannot tell us what to say. What it cannot tell us to say may nevertheless be non-vacuously said, and argued. And that to me suggests that some speculative *spielraum* remains, though it is a good deal more cramped than it seemed before the analysts went into business, and offers a somewhat hostile environment to speculators not adept with at least some of the tools of the analytical trade.

A final comment before our own business. Philosophers have always wanted to demonstrate their favourite truths. Perhaps the proposal to identify criteria of acceptability with those of non-vacuity is just the latest attempt to drag favoured conclusions down to the level of the available premises. In the same auto-biographical note quoted above, Ryle remarks, agreeably, that 'philosophising essentially incorporates argumentation', but then goes on to say: 'and so incorporates it that, whereas a weak or faulty inference might by luck put Sherlock Holmes on the track of the murderer, a weak or faulty philosopher's argument is itself a philosophical blind alley. *In this field there is no detachment of the conclusion from its premisses* .... '[1] This seems to me wholly mistaken. Faulty inferences give false readings of argumentational strength, but weak inferences are better than none, and except where philosophers are content with analytical truths—and what philosophers would be?—the most a philosopher can *demonstrate* is that his favoured account is a possible one or that a given rival account not a possible one because *demonstrably* vacuous. Ryle's view would mean that in philosophy *all* argumentation for preferred non-analytical conclusions leads to blind alleys. But a blind alley, in philosophy as elsewhere, is not one through which a chosen means of transport will not take you, any more than it is one that fails to lead you to a favourite destination. It is an alley through which there can be *no* means of transport, and which leads to *no* destination. It is the impossibility of a conclusion, not its lack of demonstrableness that prevents philosophical access to it.

Perhaps it is only appropriate that on the tour of blind alleys (in both senses) on which we are now to embark Ryle himself should lead the way.

[1] Gilbert Ryle, 'Autobiographical' in Oscar P. Wood and George Pitcher (eds.), *Ryle* (Macmillan, London, 1970), p. 7. (My italics.) Though he adds: 'if indeed the idiom of premisses and conclusions is appropriate here at all.'

II

RYLE AND THE ABSENT HOST

I. THE LINGUISTIC ILLUSION OF IMMANENCE

In *L'Imaginaire* Sartre refers to an 'illusion of immanence'. It has two parts: we think that when we see something in the mind's eye there must be an image in our consciousness, and also that the thing we imagine is in the image.[1] But we are wrong. There is no image in consciousness; and as for what we imagine, that is where we imagine it, which may be anywhere or nowhere, but certainly not literally in the mind.

In *The Concept of Mind* Ryle makes essentially the same two points.

'If a person says that he is picturing his nursery, we are tempted to construe his remark to mean that he is somehow contemplating, not his nursery, but another visible object, namely a picture of his nursery, only not a photograph or an oil-painting but some counterpart to a photograph, one made of a different sort of stuff.'[2]

And secondly,

' . . . there exists a quite general tendency among theorists and laymen alike to ascribe some sort of an other-worldly reality to the imaginary and then to treat minds as the clandestine habitats of such fleshless beings.'[3]

But however 'tempting and natural' it is 'to misdescribe "seeing things" in the mind's eye as the seeing of pictures of things',[4] there are 'no such objects as mental pictures'.[5] And 'to try to

---

[1] Jean-Paul Sartre, *L'Imaginaire. Psychologie phénoménologique de l'imagination* (Gallimard, 29th edn, Paris, 1948), p. 14.
[2] Gilbert Ryle, *The Concept of Mind* (Hutchinson, London, 1949), p. 247.
[3] Ibid., p. 245. [4] Ibid., p. 253. [5] Ibid., p. 254.

answer the question, "Where do the things and happenings exist which people imagine existing?" is to try to answer a spurious question. They do not exist anywhere, though they are imagined as existing, say, in this room, or in Juan Fernandez.'[1]

If there were such things as mental pictures, Ryle implies, our experience would differ markedly from what it is.[2] So we assume that the illusion of immanence is linguistic rather than factual. People are not mistaken when they report having imagery. In denying that there are such objects as mental pictures, Ryle is not, as he has been at pains to stress, 'denying well-known facts about the mental life of human beings'; rather, he is appealing to such facts in order to 'rectify the logic of mental-conduct concepts'.[3]

2. RECTIFYING THE LOGIC OF MENTAL-CONDUCT CONCEPTS

Ryle says that it is 'part of the function' of his book 'to show that exercises of qualities of mind do not, save *per accidens*, take place "in the head", in the ordinary sense of the phrase', and that 'those which do so have no special priority over those which do not'.[4] A prevailing Cartesian conception of the mind-body relation (the 'official theory') has led us to classify concepts erroneously, to place undue emphasis, or an incorrect explanatory force, upon some well-known mental facts—for example, that people think to themselves, feel pain or joy, have pangs of remorse, or hunger, that there is imagery—and to ignore the importance of others—for example that thinking, feeling, and imagining occur in public contexts, and that it is precisely these contexts which provide the conditions according to which we actually employ mental-conduct terms.

It is a central idea of Ryle's that we can arrive at more perspicuous descriptions of mental processes and activities than those we employ in our 'workaday thinking'. Theorists and laymen alike are misled by expressions which have the same grammatical

---

[1] Gilbert Ryle, *The Concept of Mind* (Hutchinson, London, 1949), p. 245.
[2] See ibid., pp. 248, 250, and 254–5.   [3] Ibid., p. 16.   [4] Ibid., p. 40.

pattern but are used to express thoughts of a variety of different logical types—hence with different 'logical powers'. We say, for example, that tides rise, also temperatures, and averages, but in each case 'rise' has different logical powers. You can test this by seeing whether the same predicates and other qualifications (e.g. 'vertically', 'sensibly') can apply to the different cases. If not, the word belongs to a different logical type.

It is due to the possibility of type-confusions that our ways of talking about mental processes and activities do not always mirror or represent the 'logical powers' of the words and propositions we use. For instance, we talk of the mind as if it were a something, or a kind of space in which special kinds of events occur and special kinds of acts are produced. We think of it as 'a ghost in a machine'. In *The Concept of Mind* Ryle attempts a reclassification of the words and propositions we use in talking about the mind, words like 'feeling', 'emotion', 'thought', 'thinking', 'act of judgment', 'in the mind', 'reason', 'mental image', and so on. He tries to show that in talking about minds we do not need to refer to the mind as a special kind of thing or place where mental acts take place, a hidden source of all that people do as thinking, feeling beings—nor to mental acts as the special acts of such a thing, or to events and processes 'in' it. 'Mind' connotes the actual observable things that people can be seen to do. Or in Ryle's more precise terms: 'mind is not the topic of sets of untestable categorical propositions, but the topic of sets of testable hypothetical and semi-hypothetical propositions.'[1] And a testable proposition is one that can be confirmed by observation.

3. UNDERSTANDING RYLE'S PROGRAMME FOR 'MENTAL IMAGE'

How then to deal with imaging? To answer this question we really need to know just what sort of implications Ryle thinks would have to be avoided in a satisfactory description of imaging.

[1] Gilbert Ryle, *The Concept of Mind* (Hutchinson, London, 1949), ibid., p. 46. Cf. p. 199: 'To talk of a person's mind . . . is to talk of the person's abilities, liabilities and inclinations to do and undergo certain sorts of things, and of the doing and undergoing of these things in the ordinary world.'

Unfortunately he is not quite clear on this point. He formulates his programme for 'mental image' as follows:

'The crucial problem is that of describing what is "seen in the mind's eye" and what is "heard in one's head". What are spoken of as "visual images", "mental pictures", "auditory images" and, in one use, "ideas" are commonly taken to be entities which are genuinely found existing and found existing elsewhere than in the external world. So minds are nominated for their theatres. But, as I shall try to show, the familiar truth that people are constantly seeing things in their mind's eyes and hearing things in their heads is no proof that there exist things which they see and hear, or that the people are seeing and hearing.'[1]

Now from this it is unclear whether the unwarranted, and presumably unwanted, inference is to the proposition that images are seen or heard, or to the proposition that images exist. The unclarity is pervasive. We recall that Ryle says it would be improper to describe what someone is doing when he pictures his nursery as 'contemplating' something *other* than his nursery, namely a mental image. But there are a number of different, though compatible, reasons why this description might be thought improper. For example, it might be argued that it would be as wrong to say that the picturer contemplated an image as it would to say of someone looking at a photograph of his nursery that he was contemplating a photograph. That is, if absent objects, people, events, and scenes can be counted among the objects of one's visual contemplations, then what is contemplated in both cases is the nursery, not an image or a picture.

Ryle certainly wants to deny that we contemplate mental images. Although 'the concept of picturing . . . is a proper and useful concept', he says, 'its use does not entail the existence of pictures which we contemplate . . .'.[2] Now one reason for this might be that an image, whatever else it is, is not the sort of thing that can be contemplated. However, the passage continues: 'or the existence of a gallery in which such pictures are ephemerally suspended', which seems to show that Ryle really does want to

[1] Gilbert Ryle, *The Concept of Mind* (Hutchinson, London, 1949), p. 245.
[2] Ibid., p. 247.

deny the existence of images. They could hardly exist without a domain. But now, surely, we should reject Ryle's earlier claim not to be denying well-known facts about mental life. Mental imagery is as familiar a feature of that life as are pangs of hunger, feelings of joy, or any other of the 'inner' mental occurrences Ryle wants to demote from their spurious eminence in Cartesian theory.

One would have thought that if all Ryle's programme required was a reclassification of psychological concepts that does not give special priority to such occurrences, then it would have been enough to say, first, that 'picturing' and 'contemplating' are terms of a different logical type, and then, secondly, that picturing does not, while contemplating does, entail the existence of things really seen. The sense of 'really seen' here could be captured in such logical remarks as that it is proper to speak of someone contemplating but not of their picturing something from afar, or in good light. (To picture something from afar or in good light would not be the same as to picture it *as seen* from afar or in good light.) Indeed Ryle might seem to have already provided himself with a suitable apparatus for dismissing the claims of mental images to special status. In the course of cutting sensations down to size in his preceding chapter he talks of a 'post-perceptual' use of expressions, notably of the verbs 'feel', 'look', 'sound', and the like. Someone is said to feel in a post-perceptual sense of 'feel' when, on describing his experience, he would say there was 'a gritty feeling under his eyelids', but would *not* withdraw this statement on being assured that there was no grit under his eyelids.[1] Here, Ryle explains, 'feels' or 'having a feeling' means 'feels as if', and the 'as if' clause is to be completed by referring to some state of affairs which, if it did obtain, would be discovered by feeling in another, primary sense of the terms; that is, in a sense in which a claim to feel grit under one's eyelid *would* be withdrawn if the speaker was satisfied there was no grit there.

Why then cannot Ryle go on to construe 'X's picturing his

---

[1] Gilbert Ryle, *The Concept of Mind* (Hutchinson, London, 1949), p. 241. Cf. p. 243.

nursery' in terms of a corresponding post-perceptual use of 'look'? It would seem an acceptable result, from the point of view of his programme, if a person's image of his nursery could be described as something, either a visual sensation or something like a visual sensation, which *has the look* of his nursery. If there is some difficulty in locating the thing that has this look, surely the difficulty is no greater than in locating sensations in general, and visual sensations in particular. And the fact that a description of an image has to be filled out by referring to something that can only be found in perception should effectively dispose of imaging's aspirations to be a special, even superior, brand of perception. But 'imaging', says Ryle, 'is not having a sensation of a special sort'.[1] Indeed picturing something, 'so far from having, or being akin to having, visual sensations, is compatible with having no such sensations and nothing akin to them'. In fact 'there is nothing akin to sensations'?[2]

Ryle's reasons are to be found in his analysis of sensation. First, if a sensation was to have the look of something, then it would have to possess properties of its own which gave it this look, just as a physical representation of something has properties that give it the look of what it depicts. But according to Ryle, sensations have *no* properties of their own. We can only describe them by reference to 'how common objects regularly look, sound and feel'.[3] *They* do not have sizes, shapes, temperatures, colours, smells, or *position*.[4] Not having position, of course, it is not just difficult to locate them, but impossible. I can locate the gritty feeling in my eye, certainly, but visual and auditory sensations differ from bodily sensations in not being attached to any part of the body.

That sensations have no position means they cannot be observed. But this is a consequence that follows just as much from the fact that sensations have no other properties either. For observation is an 'exercise of a quality of intellect',[5] a properly 'mental' exercise, and in so far as sensations are devoid of the properties they would have to possess if *they* were to be

---

[1] Gilbert Ryle, *The Concept of Mind* (Hutchinson, London, 1949), p. 255.
[2] Ibid., p. 266.   [3] Ibid., p. 203.   [4] Ibid., p. 207.   [5] Ibid., p. 204.

discriminable things, they are neither observables themselves, nor are they capable of being ingredients in a *mental* exercise like the observing of things that are observable.

Since an image or picture must have at least those properties that would allow it to be discriminated as a picture of something, it follows on Ryle's analysis that a mental image could not be merely a sensation. Now this in itself does not exclude the possibility that mental images have sensations as non-mental accompaniments, in the way that, presumably even on Ryle's account, is true of physical pictures. And it is interesting to note that it also follows from his analysis that if a mental image did have such an accompaniment, any attempt to find a habitat for it, clandestine or otherwise, would be pointless, for a sensation of the kind required, on his theory, does not have location. The postulation of inner sensations as such, therefore, should not be regarded as acceptance of the thin, quasi-visible end of an other-worldly Mind. However, if inner sensations also had to have meanings, then, as we shall see, on Ryle's further assumptions the postulation of inner sensations would indeed call for such a mind; though the assumptions themselves are very questionable.

Ryle finds what he calls the 'sophisticated' language of 'visual (or auditory) sensation' highly suspect. If it doesn't entail the doctrine of sense-data as observable intermediaries in our perceptions of 'common objects', it leads easily to it. And Ryle is concerned to bolster our resistance to the doctrine. In doing so he points out that the original use of sensation-terms is to 'signify perceptions' (e.g. of the rolling of the ship),[1] and that the derivative use, which is the one he calls 'post-perceptual', for pains, tweaks, twinges, itches, and tingles (aspiring sense-data?) which do not involve perception of 'common objects', still requires a reference to common objects (the *gritty* feeling in my eye). As for the sophisticated use of sensation terminology, this too is warranted only in so far as it involves 'referring in a certain way to common objects like haystacks, things that hum, and pepper'.[2] But then of course if this assumption is made, the

[1] Gilbert Ryle, *The Concept of Mind* (Hutchinson, London, 1949), p. 241.
[2] Ibid., p. 202.

postulation of inner sensations as part of an account of imaging will call for inner, private objects corresponding to 'common' objects, for it would only be as a kind of reference to these, as opposed to such things as haystacks, bees, and pepper, that the inner-sensation language could have a meaning. Inner-sensation reports will be describing ways in which inner objects look, sound, or smell like haystacks, bees, or pepper.

Our question was what Ryle thinks a description of imaging must avoid if it is to eschew the 'official' theory. We have two answers: first that imaging cannot be sensing, *simpliciter*, because there is nothing 'mental' about sensations and there is about imaging; and secondly that imaging cannot even *involve* sensing, because sensation-terms are a kind of reference to common, not private objects. How then do these answers relate to the claim that there are 'no such objects as mental pictures'?

The claim could be interpreted as a consequence of either answer. Thus, by itself, the first answer might be taken to allow that mental images had a sensory component, and to be denying simply that this made them objects. The reason would be that whatever properties they have must be borrowed from the 'mental' part of imaging, that is from the description of what a mental image was of. The substance of the claim could then be that the only objects entering into the analysis of imaging are those mentioned in such a description; the sensory component, although it is there, would not amount to an object. This might seem a not unpromising approach, though I shall argue later that it is mistaken. However, the second answer denies flatly that there is any such sensory component. And here, I think, lies one key to an understanding of Ryle's arguments for the non-existence of mental images. They are arguments which presuppose his assumption that sensation is confined to perception. If one grants the assumption that the only way sensation-terms can have any application is as a type of reference to objects other than the sensations themselves, then it follows that to refer to mental images as sensations presupposes the existence of objects of which images are ways of appearing. Ryle's line would seem to be that because we have common objects for images to be of, we can

34

dispense with the private ones. That we should dispense with them, however, depends on the assumption that for an image to be akin to a sensation it must be a way in which some *present* object appears. The advocate of mental images would then be forced to give an account of the identity of such an object apart from its 'look'—on a par with that of common objects. And of course if he thought this was the kind of thing whose existence Ryle was denying, he might very well agree: no *such* objects serve as referents for our mental-image terminology. However, there is no clear reason at all why he should agree that the logic of 'inner' sensations must follow that of ordinary or 'outer' sensations in the way Ryle's assumption implies.

If it is a conclusion from his arguments about sensations that in the absence of such referents there can be no present referents at all for our mental-image terminology, we might prefer, on pain of denying the familiar fact that people have mental imagery, to reject these arguments. Might not mental images be sensations after all? Sensations, that is, that have the look of what is imagined, not that of something that is inwardly perceived? And wouldn't this accord with what we are in any case tempted to say, namely that mental images are in some way things in their own right, and that our references to them are genuine and direct?

If our references to mental images were genuine and direct, however, nothing would seem to prevent our describing these referents as pictures that we see, in some sense of 'picture' and of 'see'. And this, says Ryle, would be a misdescription, however 'natural and tempting'. Perhaps we can find in his arguments about imaging more convincing support for this allegation than the doctrine that mental images would have to be ways in which something other than either the image itself or the object imagined looked.

4. RYLE'S ARGUMENTS

Ryle's arguments on imaging are in the form of a threefold thesis. He claims that

'. . . a person picturing his nursery is, in a certain way, like that person seeing his nursery, but the similarity does not consist in his really looking at a real likeness of his nursery, but in his really seeming to see his nursery itself, when he is not really seeing it.'[1]

That is, Ryle claims (i) that picturing resembles really seeing, (ii) that the resemblance is not that the picturer really sees a likeness, but (iii) that it is that he really seems to see. What arguments does Ryle offer?

(1) The first argument, far from being designed to support the claim, would seem to be intended to invalidate it. Ryle points out that 'when a person says that he "sees" something which he is not seeing, he knows that what he is doing is something which is totally different in kind from seeing'.[2] But if 'seeing' (seeming to see) and really seeing are totally different in kind, how can the former (as in part-claim [ii]) be, in a certain way, like the latter? Indeed the argument itself shows precisely that they are in no way similar! It is an argument by appeal to 'logical powers'. A person 'seeing' something that he does not see knows that he is doing something totally different in kind from seeing it, 'just because the verb is inside inverted commas and the vision can be described as more or less faithful, or vivid'. The person would never apply such adjectives to what he really sees. Similarly, while a doll can be called 'lifelike', a child cannot, and so with a portrait of a face as distinct from the face portrayed.

To see this quite clearly we can consider Ryle's alternative formulation. The man picturing his nursery, he says, 'is not being a spectator of a resemblance of his nursery, but . . . is resembling a spectator of his nursery'.[3] Now if a reason for not likening the man picturing his nursery to his seeing a resemblance of his nursery (part-claim [ii]) is that really seeing something is 'totally different in kind' from seeming to see it, and this is 'just because' something really seen cannot be qualified as more or less faithful, or lifelike, etc., while a picture can, then the very same consideration must weigh against a description of the man

[1] Gilbert Ryle, *The Concept of Mind* (Hutchinson, London, 1949), p. 248.
[2] Ibid., p. 246.   [3] Ibid., p. 248.

36

as *resembling a spectator* of his nursery. As far as being a spectator of the thing itself is concerned, he is just as resistant to these qualifications as he is as a spectator of a resemblance of it. If so, then on Ryle's own premiss, he should be doing something *totally different in kind* from spectating.[1]

However, Ryle's arguments in support of part-claim (iii) suggest a way of construing part-claim (i) that would preserve its validity in the face of this appeal to logical powers. These later arguments can be taken to show that Ryle is really claiming here that a man picturing his nursery resembles a spectator of it in a quite different sense of 'resembles' from that in which, to coin a convenient expression, predicative asymmetry entails a total difference in kind. The arguments concern an alleged type-similarity between picturing and other 'role' performances such as fancying, pretending, imitating, rehearsing, and demonstrating—all of them activities which 'involve the thought of' a genuine performance of some other activity which they typically *resemble*, but without themselves constituting such a performance. In that case the statement that a person who is picturing his nursery resembles a spectator of the nursery, but is not a spectator of a resemblance of it, equivocates over a type-ambiguity between two (on Ryle's criteria *totally*) different kinds of resemblance, one where 'X resembles Y' entails that X and Y are referents of expressions of the same logical type, and the other where 'X resembles Y' entails, on the contrary, that they are not. Instances of the former would be the logical resemblance between 'picturing', 'depicting', and 'seeming to see' (which can all be qualified by 'vividly', etc.), while an instance of the latter would be what might be termed the merely configurational resemblance between a portrait of a face and the face itself, or—on this interpretation of Ryle's part-claim (i)—between picturing something and really seeing it.

To bring out its logical force, on this interpretation, Ryle's statement that a person picturing his nursery is not a spectator of a resemblance of it, but resembles a spectator of it, could then be rendered: 'A person picturing his nursery is doing nothing

[1] This objection was pointed out to me by W. F. M. Stewart.

logically similar to seeing a resemblance of his nursery, but is doing something logically similar to fancying, pretending, etc. that he is someone seeing it.' Or, using 'logically resembles' for all and only references to the first type of resemblance: 'A person picturing his nursery does not logically resemble someone seeing a resemblance of his nursery, but is someone resembling someone who sees his nursery.' Ryle's expression 'resembling a spectator' would be misleading in suggesting that he means to say that the picturer is a species of spectator, when what he wants to say is that the picturer is a species of 'spectator'.

However, although this is in fact what Ryle wants to say, and his assertion that the picturer resembles a spectator might plausibly be construed to express such a claim, this is not the only way in which to construe it. In part-claim (iii) Ryle states how picturing and really seeing are to be likened. It is in so far as the person picturing his nursery is really seeming to see the nursery itself. Now quite clearly he cannot mean that *this* is something common to picturing and really seeing. The person who really sees his nursery is not seeming to see it; in seeing it he is doing something totally different in kind from seeming to see it. But there is still 'a certain way' in which the two cases are significantly similar, namely that in both his picturing his nursery and his seeing his nursery the appropriate object-term for the two verbs in question is 'his nursery'. And the point that Ryle could be making, quite correctly, is just that this is not the case for seeing when what is seen is a real likeness of the nursery for here the object-term is, obviously enough, 'a picture of his nursery'.

Now the fact that Ryle certainly wants to say this is at least an indication that it is part of what he means. Indeed it would seem an excellent argument for his claim that 'images are not seen',[1] that the answer to the question 'What is seen in seeing a likeness?' is quite obviously 'a likeness', i.e. an image (though not, of course, a mental one), while the answer to the question 'What is seen in picturing?' is 'what one pictures or seems to see',

[1] Gilbert Ryle, *The Concept of Mind* (Hutchinson, London, 1949), p. 247. Although 'imaging occurs'.

i.e. not an image. Giving, as it does, a correct account of the respective 'accusatives' of the corresponding verbs, the argument might even seem to *entail* the conclusion that in imaging one is not seeing an image.

But the conclusion is not a logical one, nor does Ryle suggest that it is. On the contrary, he allows the conceivability of counter-examples. He says that although 'there are no such objects as mental pictures . . . *if there were such objects*, seeing them would still not be the same as seeming to see faces or mountains'.[1] And indeed, given Ryle's assurance that he is appealing to and not denying familiar facts, at least some of the plausibility of his claim must be supposed to derive from experience. But there would be no empirical basis for preferring one form of words to another as a description of the facts if the alternative form of words could not describe anything.

More significantly for Ryle's own reasoning, however, the fact that 'picture' and 'see' take the same accusatives, which is surely a fact about their logical powers and hence amounts to a logical similarity, must still be maintained in the face of what, for Ryle, should be their 'total difference in kind'. For the difference between seeing and picturing is a special case of the difference between seeing and seeming to see, in so far as seeing can be described as vivid, etc., but picturing cannot. But if this similarity can be maintained in the face of their total difference in kind, why should other similarities not be maintained also— for instance in respect of there being an image that is seen?

That this is indeed possible becomes clear if we isolate the precise function of adjectives like 'vivid', 'faithful', and 'lifelike' in the present case. The point of such expressions is to describe the way in which something not presently perceived nevertheless seems to be perceived. But the fact that I seem to perceive one thing does not entail that I cannot be perceiving, or at least seeing, another. And surely even Ryle must admit the possibility of seeming to perceive something when at the same time perceiving something else, for isn't this precisely what happens

---

[1] Gilbert Ryle, *The Concept of Mind* (Hutchinson, London, 1949), p. 254, my emphasis.

when someone sees a real likeness of something, or at least sees a real likeness as a representation of that thing—which is what we must assume Ryle to mean by 'looking at a real likeness' if his denial that picturing involves seeing likenesses is to be an argument for denying that we see mental pictures? So it seems that the force we should attach to Ryle's claim that 'picturing his nursery' is like 'really seeing his nursery', but unlike 'looking at a real likeness of his nursery', must be that anything that can be called 'seeing an image' is confined to that species of seeming to see in which one sees a real likeness, for example a photograph or a portrait.

But since all that the argument from predicative asymmetry shows is that 'seeing' X and seeing X are mutually exclusive ways of addressing oneself to X, and not that 'seeing' X excludes addressing oneself to Y, Ryle needs further arguments to show why this latter exclusion should obtain when 'seeing' is picturing.

(2) He may of course argue that it is not possible to seem to perceive something and also perceive something else, even in the case of seeing a real likeness. He might argue, for example, that 'address' in 'address oneself to X' must be understood in such a way that it is possible to address oneself only to one thing at a time. Then, if 'seeing' and ' "seeing" ' connote species of addressing oneself to something, we could not at the one time both seem to see X and see something other than X. However, although there may be good grounds in usage for such a restriction on 'address' (as on related terms like 'attend', 'notice', and 'look at'), there seem to be none for confining 'see' to a sense in which seeming to see something excludes the possibility of seeing something else. After all, one should not be said to have failed to see the 'Mona Lisa' because in looking at it one always saw it as a representation of Mona Lisa (or whoever).

However, it might still be objected that when I 'see' or 'hear' something *in imagination* there are no senses of 'see' or 'hear', however broad, in which I *both* seem to see or hear something *and* also do something describable as seeing or hearing something. To *see* or *hear* something, it can be claimed, is to be able to locate the thing in public space. When you see or hear something, not only have *you* managed to see or hear it, but something has, as it were, managed to become visible or audible to you. But this cannot be true when one sees or hears in imagination; an *image* is never locatable in space, it is not *found* existing anywhere,[1] or not anywhere it would be natural to say one can find things.

But even granting the truth of these latter observations, it is not clear that there is no acceptable general description available which connotes a visual or auditory experience of objects or sounds that is common both to visual and auditory perception on the one hand and to imaging on the other. Visual experience, one might want to say, has many dimensions, and not all the dimensions in which it is conveniently and properly described as an experience of objects may be dimensions in which the objects in question are locatable in a public (or perhaps any) space. And not all the dimensions in which visual experience should *not* be so described are necessarily specific to modes of imaging. We may wonder, for example, whether a view is an object.

But one might also appeal directly to fact. A reason for denying that in picturing something we can at the same time be seeing, or in any other way attending to or being aware of, another thing may be that such a division of interests is excluded by the nature, or structure, of consciousness. Thus Ryle himself argues, and I believe quite correctly, that mental activity is to be understood as a unitary process.[2] I will try to show later that this truth is not an argument against the claim that picturing involves or is compatible with seeing a mental image. But here it can be noted that in any case the argument will not suffice as a general reason for denying that in *imaging* we see, or are in any other way aware of, something. Some imaging is not strictly, or obviously, representational at all. We see shapes, patches of colour, and so on, but without necessarily understanding them to be in any sense representations of shapes or colours of real

[1] Gilbert Ryle, *The Concept of Mind* (Hutchinson, London, 1949), p. 245.
[2] Cf. ibid., p. 262, and p. 46 below.

things.[1] But when imagery is not representational there is no need for our attention to be divided. The only 'object' is the imagery itself. So we cannot argue here that the object of our attention is something we *cannot but could* (if it was present) see, and infer from this that there is *nothing* we see. For here we have something we may well feel tempted to say we *do*, in some sense, see. And if we were still inclined to say we only 'saw' the shapes, our likely reason for this would not be that we knew we were not seeing them (on the grounds that they were not present), but that we hesitated to say outright that this was to be called a kind of seeing, or that it seemed to us to be such an unusual kind of seeing that to offer no syntactical signposts might mislead people into thinking we were talking of a quite different, and more usual, kind of case. In neither event would the disclaimer be that one saw anything; but at most that we did not see anything in an ordinary sense. And even if we decide that there are good grounds for denying that it is a species of seeing, the question remains, if it is not a *kind* of seeing, what sort of visual or quasi-visual experience is it?

Now if this is one blind alley for Ryle, another route might seem to be open. Rather than argue that it is *impossible* both to seem to see something in imagination and to see a mental picture, it would be enough for his purposes—and of course also necessary—to show the *possibility* of doing the one without the other. Ryle does offer such an argument.

(3) He says that 'we speak of "seeing" as if it were a seeing of pictures, because the familiar experience of seeing snapshots of things and persons so often induces the "seeing" of those things and persons'.[2] And continues:

'When a visible likeness of a person is in front of my nose, I often seem to be seeing the person himself in front of my nose, though he is not there and may be long since dead. I should not

---

[1] Cf. A. G. N. Flew, who points out that not all, even deliberate, visual imagery is pictorial, and says that it is 'easy to make the mistake of thinking that all imagery must be pictorial; because any descriptions of it will have to liken it to something if they are to be understood'. *Mind*, LXV (1956), No. 259, pp. 395 and 396. [2] *Concept of Mind*, p. 253.

keep the portrait if it did not perform this function. Or when I hear a recording of a friend's voice, I fancy I hear him singing or speaking in the room, though he is miles away. The genus is seeming to perceive, and of this genus one very familiar species is that of seeming to see something, when looking at an ordinary snapshot of it. Seeming to see, when no physical likeness is before the nose, is another species. Imaging is not having shadowy pictures before some shadow-organ called "the mind's eye"; but having paper pictures before the eye's in one's face is a familiar stimulus to imaging.'[1]

Now, let us assume that Ryle intends this argument to show, as in his statement of his programme (on page 30 above), that seeing things in the mind's eye *does not entail* that anything is being seen. To serve this purpose the argument would have to show that *neither* species of seeming to see is also a kind of seeing. For otherwise he would have to admit that picturing a nursery, a mountain, or a face might still have to be a kind of seeing of something. He has to show that neither species of seeming to see is also a case of a kind of seeing of something. The causal argument must therefore place the causing situation and the caused one in a temporal succession. The effect will then be one species of the genus 'seeming to see', while picturing will be another species of the same genus and differentiated from the former by virtue of the absence of the causal factor. Thus the causal circumstances will be shown to be functionally accidental to the genus, and peculiar to the case of really seeing a real likeness of something.

That Ryle means to argue to this effect is indicated by the final part of the passage in which he says that 'having paper pictures before the eyes in one's face is a familiar stimulus to imaging'. The fact that he takes 'imaging' rather than 'imagining' to be an alternative expression for 'seeming to perceive' suggests he regards the end-product of the causal process to be autonomous and no longer dependent upon the seeing of a likeness. However, this interpretation seems to be contradicted by the description in the preceding sentence, of the physically caused

---

[1] *Concept of Mind*, p. 254.

species of 'seeming to perceive' as 'seeming to see something when looking at an ordinary snapshot of it', for here the *concurrence* of the causing situation and the caused situation seems to be taken as a defining property of the species. In that case, however, Ryle apparently allows that seeming to perceive can also be a case of really seeing; and then the causal argument will not show that picturing does not need its snapshot.

The difficulty in grasping the precise force Ryle claims for his argument is compounded by his further remarks on the fact that 'seeing replicas, however accurate, need not result in "seeing" vividly'.[1] His observation is perfectly correct, of course, and raises interesting questions for the analysis of visual experience. But in the context of his discussion it is clear that Ryle is hoping to draw support from this phenomenon for his causal argument. What he says in effect is that because vivid seeming to see in the case of physical replicas is not a function of the literal accuracy of the likeness, we do not have to explain vivid picturing in terms of our seeing an accurate likeness. Vivid 'seeing' is, as it were, autonomous in so far as 'the speakingness of a physical likeness has to be described, not in terms of similarity, but in terms of the vividness of the "seeing" which it induces'.[2]

Two comments are in order. First, in this context the causal relation is supposed to obtain between *seeing a likeness* and seeming to see what it is a likeness of. But in that case both terms of the causal relation comprise species of the genus 'seeming to see', for Ryle would presumably allow that to see a portrait as of a face is a case of seeming to see a face, however pedantic and stilted the artist's work may be. However, in this version the causal argument would tend to show that picturing, too, should include a likeness *which is seen as such*. If the argument assumes that in perception we are caused to seem to see in one way by already seeming to see in another, its force is altogether lost.

Secondly, even if the argument is interpreted in the way needed to give it the required force, it is doubtful whether it achieves a separation of the terms which would demonstrate the superfluousness of the cause. Consider how the notion of 'cause'

---

[1] *Concept of Mind*, p. 254.   [2] Ibid., p. 254.

must be applied if we are supposed to come to seem to see in one way without first seeming to see in another. A physical object, or collection of physical objects, could be said to bring it about that I seem to see something that I do not really see, by virtue of its, or their, physical and spatial organization. A newspaper photograph is an organization of black dots on a white background, and if I look at it from neither too close nor too far I will see something represented.[1] If the organization was disturbed in certain ways, or I was not placed at a suitable distance from it, I would not come to see it as a representation; *it* would have failed to bring it about that I saw it in that way.

It seems clear that in picturing things in imagination not all of this can apply. But we must be careful to distinguish what obviously does not from what quite reasonably may. We can safely say, for example, that there is no object analogous to the paper with its black and white dots, about which we can say one comes to see it as a representation. There is nothing in the experience of picturing something analogous to opening the page, or controlling the distance from which I observe something so as to see it as a representation. In that case there is no empirical basis for saying that such an object is a causal factor in my seeing a physical likeness as such. However, this does not even tend to show that picturing does not *require* an object analogous to the physical representation; it shows only that such an object cannot function in such a way as to determine, by virtue of *its own* organization, what it is I seem to see, which leaves open the possibility that it is my seeming to see what I do seem to see that determines *its* organization, and that without its having this organization I would not seem to see anything.

(4) Ryle, as we have noted, sees the resemblance between picturing and really seeing as consisting in the fact that real seeing is mentioned in both activities, but in the former only obliquely. Picturing is a way of not seeing, it is like putting on a perceptual role. The model with which he seeks to explain what picturing, or imaging in general, is, as opposed to what it is not,

---

[1] An additional condition is that I am able to recognize a thing of the type represented. But here we may ignore this and other important factors.

is that of activities which 'involve the thought of (doing) something' but in such a way as to constitute no way of actually doing it. The argument for the assimilation of picturing to the adopting of roles of various kinds is in two main steps.

First Ryle formulates the logical type of activities which involve the thought of some other activity of which an activity of this type does not constitute a genuine performance. Examples of activities of this relatively sophisticated form whose description involves an 'oblique' mention of an activity not being genuinely performed are pretending, obeying an order, doing what one has planned to do, growling like a bear, repenting of what one has done, keeping a resolution, jeering at another's performance and complying with the rules. 'In all these cases, as well as in many others', says Ryle, 'the doing of the higher order acts involves the thought of the lower order acts; yet the phrase "involves the thought of" does not connote the collateral occurrence of another, cogitative act.'[1]

The force of this latter remark is that although activities of the kind listed are logically complex, the complexity is not such that in describing them we must allow for two different activities, an inner one we do not see and the outer one we do see, as if the total activity was in some way a concerted one. Thus pretending to be angry, for example, does not consist of 'one operation of meditating about crossness, shepherding a second operation of performing the quasi-cross actions'.[2] We should not be led, therefore, to suppose that picturing, whatever its complexity, is to be thought of as one operation of seeing a resemblance of the nursery shepherding *another* operation of seeming to see it.

A species of this genus of logically complex activities comprises various forms of make-believe, for example a child playing at being a pirate, or fancying he is a pirate. The former corresponds to the notion of 'acting a part', which together with 'pretend', involves the giving of an 'overt and muscular representation', while the latter belongs to the range of cases where the things people do are done 'inaudibly and invisibly because "in their heads"'. Usually we reserve the terms 'imagine' and

[1] *Concept of Mind*, p. 263.   [2] Ibid., p. 262.

'fancy' for this latter range; that is, as Ryle puts it, 'for people's fancied perceptions as opposed to their mock-actions'.[1] This distinction comprises the second step in Ryle's assimilation argument. There are, he says, two brands of make-believe. One is where an overt activity involves the thought of an overt activity that it resembles but whose fulfilment it does not constitute, as in imitating somebody, or demonstrating the movements for tying a certain kind of knot without actually tying one, because one is empty-handed; and the other is where a species of non-muscular doing involves the thought of another species of non-muscular doing, as in seeing Helvellyn in one's mind's eye.

In distinguishing these varieties of make-believe Ryle warns against assuming the logical powers of expressions referring to one case to apply automatically to another. He says we should not think that because overt pretence, or mock-action generally involves a form of overt activity, we should look for anything corresponding to this in non-muscular pretence. The difference between the two varieties of make-believe, according to Ryle, is

'. . . nothing but a consequence of the difference between perceiving something and bringing something about overtly. This difference is not between bringing something about privily and bringing something about overtly, for perceiving is not bringing something about. It is getting something or, sometimes, keeping something; but it is not effecting anything. Seeing and hearing are neither witnessed nor unwitnessed doings, for they are not doings.'[2]

Ryle is claiming that *picturing* is not to be thought of as a private way of bringing something about. He argues that this can be shown by the fact that *perceiving* is not to be thought of in this way. But can he argue this? According to the logic of the type of activities to which he wants to say picturing belongs, perceiving and bringing things about overtly are to be mentioned only obliquely in the description of non-muscular and overt pretence. But then why should it even follow from perceiving

[1] *Concept of Mind*, p. 264.　　　[2] Ibid., p. 267.

being non-muscular that picturing is, as it surely is, non-muscular? This truth should no more follow from that fact than should the falsehood that picturing is muscular follow from the fact that a child can indulge non-muscularly (i.e. 'in imagination') in the fancy that he is being muscularly piratical. And Ryle would be the first to point out that fancied muscularity was not a species of muscularity. So Ryle cannot explain the fact that picturing is not a mock *action* by noting the fact that perceiving is not a way of bringing something about overtly. Nor, therefore, can he take it to be a reason for not regarding picturing as a way of bringing something about privily that perceiving is not this either.

Then why does Ryle make this slip? It looks as if part of the explanation is that if he did not make it he would be at a loss to say anything at all about what picturing positively is. For, if we suppose, as seems fair, that Ryle means that it is in any case wrong to describe picturing as a way of bringing something about privily, the only other candidate in the field seems to be perceiving. Perceiving itself is of course excluded by virtue of being mentioned only obliquely in a description of picturing; perceiving is what picturing is *not*. Now this in itself would not prevent the possibility of picturing resembling perceiving in, say, being something like the getting of sights and hearings of things, so long as the resemblance was of the kind mentioned earlier in which a portrait resembles a face. However, Ryle himself has ruled this possibility out by not allowing that there could be anything to get in such a case. In his view, we recall, there is 'nothing akin to sensation'; sensation is peculiar to perception. But since, as we have said, Ryle apparently excludes the possibility of a covert species of bringing something about— and what could be brought about but something akin to sensations?—he seems to have categorized picturing out of existence altogether. There seems to be no operation to act as host to the oblique mention.

Perhaps we should see in Ryle's mistaken inference an implicit acknowledgment of a kind of resemblance between picturing and perceiving that he seems almost perversely intent upon denying, that is, in respect of their being something visual. That there *is* a resemblance is, of course, what he has been claiming all along. And if his general thesis is right, that is, that picturing is a sort of representation of perceiving, then this acknowledgment would be wholly edifying. But we saw that his account of sensations prevents the resemblance from consisting in any actual, as opposed to obliquely mentioned, visual experience, for example a 'post-perceptual look as if'; and have seen now that he even argues as if the truth of the general thesis excluded this possibility in any case. His unwillingness to accept that picturing is a way of bringing something about compounds the impossibility, but at the expense of leaving him with nothing to which to attach the label 'picturing', about which he can say it is a way of not perceiving.

(5) Ryle's final account of picturing as a species of ways of not doing something is in terms of 'expectations' and 'rehearsal'.

'Seeing Helvellyn in one's mind's eye . . . [involves] the thought of having a view of Helvellyn and it is therefore a more sophisticated operation than that of having a view of Helvellyn. It is one utilisation among others of the knowledge of how Helvellyn should look, or, in one sense of the verb, it is thinking how it should look. The expectations which are fulfilled in the recognition at sight of Helvellyn are not indeed fulfilled in picturing it, but the picturing of it is something like a rehearsal of getting them fulfilled . . . it involves missing just what one would be due to get, if one were seeing the mountain.'[1]

Here Ryle proposes 'rehearsal' as an analogue of the host operation and 'getting expectations fulfilled' as the obliquely mentioned activity. In doing so, however, he now openly infringes his own principle of oblique mention, for he is allowing that picturing can be a *form* of expecting. It is not the expecting that is rehearsed, but the actual seeing, the *fulfilment* of the expectations, which is clearly quite another thing. Thus the rehearsal he means involves not the *thought* of expecting, but actual, though fanciful and not genuine expecting. Perhaps we

[1] *Concept of Mind*, p. 270.

should say it is mock-expecting, except that there would be an important asymmetry between this case and those, such as demonstrating how to do something, or sparring instead of really fighting, that Ryle himself labels mock- or sham-actions. For where sparring, or sham-fighting is, as Ryle puts it, 'a series of calculated omissions to fight',[1] mock-expecting here would be at best an omission to expect ingenuously, and not an omission to expect altogether. The type-difference is therefore not, as in sham-fighting, between a way of not doing something and doing it, but between two ways of doing something, corresponding to the ways in which sparring and fighting are two forms of muscular activity.

So picturing is a form of expecting; it is expecting what one knows one will not get. Earlier Ryle has assimilated a person following an imagined tune to someone really listening to 'a moderately familiar tune' and who sometimes listens for notes 'other than those which were really due to come'.[2] Thus Ryle claims:

'To expect a tune to take one course, when it is actually taking another, is already to suppose, fancy or imagine. When what is heard is not what was listened for, what was listened for can be described only as notes which might have been heard, and the frame of mind in which they were listened for was therefore one of erroneous expectancy. . . . A person going through a tune entirely in his head is in a partially similar case. He, too, listens for something which he does not get, though he is well aware all the time that he is not going to get it.'[3]

But how, on Ryle's own terms, can there be even a partial similarity between erroneous expectancy and expecting what you *know* you will not get? For there to be a similarity of any kind there would have to be a genus, in this case 'listening for what is not got', of which both cases could constitute species. But since listening for what one does not get in the former case can be described in terms of disappointment or surprise, while such qualifications would be wholly inappropriate in the case of

[1] *Concept of Mind*, p. 265.   [2] Ibid., p. 268.   [3] Ibid., p. 268.

knowing that one is not about to get what one 'expects', the two should be regarded as totally different in kind. According to Ryle's own criteria of type-difference, therefore, mock-expectation should indeed be regarded as strictly parallel to what he himself calls mock-actions, in so far as the expectation itself is excluded as part of a direct description of the host-doing. But then since there seems to be nothing more to this 'rehearsal' than the visual or aural, etc. expectations that are known not to be about to be fulfilled, the host operation once again vanishes into thin air.

5. MENTAL CONDUCT AND THE ARGUMENT FROM WHOLE TO PART

The claim that the two cases of unfulfilled expectation are partially similar reveals both the nature of and the inherent weakness in Ryle's over-all strategy. His general purpose seems to be to refute a dualistic explanation of mental conduct by showing how in particular cases of the use of mental-concept terms we neither do, nor need to, refer to anything more recondite than the ways in which we see one another behave. Thus the point of the assimilation between erroneous expectancy (which Ryle claims is 'already to imagine') and 'listening for' what one knows one will not hear is to show that we already have a use for 'imagine' where we do not have to invoke a theory of inner attention to special objects. The correct account of erroneous expectation, according to Ryle, is not in terms of precognizings and anticipations of what has not yet come, but in terms of 'niches' which may or may not be filled.[1] Having a niche for a note is no more than being about to be unperturbed if the familiar tune runs its course and perturbed if it wanders from it. The musician with perfect pitch will wince when he hears a note that is to other less gifted people inaudibly flat or sharp, but we do not have to explain this by saying that he had the right note in mind. He simply has the capacity to tell when a

[1] Ryle says that 'following a known tune involves not only hearing the notes [but also] having the proper niche ready for each note as it comes'. *Concept of Mind*, p. 268.

note is correctly pitched and when it is not, and the only object we *have* to credit to his attendings is the culprit sound itself.

Although it would surely be an odd use of the term 'imagine' to apply it to this situation, the passage we quoted above shows that Ryle thinks that if it can properly be applied in cases of no greater complexity than this then he has shown how imagining— as a broad concept that embraces imaging—does not include as a necessary ingredient some kind of inner doing. That is, he will have shown that imagining is no exception to the rule that 'exercises of qualities of mind do not, save *per accidens*, take place "in the head" . . .' and that 'those which do so have no special priority over those which do not'.[1]

It is an argument from the whole to the parts. According to this argument, even if some of the parts, or 'species', contain elements that the case favourable to a behavioural interpretation does not contain, these should not be regarded as conceptually significant, as having that 'special priority' given them in the 'official theory'. For if some imaging does not contain these elements the anti-dualist case has been established. Accordingly one is entitled to say there is a 'partial similarity' between the two cases of imagining described as 'expecting what is not got'; for although the similarity is only partial—since in the second case the tune is running 'in the person's head'—the complement does not amount to anything serious. The important point about auralizing is its being a type of relatively sophisticated performance. It is differentiated from other such performances, not by involving a special faculty of inner hearing, or a special organ—the mind's ear—but by involving the use of a particular kind of knowledge, that is, knowledge of how tunes go and what noises things make. Similarly with smells, tastes, sights, and feels. What is important about, say, the ability to recall the smell of a smithy, or to picture Helvellyn to oneself, is the fact that one is using one's knowledge of how things smell and look when one does not smell or see them. So with all operations 'in the head': talking to oneself, for example—or as Ryle calls it, 'silent soliloquy' —is not a kind of talking but 'a flow of pregnant non-sayings'.[2]

[1] *Concept of Mind*, p. 40. See p. 28 above.   [2] Ibid., p. 269.

The weakness of Ryle's strategy in the case just mentioned is that in order to establish his conclusion he has to allow as instances of imagining cases that quite obviously fail to satisfy the criteria he lays down for type-similarity. 'Expecting what you are not going to get' is simply not a bridge that Ryle can build to link imaging, as an exercise of imagining that takes place 'in the head', to cases of imagining that do not.

However, since 'imagining' in the sense of 'erroneously expecting' is in any case a somewhat dubious representative of the overt members of the family of imaginings, we can still ask whether the strategy may be applied more effectively with regard to other members of the family.

The problem here, however, is to know what precisely the strategy is designed to achieve. If Ryle only means to show that imaging and certain overt activities, for example what he calls mock-actions, but also the mock-use of sentences in 'assuming, supposing, entertaining, toying with ideas and considering suggestions',[1] are exercises of a relatively sophisticated sort, then the gap between inner and outer is easily bridged. But then this would not seem to require the denial of mental images; it would be enough, surely, to assert that picturing, for example, is a sophisticated use of ordinary visual knowledge. The point could be put summarily by saying that picturing was a post-perceptual exercise of visual knowledge, and not a special way of perceiving.

Now it could be that, in arguing as if denying mental images was essential to the programme of flushing the Mind from its Cartesian coverts, Ryle is merely overstating his case. Perhaps all he really needs and intends to show is a certain parallel between the way in which real sights are absent in imaging and that, say, in which real pieces of string are absent when someone empty-handedly demonstrates the movements of tying a knot.[2] If this was all he meant to show, then it would not be necessary to take this analogy to show that there was nothing at all that was seen. The net Ryle casts would simply not be sufficiently

[1] *Concept of Mind*, p. 263.
[2] Cf. G. E. M. Anscombe, 'Pretending', in S. Hampshire (ed.), *Philosophy of Mind* (Harper & Row, New York, 1966), p. 295.

fine-meshed to capture such rarified facts as what an image is or whether it is seen. This could perhaps explain why the apparent truism, 'There are mental images' is among the more intrusively pregnant of *The Concept of Mind's* own characteristic non-sayings.

And yet, in the final analysis, it is impossible to regard Ryle's omission to utter it as anything but calculated. The knot-demonstrator's string, after all, is simply not there; and it seems obvious that we are meant to conclude that in imaging there is no image either. Moreover, even if the denial of mental images was not directly dictated by Ryle's programme, we have seen that he is prevented indirectly from saying anything about them. If a mental image cannot be or involve something akin to sensation, what could possibly substitute in picturing for the real likeness we see when we look at a portrait? And if there is no unwitnessable bringing-about, how could imaging be what Berkeley calls the 'framing' or 'exciting' of ideas in the mind? Whether these assumptions themselves are directly dictated by the thesis that Ryle would erect in place of the dualism he opposes is another question. It may be that he has left himself needlessly short-handed in denying himself the descriptive tools with which to account for the familiar fact of imaging. I shall argue, however, in conclusion of this examination of Ryle's account, that to avail himself of the necessary tools would lead him to weaken considerably the connection he seems to have been claiming between observable conduct and the content of psychological terms, and thus to undermine seriously his conception of mind as a topic of observationally testable propositions.

But before coming to that there is a further problem to mention in connection with the argument from whole to part. We said that if all Ryle wanted to show was that imaging belonged to a range of relatively sophisticated exercises, then the conceptual gap between inner and outer imaginings can be easily bridged. But what justification is there for regarding it as a conceptual bridge between imaginings? Or to put it in another way, how can one conclude from the fact that imaging is one of these sophisticated exercises that imagination does not involve essentially inner exercises?

Ryle is concerned not merely with ridding imaging of inner objects, he also wants to show that 'there is no special Faculty of Imagination, occupying itself single-mindedly in fancied viewings and hearings'.[1] He calls attention to all the 'widely divergent sorts of behaviour in the conduct of which we should ordinarily and correctly be described as imaginative'.[2] In describing a piece of conduct as imaginative or as an exercise of imagination we are not, he claims, attributing to its owner a specific mental operation by virtue of which his behaviour is properly so described. In particular we are not attributing (or have no justification for attributing) to him an operation of 'seeing things in the mind's eye, hearing things in one's head and so on, i.e. some piece of fancied perceiving'.[3]

This latter point is indeed an obvious one and involves no gainsaying of 'well-known facts about the mental life of human beings'.[4] And perhaps we should say the same of the former point, although it is less obvious. But there is still a problem. If all the behaviour Ryle mentions under the heading 'exercises of imagination' is properly so called but not by virtue of a specific, 'nuclear' mental operation, the only justification he provides for this is that imaging and other, in many ways quite different, exercises are all of a certain relatively sophisticated kind. He can add that they are ways of doing something 'hypothetically', or in a 'hypothetical [as opposed to categorical] frame of mind'.[5] But is this enough? Or if enough, will it support Ryle's claim that exercises of imagination do not take place 'in the head'? It is

---

[1] *Concept of Mind*, p. 257.

[2] Ibid., p. 256. Ryle mentions 'the mendacious witness in the witness-box, the inventor thinking out a new machine, the constructor of a romance, the child playing bears, and Henry Irving . . . [also] the judge listening to the lies of the witness, the colleague giving his opinion on the new invention, the novel reader, the nurse who refrains from admonishing the "bears" for their subhuman noises, the dramatic critic and the theatre goers'. They are all 'exercising their imaginations'.

[3] Ibid., p. 257.   [4] Ibid., p. 16. See p. 28 above.

[5] Ibid., pp. 263 and 269. Though the reference to 'frame of mind' might be thought to exclude some imaging from imagination. Solving a problem in geometry 'in the head' no more requires a hypothetical frame of mind than does doing it on a blackboard. Cf. p. 83 below.

significant that Ryle allows a child's 'growling somewhat like a bear' to be such an exercise. But without specifying that the growl be something more than a mere imitation, why should we take this to involve imagination? Surely a child may growl like a bear, or shout 'Yo ho ho!', just because he thinks these are bearish, or piratical, things to do, yet still be a long way from imagining or fancying himself being a bear or a pirate. And unless Ryle can indicate that these latter imaginings involve nothing done 'in the head', the conceptual bridge will not reach convincingly to the outer. Alternatively, if it does reach convincingly to the outer, the bridge itself is less convincingly a link between two kinds of imagining. Before he can argue from whole to part Ryle must assume that imaging and overt imagining are both exercises of a unitary concept of imagination. Moreover, he cannot argue from whole to part by saying that all these activities are just *called* exercises of imagination, appealing to well-known facts of *usage* as opposed to well-known facts of mental life; for there can be no appeal to usage in *rectifying* the logic of mental-conduct concepts.[1]

6. RYLE AND THE ANALOGY OF DEPICTING

We asked whether Ryle's inability to say what kind of activity imagining is, as opposed to what it stops short of, was dictated by his thesis. We can answer this question by considering a proposed emendation which would enable him to overcome this difficulty.

J. M. Shorter has proposed *depicting* as an analogue for picturing. He points out how the reasons which Ryle uses to justify the claim that seeming to see and seeing are totally different in kind can be used to justify the claim that picturing logically resembles depicting.

'The reason why we can use words like "vivid", "faithful" and "lifelike" in connexion with picturing or visualising . . . is that the logic of words like "picture", "visualise", and "see in

---

[1] *Concept of Mind*, p. 28 above.

the mind's eye" is to some extent parallel to that of "depict", and "draw a picture of".[1]

Since there is a partial parallel, the point of saying that picturing is 'depicting', with the quotation marks, is not that picturing is *no kind* of depicting, but only that it is *not the same* as depicting; it is depicting only in a metaphorical sense. This has two important advantages over Ryle's account. First, it explains why 'see an image of that mountain' is a wrong way of describing the visualizing of Helvellyn. It is wrong for the same reason that it is wrong to say that drawing a picture of Helvellyn is drawing a picture of a picture of Helvellyn. In literally depicting Helvellyn, it is the mountain itself I depict, not the picture I make while depicting it.[2] Secondly, as a piece of metaphorical depicting, visualizing shares with literal depicting the property of being a species of activity on its own account, even of (if only metaphorical) 'effecting'. That something is a doing which can be characterized in metaphorical terms does not mean that it is metaphorical doing. It is just that to characterize it we must liken it to another doing. Moreover, it and the doing that it resembles can be regarded as species of a common genus, say, 'producing likenesses of things'. In saying what visualizing is we are not restricted, therefore, to saying what it is not, i.e. perceiving. 'Visualizing is not mock-seeing.' It is '*doing* something in a way that seeing is not doing something'. This is shown, for example, by the fact that 'one can be ordered to depict or to visualize something [but not] ordered to see it'.[3]

The strength of the analogy of depicting seems clear, at least

---

[1] J. M. Shorter, 'Imagination', *Mind*, LXI (1952), No. 244, pp. 529–30.

[2] Ibid., p. 530. Note how this argument parallels the one on page 38 above for likening 'picturing' to 'seeing' rather than to 'seeing a real likeness'. It is clear, however, that there is a greater parallel between 'picturing' and 'depicting' than between 'picturing' and 'seeing', in that to see something depicted or to depict something, is, as also with picturing, not to see it, in this sense of 'see'.

[3] Ibid., p. 530. Shorter's remarks here correspond to Wittgenstein's in the *Philosophical Investigations*, cf. p. 225 below. Professor A. G. N. Flew, in 'Facts and "Imagination"' (*Mind*, LXV [1956], No. 259, pp. 392–4) has challenged Shorter's claim that visualizing does not correspond to perceiving, on phenomenological grounds. Cf. pp. 71 f. below.

for the more deliberate forms of imaging. But it is instructive to see how it would not at all suit Ryle's book.[1]

In the first place, as Miss Ishiguro has noted, Ryle would have to regard depicting as a hybrid sort of activity that falls into neither of the twin and disjunct categories of performances and achievements. To depict something is not only a doing, it is also, in a sense, a getting, as we shall see more clearly later.[2] The 'ambiguity' of the concept, as Ishiguro points out, 'derives from the complex nature of the fact itself, which involves elements that depend on my intention and elements which do not'.[3] The complexity of the facts must, of course, throw doubt on the general utility of Ryle's system of classification, at least if its categories are to be regarded as descriptive and not merely as useful heuristic devices.

But secondly, it is hard to see how, even if his system of classification could be adapted to accommodate an activity like depicting, such an activity could, in Ryle's terms, illuminate the notion of picturing at all. Those terms state that 'when we characterize people by mental predicates, we are not making untestable inferences . . . we are describing the ways in which those people conduct parts of their predominantly public behaviour'.[4] What a person does, on this view, is what we are entitled to say on the strength of what he is seen to be doing and of what we are entitled to expect him to do on the basis of his known 'powers, and propensities'.[5] The cash-value of a mental predicate, therefore, will be actual and anticipated conduct. In

[1] This despite Ryle's verbal assurance that he regards Shorter's proposal an improvement on his own.

[2] See pp. 79 ff. below.

[3] Hidé Ishiguro, 'Imagination', in Bernard Williams and Alan Montefiore (eds.), *British Analytical Philosophy* (Routledge & Kegan Paul, London, 1966), p. 169.

[4] *Concept of Mind*, p. 51.

[5] Loc. cit. Cf. Stuart Hampshire's claim that 'Ryle is not really arguing that all or most statements involving mental concepts are (or are expressible as) hypothetical statements about overt behaviour, but (and it is very different) that to give reasons for accepting or rejecting such statements must always involve making some hypothetical statements about overt behaviour'. (Critical Notice of *The Concept of Mind, Mind*, LIX [1950], No. 234, p. 245; in O. P. Wood and G. Pitcher, op. cit., p. 30.)

that case the descriptive content of predicates like 'depicting', 'drawing a picture', and 'drawing an object' will derive from the visible events of the depicter's plying pencil to paper or brush to canvas. But since Ryle would evidently object as much to the notion of inner manipulation as to that of inner representation, the analogical possibilities of 'depict', etc. will be even less than those of 'see'. For, as a 'non-effective', 'see' has at least the advantage over 'depict' of having none of the latter's overt manipulative content to place on the debit side of the analogy. Consequently, no less than with 'see', Ryle will have to reserve 'depict' for that part of the complex description of picturing which mentions what is not, rather than what is, being done. We should expect the Rylean objection to the proposal to use 'depict' as an analogue of the host operation to be phrased in terms of 'brushless artistry' and 'clandestine studios'.

We have seen hints of Ryle's own preference for what can be termed the spectator role. Recall his claim that picturing is, despite a total difference in kind, 'in a certain way' like really seeing, the slip by which he infers that because perceiving is not a form of effecting anything, then picturing need not be so either, and finally the idea of rehearsal itself, where, despite the logic of oblique mention, picturing begins to look like a kind of incipient but not-quite perceiving. We should expect this. Given Ryle's view of the content of mental predicates picturing is much closer to perceiving than to depicting. If to be bringing anything about privily the man picturing his nursery must be doing something like manufacturing an image of it, then it is quite obvious that he is not bringing anything about privily. Mental images are not products of skill, and since real pictures are, picturing and depicting are not, in Ryle's terms, 'exercises of the knowledge of the tricks of the same trade'.[1] If in special cases, as in imagining oneself tying knots correctly, picturing does involve a skill, it is in so far as what one pictures is skilled; skill is mentioned here only obliquely. The knowledge one exercises in picturing is visual not manipulatory knowledge; picturing oneself tying the knot is not picturing oneself making a picture of oneself tying

[1] *Concept of Mind*, p. 55.

59

the knot. Since Ryle's concept of mind seems to be deliberately intended to preclude any inner doing that is *not* analogous to manipulation, all that remains to picturing is the exercise of visual knowledge. So at least Ryle has no reason for denying that picturing and *perceiving* are exercises of knowledge of the same, non-manipulatory, powers or propensities.

III

SHORTER'S EXCUSES

I. THE NEGATIVE CLAIM

Philosophers dissatisfied with their own arguments cannot always count on making do with the arguments of others. For in one very important sense Ryle's claim that a philosophical conclusion is never detachable from its premisses is indeed true. By subscribing to an alternative argument for his conclusion a philosopher can well find that he has unwittingly shifted his ground, perhaps even changed philosophical camps altogether. For example, as we shall see in the next chapter, if Ryle were to adopt Sartre's arguments for the conclusion that mental images are not objects, he would find himself stoutly defending a tradition he is explicitly out to demolish. But even to adopt the relatively simple terminological amendment proposed by Shorter would involve him in a fairly major shift in position. I think the move is clearly one he must make. Picturing is indeed, like depicting, a *doing*, and any theory of mental reference that denies this amount of parallel between them must be rejected.

Although in their anti-Cartesian slant Shorter's arguments have a programmatic affinity with Ryle's, they are in fact very different. Shorter claims:

'The analogue of "seeing" and picturing is not seeing, but depicting. . . . [However] seeing in the mind's eye or picturing, what might best be called "depicting", is not the same thing as depicting. It is depicting only in a metaphorical sense and is not even metaphorical seeing.'[1]

We shall concentrate on the negative claim, that picturing is not even metaphorical seeing, since this shows the way to problems

---

[1] 'Imagination', op. cit., p. 530.

I shall draw attention to in the positive claim, that the analogue of picturing is depicting. The negative claim has two parts: that picturing is not metaphorically seeing an image or picture, and that it is not metaphorically seeing what is imagined or depicted. We shall see that Shorter's argument for the first involves an unnecessarily strict requirement for metaphorical seeing. It is a consequence of this requirement that images do not exist, though unlike Ryle, Shorter allows the expression 'mental image' has a use. His argument for the second part is tenable so long as what is denied is understood to be that picturing is metaphorically *perceiving*. But then this leaves it open as to whether picturing, and especially other, less 'active' forms of imaging, might not be correctly described as a genuine kind of seeing that is not a kind of perceiving. This possibility raises doubts about the claim that seeing is not an analogue of 'seeing', and even about whether the analogy of depicting is all Shorter thinks it is.

2. THE NATURE OF THE FACT THAT IMAGES ARE NOT SEEN

Shorter describes the following facts as being both logical and empirical: that mental images are not seen,[1] that they are not objects,[2] and that they do not exist.[3] They are logical facts in so far as expressions like 'see a mental picture'[4] and 'that image no longer exists'[5] have no use;[6] and they are empirical facts in so far as 'it is a fact about the non-linguistic world that it is not of such a nature that it would be convenient to give a use to expressions like "see a mental image" '.[7]

By an expression's having a use Shorter clearly means more than that the expression is an actual expression in the language. For this would make the nature and existence of images depend on facts about the linguistic world alone, about what people *say*. Moreover, Shorter himself allows that 'see a mental picture' is an actual expression, though, as he claims, not a normal one; it has been introduced by philosophers as a synonym for 'visualize

[1] 'Imagination', p. 530.   [2] Ibid., p. 540.   [3] Ibid., pp. 531–2.
[4] Ibid., p. 530.   [5] Ibid., p. 532.   [6] Ibid., p. 532.   [7] Ibid., p. 531.

something' in an attempt 'to elucidate what we mean by this phrase'.[1] Thus although the expression both can be and is used, the question as to whether it *has* a use asks something else. It asks whether we do anything that it 'is natural to describe' in such terms.[2]

How are we to decide whether a description is natural or not? Shorter's own procedure can be presented briefly as follows. In order to describe imaging we have to 'use familiar words in an extended sense',[3] that is words for which we already have a use. We have uses for expressions of the form 'X exists', 'X is in a space of its own', 'notice a feature of X', and so on. For the uses of such expressions there are established criteria, and it is the fact that these criteria can be satisfied that gives the words their 'point'.[4] For the facts of imaging (or to use the case Shorter concentrates on, visualizing) to be describable in these terms the same criteria would have to be satisfied. Only then would the point of the familiar terms be preserved.

Thus, in order for expressions of the form 'X exists' and 'X is in a space of its own' to be applicable to imaging, it would have to be 'convenient to ask questions that it is in fact not proper to ask . . . [like] "Is that mental picture you produced yesterday still in existence, or have you rubbed it out?" [or] "Where is it?"'[5] That is, our experience of imaging would have to duplicate the conditions in which the expressions have a point. This would be the case if, for example, 'when we visualised anything the image stayed put until we visualised it being rubbed out . . . [or if] there is a limit to the number of things we can visualise, if we go on visualising new things without "rubbing out" the images of the old ones'.[6] It is because the facts are not of this nature that 'X' in 'X exists' and 'X is in a space of its own' cannot be replaced by 'mental image'. And yet, because the facts conceivably might be of this nature, we should say that it is an empirical as well as a logical fact that mental images do not exist and that they are not in a space of their own.

Given this account of an expression's having a use, we should

[1] 'Imagination', p. 530. [2] Ibid, p. 531. [3] Ibid., p. 531.
[4] Cf. ibid., p. 538. [5] Ibid., p. 531. [6] Ibid., p. 531.

be able to state Shorter's thesis now as follows: The expression ' "depict" ' (in inverted commas) has a use, which is to say that it can be introduced as a synonym to elucidate what we mean by 'visualize', which is also to say that it is natural to describe visualizing as a kind of depicting; and the same is not true of the expression ' "see a picture" ' (in inverted commas).

3. A USE FOR 'MENTAL IMAGE' BUT NOT FOR 'SEE A MENTAL IMAGE'

We recall that Shorter argues for 'depicting' as the analogy for 'picturing' on the grounds that 'the logic of words like "picture", "visualise", and "see in the mind's eye" is *to some extent* parallel to that of "depict", and "draw a picture of".[1] That is, it is enough that 'depicting' presents only a partial parallel with 'picturing'. One might think, then, that the reason for rejecting 'see a picture' as an analogy for 'picturing' is that the parallel between the two is even more partial. In fact, however, Shorter's reason for denying that 'see a mental picture' has a use is no more than that the logic of 'see a picture' fails to be *completely* parallel to that of 'visualize', i.e. is no more than the justification he permits himself for *accepting* 'depict', or 'draw a picture', as the appropriate parallel. The apparent anomaly is one of two that are direct consequences of the way in which Shorter interprets the results of his method. What that method is we shall now see in its application, with regard first to 'mental image', then to 'see a mental image'.

(1) We note first that he claims that although 'quite clearly a mental image is not an object . . . it may be in some way analogous to one in that it is useful to have a way of talking about visualising that does not refer to the representative aspects of visualising'.[2] Shorter mentions two kinds of ways in which the facts make this way of talking useful.

One is where, when people describe their not always successful attempts to visualize the faces of people they know very well, they find it useful to say such things as 'All I got was a blur',

[1] See pp. 56f. above, my emphasis.   [2] 'Imagination', p. 540.

'His face was a blur', or 'It was a blur'; and they do not mean that the face they try to visualize is blurred, or that the face is visualized *as* blurred.

'What we are referring to is something analogous to the "face in the picture", the picture-face . . . [The blur] is, so to speak, a feature of the image in its own right.'

Secondly, and somewhat similarly,

'. . . there is such a thing as visualising a scene in black and white, as opposed to visualising a black and white scene. If we do this and are asked what colour we visualised the sky as being, we may say "I didn't visualise it as any particular colour, the whole thing was various shades of grey". The "whole thing" is not the scene but what is best called the image of it, or the mental picture of it.'[1]

However, although Shorter says of his discussion that it 'illustrates a method of answering questions like "Are there mental images?" ',[2] a positive answer does not imply that mental images are objects. (Recall Ryle's claim that 'there are no such objects as mental pictures'.)[3] The results of his investigation are comparative rather than categorical; the implications of 'mental picture' having a use are to be seen by matching the descriptive needs in picturing against those in related activities. Thus we can begin 'by asking why it is we need a word like "picture" to which nothing corresponds in *describing*, and then seeing if there is any similar need in the case of visualising'.[4]

'Describing' serves as a useful starting-point. In the first place, to describe is to *do* something, in a way that seeing is not a doing

---

[1] 'Imagination', p. 541.   [2] Ibid., p. 542.   [3] Ibid., see p. 27 above.
[4] Ibid., p. 540. My emphasis. The procedure is an example of Wittgenstein's 'tea-tasting method', aptly so called by Ryle. 'Tea-tasters do not lump their samples into two or three comprehensive types. Rather they savour each sample and try to place it next door to its closest neighbours. . . . So Wittgenstein would exhibit the characteristic manner of working of a particular expression, by matching it against example after example of expressions pro-pressively diverging from it in various respects and directions.' 'Ludwig Wittgenstein', *Analysis*, XII (1951), p. 7.

but a getting.[1] Secondly, we can describe in more or less detail, vividly or unvividly, accurately and inaccurately, and so on, just as we can picture or visualize in these ways. But thirdly, and more significantly, in the case of describing we have no basis for attributing non-specificity, vagueness, etc., to something to which we may also find it convenient to ascribe physical-object properties, as if it were a thing in its own right. 'Describe' does not demand anything even analogous to a physical object as a necessary condition of the descriptum's being mentioned in an account of describing. Certainly, we talk of a description, as something that we 'give' when we describe, but it is only in special cases, such as when we refer to a picture as a description,[2] that we apply physical-object predicates to the description as opposed to what is described.

Compare this with depicting. Here, too, we have a *doing*; and we can depict in more or less detail, vividly or unvividly, correctly or incorrectly, and so on; but in this case we clearly do have a basis for attributing non-specificity, vagueness, etc. to something to which we may also find it convenient to ascribe physical-object properties as a thing in its own right. There is the physical object we refer to as a picture, and although it is not a *necessary* condition of the descriptum's being mentioned in the account we give of the action of depicting (I can depict something by a gesture in the air), in the typical case it *is* such a necessary condition. The picture is a thing in its own right.

The claim is now that picturing, or visualizing, falls somewhere between describing and depicting. It is not describing plus what differentiates depicting from describing, namely the presence of a picture-thing in its own right; nor is it depicting minus this factor. Where picturing fits can best be seen by why we need to introduce the word 'picture' in the first place, in the case of depicting.

'A statue can have no hand, and this does not mean that it is a statue of a man without a hand. In saying that a statue has no hand we are not thinking of it in its representational aspect, but,

---

[1] 'Imagination', p. 530. [2] Cf. ibid., p. 540.

so to speak, as a thing in its own right. We cannot do this in the case of a description. The case of a picture is rather more complicated. We can speak of a picture as a thing, as when we say that it is brightly coloured, and do not mean it is a picture of something brightly coloured. Also we have phrases like "the man in the picture" where the object is thought of as a man (a picture-man). We may say "this (picture) hand is delicately drawn" or "this (picture) hand has blurred edges" and we do not mean that it is a picture of a hand with blurred edges. A statue may be regarded as a stone man, as well as a statue of a man in stone. For all these reasons we need a word like "picture" or "statue" to which ordinary material object adjectives may be applied.'[1]

The point of introducing the term 'picture' for depicting is to account for needs that arise when we move from one kind of activity, describing, to another, depicting. The justification for introducing the term 'mental image', in Shorter's view, is that similar needs arise in the case of imaging. Thus the introduction of a term into a secondary context is permitted if the new context can generate needs analogous to those which the term serves in the original context. If there is an analogous *need*, there can be an extension of the use of the *term*. The way we describe the new phenomena is therefore governed by the possibility of duplicating in the new domain not the 'logical powers' of the words (as in Ryle) but the empirical 'excuses'[2] for making the distinctions that justify their introduction in the first place.

The excuse for using 'mental picture', then, is that part of the logic of 'picture' has to be invoked to cover our descriptive needs in picturing. Significantly, the part in question is not a consequence of a picture's being a physical object. 'Mental image' has a use even though mental images are not things we can examine, locate, rub out, or store away. But then this looks rather strange when we examine Shorter's argument for denying that we have any use for '*see* a mental image'.

(2) If any kind of imaging were to be analogous to seeing a picture, according to Shorter, it would have to reproduce the

---

[1] 'Imagination', p. 540.　　　　[2] See ibid., p. 541.

conditions that give the word 'see' its point. And he rejects a use for 'see a mental picture' because he takes these conditions to include the possibility of examining what we see. It would be to 'press the analogy [with 'picture'] too far . . . to talk of seeing mental images as though having produced them one could afterwards do something analogous to examining them'.[1] Similarly with 'noticing a feature of X'; for where one can

'. . . notice that the wallpaper is red without noticing what particular shade of red it is . . . [not] only have we got no established use for expressions like "notice a feature of my mental image", but if we did decide to apply it in the situation [of visualizing something as red, but no specific shade of red, e.g. crimson or scarlet] . . . we would still be unable to give criteria establishing what the overlooked feature was like, what the colour really was. But we do have such criteria in the case of the wallpaper, and this is just what gives the word "notice" its point.'

To this extent, therefore, one cannot 'preserve the analogy between images and things';[2] that is, because the conditions of 'noticing' are not satisfied in imaging,[3] and because the conditions of 'thing' (presumably 'physical object') include a thing's having properties that may be noticed or unnoticed, images are not things and they are not seen.

Now the strangeness we referred to is that a sufficient condition

---

[1] 'Imagination', p. 541. It is not clear that the analogy of 'examining' does not fit cases of eidetic imagery (cf. E. R. Jaensch, *Eidetic Imagery* [Kegan Paul, London, 1930]), though if one requires of 'examining an image' that one examine it *after* having *produced* it, the analogy would be inappropriate. In the sense in which one produces eidetic imagery, one is producing it as long as it is there. Cf. Alan Richardson, *Mental Imagery* (Routledge & Kegan Paul, London, 1969), p. 29: 'Jaensch coined the word *eidetic* . . . to describe a form of percept-like imagery differing from after imagery by persisting longer and not requiring a fixed gaze for its formation.' For Flew's criticism of Shorter in this connection see pp. 71f. below.   [2] Ibid., p. 538.
[3] Once again, eidetic imagery might prove an exception. When such imagery is repetitive I may find a use for such expressions as 'It disappeared before I could see everything in it' or 'If it comes back I'll attend to the bottom left corner'. This would depend, of course, on the 'convenience' of talking of two occurrences of imaging as involving the same image.

of 'Is there an image?' or 'Is there a mental picture?' being answered affirmatively is that part of the logic of 'picture' *not* entailed by a picture's being a physical object should apply to imaging, while a *necessary* condition of answering 'Is an image seen?' and 'Is an image an object?' affirmatively is that part of the logic of 'see' and 'object' that *is* entailed by seeing an object's being the seeing of a physical object should apply to imaging. Or to put it in another way: even if we grant that what justifies the use of 'mental image' is that *some* of the logic of 'physical picture' applies to imaging, and that it is precisely because (if it is indeed the case) *nothing* of the logic of 'notice' and 'examine' applies to imaging that it is wrong to say that mental images are objects, why should 'see a mental picture' be denied a use simply on the grounds that imaging does not reproduce conditions which give 'notice' and 'examine' a use? Surely, if 'see' and 'object' are treated equally we should require only that *some* of the logic of 'see a physical object' be applicable to imaging. Or alternatively, if 'see' and (the noun) 'picture' are treated equally, then 'picture', too, must be denied a use in the new domain.

We noted the other anomaly. Shorter says, on the one hand, that the parallel between 'visualize' and 'depict' which makes the latter the correct analogy for the former, is not a complete parallel; but on the other hand, that if there was a complete parallel it would be a combined logical and empirical fact that we saw mental images just as we see real pictures. That is, that the expression ' "see a mental picture" would have a use'[1] if and (it is clearly implied) *only if* the parallel was complete. An interpretation of what Shorter means by a 'complete' parallel shows, however, that this anomaly is only apparent. Rather it is an expression of the same false assumption that leads him to treat 'object', 'see', and 'exist' in one way, and 'picture' in another.

4. THE REQUIREMENT OF A COMPLETE PARALLEL

By a complete parallel it is clear that Shorter cannot mean that the inner world must correspond to the outer in *all* particulars,

[1] 'Imagination', p. 530.

for there are *logical* consequences of a world's being 'inner' that would preclude that, and that would mean that the radical differences demanded by the new uses were unthinkable. For example, whatever basis we might conceivably have for using expressions like 'my image isn't there any more' or 'I can't get my image out of the way', we could never give the component expressions 'there' and 'out of the way' the same force that they have in their primary use. A mental image could never be directly locatable by others, for instance; and I could never tip my mental screen as I can my hand at cards. Thus, and as the very notion of a 'parallel' implies, there must be *some* debit to be placed to the secondary use's account. But in that case how large a debit does Shorter mean it to be before we can no longer accept that a parallel is complete?

A plausible suggestion here might be as follows. By requiring the parallel to be complete before a secondary use is in order, what Shorter means is not that there must be a complete parallel in all particulars, but that there must be some parallel—not necessarily a complete one—in respect of what, in the primary context, gives the expression in question its point. Thus we might say that for 'see a mental picture' to have a use, there would have to be some parallel to the descriptive needs which the expression 'see a picture' is introduced to fulfil in the context of seeing portraits, snapshots, etc. On this interpretation of 'complete parallel' one might even allow that the way in which Shorter sanctions a use for 'mental picture' (or 'mental image') fulfils the requirements of a *complete* parallel; for this sense of 'complete' only requires the descriptive needs to be *somewhat* reproduced in the secondary context. And the reason why '*see* a mental picture' has no use can now be that the descriptive needs of '*see* a picture' are *not* reproduced in that context. In order for the parallel which could sanction the use of the expression 'see a *mental* picture' to be complete, one would have to find analogues of the descriptive needs which each of the component expressions 'see and 'picture' were introduced to fulfil in the primary context.

But although this is a plausible suggestion, and looks like a reasonable criterion for introducing secondary uses of terms, it

merely shifts the oddness of Shorter's conclusion from the requirement itself to his claim that it is not satisfied in the case of the
expression 'see a picture'. For the anomaly now is not that for
'see a mental picture' to have a use there must be a complete
parallel between depicting and visualizing, but that for the requirement of a complete parallel to be satisfied the depicter would have
to be able to do things that it would be natural to describe as,
e.g. standing back from his image, rubbing it out, and turning it
so it faces away from him. Or alternatively, to suppose that for it
to be satisfied, the image would have to *behave* like an ordinary
picture, that there would have to be point to questions like 'Is
that mental picture you produced yesterday still in existence, or
have you rubbed it out?' On this interpretation, then, as I shall
argue, Shorter's error is to suppose that the common experience
of imaging does not satisfy his requirements. But before locating
his mistake, there is one other aspect of his negative thesis to
discuss.

5. A USE FOR 'SEEING IN THE MIND'S EYE'?

Shorter's denial that mental images are seen is necessary for his
negative thesis that imaging is 'not even metaphorical seeing'.
But it is not sufficient. He must also deny that imaging is metaphorically seeing the imagined. To see what this involves we can
begin by considering Flew's criticism of Shorter.

Flew has suggested kinds of occasions where 'see' would be
an appropriate expression for imaging: first, where our imaging
contains 'unwelcome' elements which cannot 'be got rid of at
will'; in such cases, he says, 'the word "see" would be appropriate
and "visualise", "picture", or "depict" would be inappropriate:
precisely in as much and insofar as it does not, whereas the
others do, suggest doing'.[1] And secondly, where the nature of
the achievement involved in some seeing is, on the contrary,
shared by visualizing. To keep a distant object distinct from its

---

[1] Antony Flew, 'Facts and "Imagination"', *Mind*, LXV (1956), No. 259,
p. 395. His example: 'When anyone mentions Clogwyn Du I see Manx Wall in
my mind's eye: and shudder.'

background is similar in difficulty and achievement to some cases of picturing a thing in our mind's eye, as when we continue only with an effort to keep the picture before us, and can say: 'I've got it now, I can see in my mind's eye how it would look.'[1] As an objection to the claim that visualizing is not even metaphorical seeing, Flew notes that the expression 'see in the mind's eye' itself seems 'a clear case of a metaphorical use of a word used literally in "I can see the overhang" '.[2]

Now it is significant that Shorter himself never raises the possibility of using 'see' in 'see X in the mind's eye' or 'see X in a mental picture'. He rejects 'see' as a metaphor for picturing on the grounds that the mental image is not an object, that is because the *image* is not something that can be seen. There seem to be two reasons for this. First, his principal objective is to correct a philosophical assumption that 'seeing' connotes a genus of which seeing material objects and seeing mental pictures are species. This is the assumption that has led philosophers to introduce 'see a mental picture' as a synonym for 'visualize something' in an attempt to 'elucidate what we mean by this phrase'.[3] The task is achieved by pointing out the big differences and only partial similarity in the descriptive roles of the expressions 'picture' and 'mental image'. A picture can be located, scrutinized, overlooked, and so on, but a mental image cannot; it is like drawing a picture. But not to the extent that there is an object we can see as we can see the picture that someone draws. Thus in denying that the analogue of seeing applies, he devotes his efforts to showing how we do not need to incorporate the notion of 'picture' in our account of imaging to the extent of introducing also the idea of something that is seen. To this end his method is perfectly adequate. It is 'to try to talk about visualising in the same sort of language as we talk about depicting and about pictures, and to see how far such a way of talking is possible and useful'.[4]

The method ensures that we do not force upon ourselves unnecessarily questions that only have their point in the context

[1] Antony Flew, 'Facts and "Imagination" ', *Mind*, LXV (1956), No. 259, p. 395.
[2] Ibid., p. 393.   [3] See p. 63 above.   [4] 'Imagination,' p. 532.

of the physical world. It shows that whatever excuse image-experience provides for the use of the term 'mental image', that excuse does not bring with it others corresponding to needs that only arise in the case of *physical* images.

The second reason why Shorter ignores the claims of 'see in the mind's eye' to be a legitimate metaphorical use of 'see' is that he can reject them on principle. It is not a lacuna, nor I think a damaging limitation, in Shorter's account that he apparently confines it to cases obviously favourable to the analogy of 'depict'. Even in mentioning cases where the activity implied by 'depict' has either little or no place at all, such as hallucinatory 'seeing', cinema 'seeing' and the mirage 'seeing' of oases, in which the term 'see' fits because the experiences are very like really seeing, and the disclaiming commas are in order precisely because they are not really seeing, Shorter says they are cases of *thinking* that one sees something when one does not.[1] The presumption is that even here he would deny that there was anything *logically* like seeing. So, although he does not say so explicitly, he apparently argues that even if imaging is often visually like seeing and may at times be mistaken for it, this in itself is no indication of the extent of the logical parallel between seeing and imaging. That, according to the method, is to be found out by seeing how far it is possible to *talk* in the same way about seeing something and about having an image of it.

Now it is clear that although there are many types of utterance (e.g. 'I can see it now', 'That's Peter', 'It's green all over', 'I've got it now') that can occur in both contexts, the force or 'point' of the term 'see', 'that', and 'it' is lost if the contexts are taken as parallel. Before one can understand the significance of the expressions when they are used in the context of imaging one has to be aware that the context is of this kind. But this is not the case with expressions like 'I am depicting' and 'I am picturing'. Here the implication that the visual experience is a product of *mine* is a part of the point, and therefore of the grammar or logic, of the expressions themselves. That the visual experience is shareable, or an experience of the same piece of public space, on the other

[1] 'Imagination', p. 532.

73

hand, is part of the grammar or logic of only a limited range of such expressions, notably 'depict', 'portray', 'draw', and 'sketch'. Consequently, in so far as depicting, visualizing, and imaging in general are, like describing, all things that a person *does*, though not always in the same sense of 'does', there is a parallel between them. And this is a fact wholly independent of the extent of any purely visual correspondence between imaging and seeing. In this respect, therefore, 'see' in '*see X* in a mental picture' (where 'see' is used as a synonym for 'perceive') lacks any parallel with 'see *X*', while 'imaging' has some parallel with 'depicting'.

Shorter's point here would be Ryle's.

'The fact that in certain conditions [a person] fails to realise that he is not seeing, but only "seeing", as in dreams, delirium, extreme thirst, hypnosis and conjuring-shows, does not in any degree tend to obliterate the distinction between the concept of seeing and that of "seeing", any more than the fact that it is often difficult to tell an authentic from a forged signature tends to obliterate the distinction between the concept of a person signing his own name and that of someone else forging it.'[1]

Its significance is that in respect of what gives the term 'see', as a synonym of 'perceive', its point there is no parallel at all between 'seeing' and 'imaging'. Which, provided one confines oneself to this use of 'see', is a sufficient reason for saying that imaging is never even metaphorical seeing.

If Shorter accepts this argument, incidentally, a consequence of his view will be that one more level must be added to his hierarchy of 'excuses'. For the conditions that allow us to say that we saw something in the mind's eye would require either that we perceive things by visualizing them or that the term 'perceive' cease to have its point, that is that seeing no longer be a way of experiencing a piece of public space. And while the conditions that would allow us to say that we saw a mental image could, as Shorter acknowledges, conceivably be satisfied, it would certainly be much more difficult to satisfy these other conditions, if they can be thought to be satisfiable at all.

[1] *Concept of Mind*, p. 246.

6. CONSISTENCY AND ERROR IN SHORTER'S ACCOUNT

Shorter's strictures on 'seeing something in the mind's eye' are amply justified, I believe, on the grammatical grounds we have attributed to him. To say that seeing Helvellyn in the mind's eye was an approximation to *perceiving* would be tantamount to ignoring the logical difference between genuine and fake, between being a spectator and only a 'spectator'. If a visual experience is due to our agency alone, then it *is* a kind of forgery. It only *resembles* a perceptual experience. On the other hand, there would be nothing against introducing the word 'see' in another sense to refer to these resemblings or resemblances of perceptions. A counterfeit signature has in common with a genuine one that it is a written name, and we *could* call it a signature. Similarly an imagined sight has in common with a genuine one that it is a visual experience, and we *might* call it seeing. Shorter gives no indication that he would accept such a use, though in adopting the expression 'see in the mind's eye' as a manner of speaking, he would in any case be accepting it in practice. But he would then, as Flew suggests, be committed to accepting that imaging was metaphorical seeing; to see something in the mind's eye would be a genuine way of seeing, though not any way of perceiving.

However, the same does not apply to 'see a mental image'. If Shorter gave any sense or use to this expression, he would indeed be forced to retract his denial that imaging is metaphorical seeing. For the image must be regarded as part of, perhaps identical with, the visual experience itself. The visualizer would be a genuine spectator of his image, not a 'spectator' of it; visualizing would be parallel to seeing real pictures, and the image itself parallel to the real picture. And since it is, we now assume, the presence of a parallel that justifies an analogy and thus the introduction of a metaphor, it would follow from imaging being or involving the seeing of an image, that it *was* metaphorical seeing—as well as metaphorical depicting. Shorter's strictures on 'see a mental image' are therefore essential to his thesis. Are *they* justified?

His argument is that imaging does not in fact reproduce conditions that give point to questions like 'Is that mental picture you produced yesterday still in existence?' or 'Where is it?' To talk of mental pictures our imaging experiences would have to be such that 'when we visualised anything the image stayed put until we visualised it being rubbed out', which it clearly is not.

One might argue that this fact weighed as much against the analogy of 'depict' as it did against that of 'see a picture', since it is only in real depicting that pictures stay put, can be there since yesterday, and have been taken away. But 'depict' survives because it is a *doing*. Our question is whether 'see a picture' can survive only if mental pictures behave like real ones.

The answer surely is no. Shorter assumes that the logical parallel must be generated in the terms with which the visualizer describes his own performance. That is to say, he thinks it is sufficient to dispel the idea that visualizing parallels seeing a picture that no such parallel is revealed in an analysis of what we *mean* by 'visualize'. This is a fallacy, though one that is common enough in the recent literature on imaging. Because the *sense* of 'visualize' cannot be captured in expressions like 'see a picture', or 'produce a picture', let alone, in Ryle's parody, 'regarding [and even less *producing*] a variously illuminated sheet of "mental" linen',[1] it is argued that such expressions have no place in the analysis of imaging. Shorter's own adherence to this belief is evidenced in his easy assumption that everyone else must hold it too. He alleges that philosophers have sought to introduce 'see a mental picture' as a *synonym* for 'visualize something' in an attempt , as he says, 'to elucidate what we mean by this phrase'.[2] But surely what *some* of them have been trying to do by using such expressions is to convey not what someone ascribing the mental predicate 'visualizes' wishes to say, but what facts he is committed to if what he says is true.

We can now see the initial disparity between Shorter's excuses for 'mental image' and 'see a mental image' as an instance of the same mistake. He assumes the expression 'mental image' has a use only because the *visualizer* needs to talk of what he does in a way that does not refer to what he visualizes. We saw that he regards

---

[1] *Concept of Mind*, p. 255.   [2] 'Imagination', p. 530. See p. 63 above.

his discussion as illustrating a way of answering questions like 'Are there mental images?' Undeniably it throws much light on the notion of a mental image, and this light would be obscured rather than transmitted were the answer given in the unqualified categorical pronouncement 'Mental images exist'. This would sound as if mental and physical pictures belonged to the same ontological club. Shorter's matching method therefore ensures that a need to refer to mental images is not taken to mean that 'Mental images exist' has the same logic as 'Physical images exist'. The most informative and so least misleading answer to the question 'Are there mental images?' is not that there are, but rather what an image is. Shorter's own apposite answer to it is that it is 'a sort of half-way house between pictures and descriptions'.[1]

But it is just as misleading to say that mental images are not objects as it is to say that they are. Shorter assumes that because picturing falls between describing and depicting he has shown how the expression 'mental image' lacks full designating force. Because, like descriptions though in less degree, mental images lack some of the determinations of physical pictures he seems to think he can assign them to an ontological twilight zone half-way between pictures and descriptions. But here Shorter is twice wrong. First, he is wrong to suppose that the determinations that an image does have in common with a picture are to be found in the vocabulary that the visualizer himself calls on. In that case if our visualizing was never blurred, or we never had occasion to refer to the 'whole thing', there would be no need to call on the logic of pictures at all. Provided we were adept imagers and did not stop to appraise our performances there would presumably be no mental images—just as if we never visualized at all—unless 'mental image' could somehow refer to the permanent possibility of the need to call on the logic of 'picture'. Secondly, he wrongly supposes that the logic of 'picture' exhausts the possibilities, that the *only* determinations the image may have are those of the picture. It is as though the image must aspire to picturehood, but that if it failed altogether in its attempt it would have nothing

[1] 'Imagination', p. 542.

77

of its own to fall back on. It must cleave to the picture or perish. But clearly there *are* questions to ask of the image, or even of the blur, which we would not expect to be answered in the way appropriate to questions about physical representations. For example, although it is inappropriate to ask 'Where does the image of Helvellyn go when I am no longer picturing Helvellyn?', as if the case were similar to that of objects that come and go before our field of vision, there is surely still a question of where the image is when I do picture Helvellyn. To say, for example, that it is where it seems to be—if in fact it does seem to be anywhere—is not sufficient, and misleading. Imaging, one might say, discloses a new problem, namely that of explaining the real relation of an image to the things about which it *is* proper to ask questions like 'Where from?' and 'How many inches from my nose?'

7. THE POSITIVE CLAIM AND THE FORCE OF THE ANALOGY OF DEPICTING

So far we have said little of Shorter's positive claim, that the analogue of visualizing or picturing is depicting. This is partly because Shorter's own stress is on the negative side of his thesis. But the positive claim, too, needs defending, as the objections of Flew show. Flew claimed, we recall, that in some cases 'the word "see" would be appropriate and "visualise", "picture", or "depict" . . . inappropriate . . . precisely in as much and insofar as it does not, whereas the others do, suggest doing'.[1]

Now we argued on Shorter's behalf that such cases would go nowhere towards disconfirming his claim that imaging is 'not even metaphorical seeing', taking 'seeing' here to be a synonym of 'perceive'. For however much seeming to perceive resembles really perceiving, it cannot in any degree approximate to it; we cannot do in imagination what the word 'perceive' was introduced to describe. Thus, we said, if 'see' is to be applicable in the cases Flew mentions, it must be in another sense, and then not a metaphorical sense. But of course his objection still

[1] See p. 71 above.

78

holds with regard to the positive claim, since the very appropriateness of such a usage must call in question the appropriateness of describing imaging as a kind of doing. If we take the extreme case of dreaming, for example, what 'excuse' have we here for saying that our imaging is something we do? Surely only that it somehow originates with us; it is *ours* because it is nobody else's and it is a *doing* because it is not perceiving. In fact this kind of case, as well as others, might indicate that an adequate analogy for imaging would have to be depicting in a sense in which it was not specified that the imager *himself* is also the depicter. Picturing and visualizing would come close to depicting in the normal sense, but other instances would come closer to seeing things depicted, as when a picture is presented to us or made for us. And note here that we could say that in approximating to seeing things depicted, these latter instances could quite legitimately be characterized as 'metaphorically seeing things depicted', since the sense of the primary expression 'see something depicted' is not that of 'perceive something depicted' (what is depicted is *ipso facto* not perceived), and it is at last unclear that to see something depicted entails that one perceives something else which depicts it.

But depicting may be a better analogy than these objections suggest. 'Depicting' denotes neither one clearly demarked kind of activity nor a range of activities that are all clearly distinguished, or understood. One of the more interesting aspects of its variety and unclarity is precisely that in which the notion of 'action' or 'activity' can be applied to depicting. We tend primarily to think of simple cases of drawing objects we have seen, and of depicting as essentially similar to describing in that the content of a picture, as of a description, is no more, and usually less, than what we mean—have had in mind—to include in it. But there may be reason to believe that the activity of drawing something can have a function quite different from that of describing it. In his illuminating discussion on drawing an object Wollheim has indicated how drawing may have a revelatory or self-revelatory function. He points to two factors underlying this possibility: first, the empirical basis for a sense of knowing something in which we can come to realize what we know,[1] and secondly, an important distinction concealed in the expression 'what we have seen' between 'what *thing* we have seen' and 'how we saw whatever it was or what it looked like to us'.[2]

The sense of knowing here (which Wollheim calls dispositional) covers any case in which we can come to realize, for example, what we have been wanting without fully realizing it. 'We can', says Wollheim, 'be conscious to widely differing degrees of what knowledge [in the dispositional sense] we possess. So that for instance, when some dispositional form of knowledge about what we have done or felt or experienced becomes actualized, the shock or surprise can be so great for us that it seems perfectly appropriate for us to describe the situation as one in which we *come to know* such-and-such a fact about ourselves. . . .'[3] He mentions such cases of discovery as 'that we wished someone dead, that we desired a certain person, that we helped only in order to dominate'. Applying this to visual experience, Wollheim accepts that the representation we make of something can be the 'criterion of the visual experience'[4] which it is an attempt to reproduce.[5] Thus, by drawing something we can come to realize how we saw it, how it looked to us, and in this sense 'what we have seen'. That is, the criterion of what we saw can be how we have represented what we, in some degree, did not fully realize that we saw.

If Wollheim is right then the content of a drawing can be to some extent unpremeditated, though not necessarily at the same time unfamiliar or even unexpected. Seen in this light, then, drawing something and describing it are significantly dissimilar activities, at least where the description is of what the describer actually sees. For the describer here is no more than a recorder, whereas the person drawing what he no longer sees may be activating his knowledge of how it seemed to him. One might

---

[1] Richard Wollheim, *On Drawing an Object*, Inaugural Lecture, University College, London 1964, p. 10.

[2] Ibid., p. 5. [3] Ibid., p. 10. Wollheim's emphasis.

[4] Cf. Ludwig Wittgenstein, *Philosophical Investigations* (Blackwell, Oxford 1958), p. 198.

[5] *On Drawing an Object*, p. 14.

even be led to consider ordinary cases of drawing something in the light of more complex and specialized cases, for example the alleged process of what analytical psychologists call 'active imagination'.[1] By this they mean a supposed means of 'creative integration' of the personality. The method includes both drawing and imaging, and is said to operate through the patient's own concentration on an emotionally significant theme. He deliberately provokes an 'image development',[2] over which he exercises no direct control.

The interest of such specialized cases in the present instance is, in the first place, that they might in principle provide some basis for extending the notion of 'what a person does' to cover even things that, in the very nature of the case, would not normally be attributed to a person as an action of *his* but of some alien part of his as yet unintegrated personality. They could give a theoretical justification for treating image-contents *in general* as products of the imager's activity—of his doings rather than his sufferings.

This would take some of the disjunctive force out of objections like Flew's. We would be less inclined to say that the more our imaging resembled seeing, the less it could be characterized as any kind of doing of ours. More will be said of this later. Secondly, these contexts stress a feature of the activity of imaging about which Shorter says nothing, but which differentiates this activity from that of describing, or of stating or reporting. For granted that there is always a description under which we intend to visualize something, if we allow a dispositional sense of visual knowledge, then we can, without undue strain, talk of the intention to visualize something under a certain description in anticipation of the realization of how we saw it. Taking the realization here to cover something more general than what is suggested by the phrase 'how we saw it', we might talk, with even less strain, of the intention to visualize something in anticipation of the realization of our visual knowledge of that

---

[1] See Gerhard Adler, *Studies in Analytical Psychology* (Routledge & Kegan Paul, London 1948), pp. 45 ff.

[2] Ibid., p. 48.

thing. This account seems an apt one even for typically 'active' imagings like those Shorter discusses. It is apt if it is correct to say for at least some property F, that our picturing X as instantiating F is not a mere translating into pictorial form of our conscious verbal knowledge that XF; that is that rather than informing our contention to picture X, whatever knowledge we have that XF unfolds or realizes itself in the actual picturing of X. This sounds like a correct account, particularly if we reflect that any knowledge *that* XF where 'F' designates some visual property, such as 'blue-eyed' or 'beetle-browed', implies the possibility of knowledge of *how* X (as opposed to Y, etc.) instantiates F. Since this latter knowledge is essential to recognition of particulars, it is also essential to picturing a particular individual among all those that, perhaps to one's knowledge, instantiate F; and because this is knowledge that does typically enter into one's purely verbal or pre-visual considerations of X, one may reasonably conclude that when we picture something to ourselves we are to some extent *realizing* our knowledge of that thing, not *using* that knowledge in the way that we are when we describe what we presently see.

These considerations invite us to raise, gingerly, and for the first time, a question of the 'nature' of imagination. Let us do this by recalling Berkeley's remark that it was 'no more than willing' and 'straightway' this or that idea arose in his fancy.[1] It is a perfectly apt remark; we *can* picture things—at least some things—more or less at will. But our discussion above should make us wonder whether this observation picks out a feature that is at all genuinely characteristic of imaging. In the first place, of course, many imagings do not originate in acts of will, but are triggered or induced by a chance remark or an unpredictable turn in a train of thought. The most we can say about willing in this kind of case is that since we are nevertheless in some sense acquiescing in the succession of images we can be said to be imagining what we imagine *willingly*; that is to say, the stream of our ideas is at least not running counter to our wishes. But then secondly, there are other kinds of undeliberate imaging in which

[1] See p. 20 above.

it would be absurd to say that we were willingly imagining what we imagined. The hallucinator, for example, must surely often wish that his snakes and elephants would disappear; what he wills to do is *not* to imagine what he imagines. But now thirdly, it looks as though even where we would be most inclined to accept that a case of imaging originates in an act of will, the outcome of this act, the visual presentation of the topic, is not something of which the imager can be regarded as the fully conscious author— in a sense in which he *is* the fully conscious author both of the fact that he is imaging and of the fact that the visual presentation of his image has the topic that it does have.

One might suspect, then, that it is unilluminating to link 'imagination' with 'will'. And Shorter seems to be entertaining this sort of suspicion when he correctly criticizes Ryle for failing 'to make any distinction between the various senses of the word "see" when it is used with inverted commas'.[1] Shorter himself denies that all cases of 'seeing', such as 'seeing' the posse ride out of town in the Odeon, are *imagining*, while with regard to those that are he observes that 'the concept of imagining is to be illuminated by distinguishing visualising or picturing from [say] the sort of imagining that a drunkard does, not by identifying the two'.[2]

How illuminated? According to Shorter, among other ways the following: first, 'to visualise is to *do* something, whereas to "see" snakes is not to do something';[3] secondly, 'seeing' snakes, in hallucination, is not, as visualizing is, seeing anything in the mind's eye; it is 'making a mistake about whether I see or whether I do not see';[4] and thirdly, visualizing, *unlike* the kind of case *where the term 'imagine' naturally fits*, need contain 'no element of pretence or deception';[5] it can simply be doing something, for example solving a simple problem in geometry, 'in the head' rather than with pencil on paper or finger in air.

Now this indeed casts light where Ryle casts none. But the illumination is still very patchy. Consider the first point. Visualizing is a doing, but 'seeing' snakes is not. Why? Because it can

---

[1] 'Imagination', p. 529.   [2] Ibid., p. 529.   [3] Ibid., p. 536.
[4] Ibid., p. 532.   [5] Ibid., p. 533.

be done deliberately.[1] We cannot be deluded or mistaken on request. But now the second point. The word 'imagine' comes into its own *where there is a tendency to be mistaken, or to pretend*. Thus in pretending to see a boat I may well visualize a boat, but at least in simply visualizing it I am not *imagining that* I see it. However, I can begin so 'to enter into the spirit of the thing, I may almost take myself in'.[2] The pretence is entered into deliberately, just as the visualizing; but what about the *imagining*? In a sense it is deliberate, if it is what I thought to do. But is my entering into the spirit of the thing itself deliberate? Of course, I may deliberately do various things to make it easier to make-believe, like turning the lights low, removing obtrusively fancy-resistant objects from view, and so on. But this is not my actually submitting to the fantasy. If that was deliberate, then as I proceeded step by step into the spirit of the thing, it should be as easy to snap out of it as it is to change programmes on the radio. But as Shorter himself says, it may be 'hard to return from the world of fancy to that of reality'.[3] The world of fancy exerts some kind of pull, even though it is my own world of fancy. But then if Shorter is right to associate imagining with mistakenness, surely what he should be illuminating is not the doing that is exciting an image, but rather the doing (if a doing) that consists in the image, attracting, even exciting me. In fact Shorter says absolutely nothing about *imagination*, only that one sample of it, drunken imagining, involves no doing. And since, according to the third point, all he says of this sample is that it involves no seeing either, he tells us no more positively about imagining than Ryle does about visualizing.

As for this third point itself. Here again the light is only partial. It is true that the drunkard does not see things in his mind's eye in the sense that the visualizer does; he sees them all too plainly in front of him. But if the hallucinator 'only' thinks he sees something, then there is something he certainly sees though not in the sense of 'see' that he thinks. He sees it in a genuine sense of 'see', but not the genuine sense in which he thinks he sees it. But to do that, as I shall argue, later, he must also

---

[1] 'Imagination', p. 532.   [2] Ibid., p. 533.   [3] Ibid., p. 533.

be seeing something else in a sense corresponding to the sense in which he thinks he sees. In that sense there is still something in his mind's eye, though perhaps 'in the mind's eye' is not the idiomatic expression here, suggesting that in 'the mind's eye' is where the drunkard himself would locate the things he saw when he was 'seeing' them.

IV

SARTRE'S ILLUSION OF TRANSCENDENCE

I. IMAGING AND DOING

We saw that Ryle said nothing of the imaging *experience* except that it is a way of not seeing. We also saw that he could provide nothing for imaging, even of the most deliberate kind, to be a *way* of not seeing. Now although Shorter allows the deliberate kind of imaging we call 'visualizing' to be a 'doing', he still hasn't said anything about the doing, if doing, that is *imagining*—in his 'natural' sense—and which, in saying only that visualizing *need* not contain any element of pretence or deception, he grants may also enter into visualizing. Nor has he told us how to describe the drunkard's, or any other imager's, experience.

It is not the least of the merits of Sartre's account of imaging that it offers both a description of the experience and an explanation of how it might be proper to describe imagining, in Shorter's sense, as a kind of doing. Further, the explanation it gives, if true, would also explain how this kind of experiencing and doing can be regarded as an action of the visualizer's when that kind of doing does—as Sartre claims that to some extent it always does—enter into visualizing.

There are certain features of Sartre's account that we shall return to later. Here, however, we focus on his argument for denying that mental images are objects, an argument which, unlike those of Ryle and Shorter, is at the same time straightforwardly an argument for a certain view of the over-all nature of mental activity. Because a principal demerit of Sartre's discussion is that it lacks the relative preciseness and organization of the more analytical approaches we have examined so far, I shall devote some space to an interpretation and defence of Sartre's arguments and claims.

2. DIFFICULTIES OF INTERPRETATION

(1) Sartre's point that mental images are not objects can be expressed by saying that if they were we would have to make an unjustified claim about how imagining and perceiving are distinguished. But there are two distinct ways in which we have to understand Sartre's claim if we are to catch the full force of his denial that mental images are objects.

The first way of understanding it is as an argument against the 'immanentism' of philosophers like Berkeley and Hume who distinguish perception from imagination in terms of properties contingently belonging to elements common to both—traditionally 'ideas'. Berkeley is a good example. For him ideas of imagination (mental images) are a species of the same genus as ideas of perception, since in each case their *esse* is *percipi*. They are distinguished, first by being less 'strong, lively, and distinct'[1] than ideas of perception, and secondly by the manner of their production: ideas of imagination are entirely dependent on the will[2] and are 'excited at random',[3] or 'at pleasure';[4] they are 'formed by help of memory and imagination',[5] and are 'of our own framing'.[6] We should note, however, that for Berkeley being willed is not itself a sufficient condition of an idea's being an idea of imagination, since he holds that ideas of perception, or sense, are also due to an active agency, they are imprinted on my senses by God.[7] But in any case the immanentism of Berkeley emerges clearly when he says that ideas of the latter kind are what we know as 'real things', while the ideas that I myself activate should 'more properly be termed *ideas or images* of things, which they copy or represent'.[8]

---

[1] *Principles*, ibid., p. 72. Berkeley also distinguishes ideas of imagination as being 'less regular . . . and constant' and as less 'orderly and coherent' than ideas of perception. (Ibid., p. 73.) See Roger Woolhouse's discussion of Berkeley's criteria for distinguishing the imaginary from the real in 'Berkeley, the Sun that I See by Day, and That Which I Imagine by Night', *Philosophy*, XLIII (1968), No. 164, pp. 152–60.

[2] *Dialogues*, op. cit., p. 197.   [3] *Principles*, ibid., p. 72.   [4] Ibid., p. 72.

[5] Ibid., p. 61.   [6] Ibid., p. 74. Cf. Commentaries, ibid., p. 365, Entry 823.

[7] Ibid., p. 72. Cf. also *Dialogues*, ibid., p. 197.

[8] Ibid., p. 73, Berkeley's emphasis.

Now why should the rejection of this kind of view lead one to deny that mental images are objects? The answer is surely that if one rejects the view that all the mind directly apprehends in perception is at best an intermediary world of mental, therefore private objects, and replaces it with the view that the mind directly apprehends a world of common objects, then one has licensed a domain of paradigmatic objects of perception—paradigmatic because the objects of the public world are truly distinct from the mind; that is, they are objects *par excellence*. Since it is these objects that one perceives and, by the same token, when imagining imagines, the mental image itself inevitably loses some of its standing as an object. Not only is it no longer the best kind of object available in sensory intuition, it is not even the kind of thing we imagine.

But does the mental image thereby lose all its standing as an object? The special significance of the denial that mental images are objects for Sartre is that they cannot even be degenerate objects. This is a consequence of his view of the nature of the radical opposition of mind and object. To understand the implication we must see what else Sartre means when he says that to regard mental images as objects would be to misconstrue the distinction between imaging and perceiving.

We can best approach this by asking how one can distinguish imaging from perceiving if imaging is sometimes indistinguishable from perceiving, as one might plausibly claim it was, for example in dreams and hallucinations. The answer we extract from accounts like those of Ryle and Shorter is that even here the distinction is obviously preserved. In terms of the logic or grammar of 'perceive', what one perceives must in principle be perceptible by others, seen only partially by any one person, have been noticed, not overlooked, and so on. Since this is not true of what one only imagines, the fact that one believes one is seeing when one is not is of no consequence. For Sartre, however, it would be of the utmost consequence. His distinction between perceiving and imaging is phenomenological, not conceptual or logical; that is to say, it is a distinction to be made exclusively in terms of features available to reflection upon the content of the perceiver's or imager's own consciousness. There are three options open to Sartre. Either the phenomenological criteria for distinguishing imaging from perceiving are not adequate for all cases covered by the ordinary uses of the corresponding terms, and must be supplemented accordingly with non-phenomenological criteria; or the phenomenological criteria are adequate because he does not intend the phenomenological distinction to be extensionally equivalent with the ordinary one—what *seems* to be perception *is* perception from the mind's point of view; or, thirdly, the phenomenological criteria are adequate and the phenomenological distinction is extensionally equivalent with the ordinary one.

The first option must be rejected precisely because it admits the possibility of an image being, from the mind's point of view, an object. An object for Sartre is that to which consciousness is directed, in Brentano's sense,[1] that is in so far as consciousness is always consciousness *of* something, whether or not there is such an object as consciousness intends. Now although from the phenomenological viewpoint an object is by definition, as what is intended, outside consciousness, that is, in Husserl's term, 'transcendent',[2] there is something immanent *that* consciousness intends as such an object, namely an experience of an object—roughly, and in a sense to be explicated more fully below, a felt passivity in the face of something external. And from the phenomenological point of view there is nothing more to there being an object than this experience together with the 'thetic' act of intending the experience as one of an object.[3]

---

[1] See Franz Brentano, *Psychologie vom empirischen Standpunkt*, Vol. I, Bk. 2, Ch. 1, Engl. trans. of the chapter by D. B. Terrell in Roderick M. Chisholm (ed.), *Realism and the Background of Phenomenology* (Free Press, Glencoe, Ill., 1960), p. 50; cf. Dagfinn Føllesdal, 'Husserl's Notion of Noema', *Journal of Philosophy*, LXVI (1969), No. 20.

[2] Edmund Husserl, *Ideen zu einer reinen Phänomenologie und phänomenologischen Philosophie* (Martinus Nijhoff, The Hague, 1950 edn), I, pp. 100 and 238 ff.; cf. J.–P. Sartre *L'Imagination* (P.U.F., Paris, 1956 1st edn, 1936), p. 144, and Føllesdal, op. cit., p. 686.

[3] Acts of intending an object have different 'thetic' characters in so far as they are, for example, acts of memory, imagination, or perception. Thus, acts of different thetic character can intend the same object. Cf. Føllesdal, op. cit., pp. 682 and 683. My formulation 'the experience together with the thetic act of

But if, as the first option hypothesizes, it is possible for the same experience, together with the thetic act which makes it an experience of a transcendent object, to be reproduced in imagination when (as should in any case always be possible from the phenomenological viewpoint) in fact there is no such object, then what one experiences must be construed in extensional terms on the one hand as an image, and in phenomenological terms on the other as an object. It is an image because although the experience, by virtue of the thetic character of the act involved in it, is an experience of a transcendent object, it is not an experience of a real object; and it is nevertheless an object because, in terms of what an object is for the mind, there is nothing more that the experience of an object can be. So even if Sartre has disposed of the immanentism of 'ideas' by making transcendent objects available for perception, the present option would not enable him to rule out the possibility of immanent replicas of *these* objects.

The same argument applies to the second option, except that here it must be rephrased to account for the possibility, envisioned by this alternative, of the non-existence of what is perceived. But quite apart from this, it will in any case become clear that Sartre himself would not envision this possibility, and that he means his analysis to account for what we normally refer to and distinguish by means of the terms 'perceive' and 'imagine'.

Sartre therefore must, and does, accept the third option. He accepts it by allowing that the mind must always be aware of its imaging as such, where 'imaging' is used in the normal way. And it is because of the basis of the mind's awareness of this, Sartre argues, that even the most object-like image will not be grasped as an object, that is, as something outside consciousness. Consequently there will be nothing object-like, not even the illusion of an object, that ever enters *into* consciousness. Since the very same argument applies *a fortiori* to the more usual cases of imaging where there is no tendency to be mistaken, that is, no tendency for one's thetic acts to be misdirected, we may assume that it is indeed this argument, rather than the provision

intending it as one of an object' suggests the latter can be added to the former. But Sartre rejects this idea. See p. 100 below.

of transcendent objects, that captures the force of Sartre's claim that mental images in general are not objects.

Having identified the argument, and before we examine it in more detail, there are some further interpretational problems to resolve in connection with its premisses.

(2) First we must consider the assumption that what it is for a mind to be related to an object is to be explicated exclusively in terms of the contents of consciousness. A difficulty here might seem to relate to the determination of the concept of an object. According to this assumption, what we mean by an object can only be determined by reflective analysis of consciousness, that is, by whatever is actually disclosed to consciousness. But if consciousness is aware of all and only those properties that an object appears to have, the distinction between an object, on the one hand, as something transcendent, and therefore as having more determinations than those of its determinate appearance, and an image, on the other, as allegedly having only those of its determinate appearance, is impossible. Simply to say that consciousness *intends* whatever it takes to be an object as having more properties than it appears to have would be no solution, for without any basis in the experience itself for distinguishing objects from images the intending would be merely arbitrary and therefore inadequate as a criterion.

However, Sartre, following Husserl, avoids this difficulty by allowing that objects present themselves *as* transcendent, that is as capable of further determinations than those given in experience.[1] He accepts that, as C. M. Myers has put it, a physical object

'. . . is apprehended incompletely but is not apprehended as incomplete . . . If anything is to appear to be a physical object it must appear to have undisclosed properties. An exhaustive list of the properties specifically disclosed in a physical object experience is not an exhaustive list of everything disclosed by the experience.'[2]

---

[1] *L'Imaginaire*, pp. 20–2, 27, and 156 f.
[2] C. M. Myers, 'Determinate and Determinable Modes of Appearing', *Mind*, LXVIII (1958), No. 265, pp. 34–5. Cf. J. N. Mohanty, 'Edmund Husserl's

If one of the properties of which consciousness can be aware is that there are further properties than those disclosed, the distinction between objects and images will be possible. But a difficulty remains; for it is no good consciousness knowing that what it intends is an object unless what it intends as an object (sees as having more determinations than it appears to have) is in fact an object (does have more than it appears to have). If 'object' in Sartre's account is to have the same denotation as 'physical object' or 'object in the external world' in the ordinary senses of these terms, and is at the same time to have no content other than that derived from the description of *experiences* of objects, there will have to be some guarantee that whenever something is seen as capable of further determinations, what is seen does in fact have that property. Otherwise 'object' could refer to other things than objects in the world. Now clearly there is no *logical* guarantee. It is not contradictory to say that X is seen as capable of further determinations but it may not be so in fact. Nor does Sartre claim that it is. But what else will enable him to assume that what he refers to as an object is something that is indeed capable of further determinations?

There is, so far as I can see, no satisfactory answer to this. Sartre, like Husserl, seems simply to assume that what is in fact capable of further determination presents itself as such in experience. Sartre, indeed, goes further than Husserl and assumes that *only* what is in fact capable of further determinations appears as such (though not, it is important to note, that whenever a physical object is sensibly before us [as opposed to being intended as such] we must see it as such). As we have seen, this latter assumption, that we can never mistake for an object what is not an object, is not simply a rider to Sartre's conclusion that images are not objects, but is part of his argument for the conclusion.

(3) Let us now consider a further assumption of Sartre's argument; namely that there is a sense in which the mind is always aware of its own content. Sartre expresses his own version of this Cartesian view by saying: 'The great ontological law of

Theory of Meaning', *Phaenomenologica*, Vol. 14 (Martinus Nijhoff, The Hague, 1964), pp. 140 ff.

consciousness is this: the only way in which consciousness can exist is for it to be conscious of its own existence.'[1] Now, the view that consciousness is always self-consciousness might be thought to exclude, gratuitously, from the field of consciousness such common instances of human behaviour as rushing to catch a bus, trying to head a ball into goal, reading an exciting novel, or 'losing oneself' in the sounds of an orchestra. And indeed what we have in such cases is not, according to Sartre, a consciousness *of* self.

'When I run after a streetcar, when I look at the time, when I am absorbed in contemplating a portrait, there is no *I*. There is consciousness *of the streetcar-having-to-be-overtaken*, etc . . .'[2]

In such cases I am

' . . . plunged into the world of objects; it is they which constitute the unity of my consciousness; it is they which present themselves with values, with attractive and repellent qualities— but *me*, I have disappeared.'[3]

But however other-directed one's activity may be, for Sartre there is always a sense in which one's consciousness is conscious of itself.

This is Sartre's explanation (or way of describing) the fact that to be conscious of, say, a book, or of a series of events narrated in the book, cannot be a relationship of something, the mind, to the book or the events as narrated, without also being a relationship of that thing to itself. When one reads a book, however absorbed one is in the story, the fact that one is reading a book is not something that one discovers about oneself by any kind of recognition, inference or judgment. One *knows* that that is what one is doing although one is not conscious of *oneself* in the act of doing it, that is to say, of the doing of it as a relation-

---

[1] *L'Imagination*, p. 126. Translations from this work are my own.

[2] *The Transcendence of the Ego*, trans. of 'La Transcendance de l'Ego: Esquisse d'une description phénoménologique', *Recherches Philosophiques*, Vol. VI, 1936–7, by Forrest Williams and Robert Kirkpatrick (Noonday Press, New York, 1957), p. 49.

[3] Ibid., p. 49.

ship between oneself and the book. Unless there was this 'non-positional'[1] consciousness of itself accompanying all consciousness we would have to *infer* that what we had just been doing unreflectively was what we had just been doing; by, as it were, catching ourselves *at* reading, which we clearly do not have to do. That this non-positional consciousness amounts to *self*-consciousness is because, in Sartre's view, the self is nothing other than the subjective correlate of an intentional act—that is, that which *is* conscious of something. The self does not disappear in unreflected activity, like an occulting light, to reappear in consciousness addressed to the self; if I disappear it is only because, as Sartre says, '*I* have annihilated myself'.[2] It is not by a momentary lapse of attention that my self disappears, but because *I* cease to be the *objective* correlate of my acts of consciousness.

We said that unless we were aware of what we were doing when we were absorbed in some other-directed activity, the only way we could come to know what that activity had been would be by recognition or inference, by catching ourselves in the act, or by putting two and two together. That we do not have to do this is fairly obvious in the kinds of cases mentioned so far. And it is in so far as we do not have to infer what we have been doing in such cases that we hesitate to say we did not know what we were doing at the same time. Simply because to do so would misleadingly suggest that all we have at the time, when engaged in such activities, is the basis for *future* knowledge.

But compare these cases with those we mentioned in the preceding chapter, and with Wollheim's observation that 'we can be conscious to widely differing degrees of what knowledge we possess', for instance, of whether we wished someone dead, whether we desired someone, or helped in order to dominate.[3] The lower the degree of consciousness the greater the feeling of realization, shock or surprise on coming, as Wollheim allows, 'to know such-and-such a fact about ourselves'.[4] But are we to

---

[1] Non-positional because not directed consciously *at* the unreflected consciousness as an object.

[2] Ibid., p. 49.   [3] See p. 80 above.   [4] Wollheim, op. cit., p. 10, his emphasis.

say even here that consciousness is always concurrently *aware* of its content, that we already know, in some incipient way, such a fact about ourselves? The only basis for using the term 'knowledge' here seems to reside in whatever content can be given to the notion of 'coming to realize', but coming to realize something about myself is more like acquiring knowledge than becoming aware of something I already knew. The basis for saying we were to some extent *aware* of what we subsequently realized is no longer that we must have *known* what we subsequently realized, for here it is our previously being aware of that which we come to know. We could talk of dispositional knowledge, certainly, but as Wollheim points out, to describe the facts in terms of dispositions seems to be doing little more than redescribe them.[3] And it is just to the extent that one could, without loss, redescribe them in this way that these particular facts might seem to resist a description in terms of consciousness being aware of itself in *any* sense; just as it is precisely because cases of the other-directed kind would be underdescribed by a merely dispositional description that they do not seem to resist the terminology of self-consciousness and knowledge. The man rushing for his bus certainly knows what he is doing, and so does the avid novel reader. They do not have to *do* anything to find out, because they do not have to find out. It is possible, of course, that the novel reader and the music lover become so lost to the world that it is only with a shock that they come to realize that this, i.e. sitting in a chair reading or listening, is what they are doing. But this shock differs in its implications from the shock of self-discovery where, for example, I realize I wished someone dead. The latter is a discovery, the former, a recovery of knowledge.

The significance of these considerations is that for Sartre, in so far as every case noted so far is an instance of a mental phenomenon, we would have to describe them all as cases in which consciousness is, in his sense, continually aware of itself. If I come to discover that I have been wishing someone dead, there is a sense in which my consciousness, and therefore myself, must have been

[1] Wollheim, op. cit., p. 10.

aware of this all along; and if I lapse into musical oblivion, there is a sense in which I am aware that this is what I am in. Both kinds of case, and in the latter Sartre includes dreams and psychoses, are to be understood as essentially similar to that in which my ordinary unreflective activity is activity that I am aware I am engaged in.

We might accuse Sartre here of gratuitously promoting to the status of a generic property of mental life a feature that serves merely to identify one, or some, of its species. But rather than throw ordinary distinctions in his way, we would do better to consider directions in which a tenable interpretation of his claim might lie. If we can talk of dispositional knowledge, it is perhaps just because we may come to know something fully that we only knew indirectly. The fact that we do not realize something need not mean that our conscious experience does not to some extent suggest it. The literature on artistic appreciation as well as clinical evidence in psychoanalysis and psychiatry indicate the kind of mechanisms that could make this possible.[1] Objects and situations of emotional significance may express half-realized understandings in various more or less indirect ways, and it may take a certain event or conjunction of events to bring about recognition of what was at first only vague, or ambiguous, or suppressed. It is possible that no such interpretation will bear closer analysis, but rather than assume unquestioningly that Sartre simply fails to distinguish between significantly different kinds of case, one should in any case consider another possibility: that it may be misleading to identify the property Sartre takes to be generic to mental phenomena as the one we find it natural to describe as specific to one kind of case. After all, it is far from obvious that the notion of 'conscious (or therefore, self-conscious) activity' can be used—as we often assume it can be—to make any precise distinctions in terms of *kinds* of mental activity, if one allows, as seems justified, that one *can* be conscious *in varying degrees* of one's own beliefs, intentions, and feelings.

<hr>

[1] See, e.g., Anton Ehrenzweig, *The Hidden Order of Art* (Weidenfeld & Nicolson, London, 1967), and *The Psychoanalysis of Artistic Vision and Hearing* (2nd edn, Geo. Braziller, New York, 1965), and Adler, op. cit.

This seems to indicate at the very least that it is difficult to identify that property by virtue of which an activity is to be described as involving knowledge of what one is doing. Just the same consideration makes it difficult, in the absence of theoretical or logical reasons, to distinguish one case of mental activity from another in respect of the aptness or otherwise of a merely dispositional account.

(4) There is another dimension, however, in which Sartre does suppose that mental activity lends itself to specific distinctions, namely into clearly separable *modes* of consciousness. This is related to his assumption that all mental activity is self-conscious, and can be seen to follow directly from the principle, which Sartre accepts, that intentionality—in Brentano's sense—is a defining characteristic of the mental or psychological. Being intentional in this sense is a property of acts. Since an act, in the ordinary sense which is implied here, is that which is consciously undertaken by an agent, it follows that one who holds the principle must accept that the model of agency is in some way applicable to the full range of what we ordinarily refer to as mental phenomena. And just as in the case of action generally, we are able to say, if not immediately at least by immediate reflection, what we are doing, so for Sartre are the contents of consciousness in principle always accessible to an act of reflection. Sartre adopts the phenomenologist's principle that by reflective concentration we can always find out what consciousness is actually like, phenomenology being essentially the analysis of what *general* features are available to such reflection, independently of any knowledge of causes or of natural laws applicable to the world of which we are conscious. And the general features in question are the characteristics that distinguish one kind of consciousness from another, imaging, for example, from perceiving.

It is not clear whether there are any definite limits to the identifying of specific differentiations in consciousness. But at least this uncertainty cannot support an argument against this second assumption of Sartre's parallel to that just offered in favour of the first. If we ask, What better reason is there to suppose that consciousness reveals itself in distinct modes than there is to deny that mental phenomena are distinguishable in terms of whether they are conscious or unconscious?, the adequate answer is that whatever is distinguishable is to be distinguished in some respect and the distinction can always be formulated in words. If there is something in experience that we pick out as (at least part of) what we mean by, say, 'imaging', then something we can call 'imaging' can be distinguished in general terms from other modes of consciousness. If we take 'perceiving' to refer to a certain phenomenologically distinguishable type of relationship to an object, then there are formulated features which go into our 'essential' definition of perception, and so also in the case of whatever other immediately and qualitatively distinguishable moments of consciousness there may be. The classification into modes of consciousness is therefore, at least in principle, a kind of deduction from experience; the only hypotheses concern the conventional appropriateness of the descriptive terminology. The definitions given of the general features may be aptly or inaptly, consistently or inconsistently expressed descriptions of immediately given data; but they cannot be, or be deduced from, true or false hypotheses about the data themselves. If we then ask why a similar procedure is not possible in respect of the classifying of mental phenomena into conscious and unconscious modes, the answer is that to pick out anything as a case of an 'unconscious' mental process is either question-begging in a way that picking out an *experience* as a case of, say, emotion is not, or it is to use the word uninterestingly to refer to nothing more than those overt features of mental life which provide our method of identifying it.

3. THE IMAGING RELATION

It is in terms of their relationships to their objects that the alleged differences between modes of consciousness are revealed to immediate reflection. For Sartre reflection reveals four general characteristics of imaging-consciousness.

(1) The image is a consciousness. By this he means that

imaging-consciousness is consciousness directly of the imagined object and not of the image. Pierre can be perceived or imagined,[1] but in the latter case we are not perceiving, instead of Pierre in person, a picture of Pierre. In imagining Pierre there is nothing in mind analogous to a portrait of him on the wall. This point is obvious, thinks Sartre. It would, of course, be patently absurd to say that a chair, say, was in my mind when I perceived it, at least in any literal sense, for what is meant by an object of perception is precisely something that in principle transcends any one perception or the perceptions of any one person. The fact that it does not seem equally absurd to say that when I imagine a chair there must be an object in my mind, namely a copy of the chair, is due to the illicit transference in thought of a relationship peculiar to seeing physical objects to the case of forming a mental image. This is not only wrong, it is obviously wrong; and the mistake can only be made because the transference occurs at the level of language, or as Sartre says, because the 'illusion of immanence' has remained in the implicit state.[2] The object of imaging-consciousness, he says, is not the image itself,[3] but that which has a certain way of appearing to consciousness. The term 'image' itself should be used to refer to the way the object appears, or rather, to the way in which an imaging-consciousness 'gives itself an object'.[4]

The remaining three characteristics determine the way imaging-consciousness has of giving itself an object.

(2) The first of these Sartre calls 'quasi-observation'. In perception I observe objects, and in observing something I am always, in the way we have already pointed out, prepared to find further determinations of it; my knowledge (*savoir*) of it increases as I look;[5] the object *precedes* my consciousness of it. We can put this by saying that the description of the objects

---

[1] The transitive form 'imagining X' comes more naturally than 'imaging X' and I shall prefer it to the latter when referring to imaging in general, rather than, say, to visualizing or dreaming specifically.

[2] *L'Imaginaire*, p. 16.

[3] Sartre says: 'What, really, is the image? It is clearly not the chair: in a general way, the object of the image is not itself (the) image.' Ibid., p. 17.

[4] Ibid., p. 18. [5] Ibid., p. 19.

of perception are to a degree opaque. The object of imaging-consciousness, however, is bounded by the moment of that consciousness. The knowledge I have of it is 'immediate'; it does not precede the latter, as in perception; nor does consciousness precede it, like some light that finds out its object, as when I think an object.[1] The object is contemporaneous with the consciousness of it, and exactly determined by it.[2] In other words its description is transparent. This makes it a distinctly poorer object than that of perception. Whereas the latter 'overflows' the consciousness one has of it,[3] in imaging-consciousness there is no risk, no expectation,[4] not a second of surprise.[5]

(3) Sartre then notes the way the unreflective imaging-consciousness posits its object. In perception we intend the object in the space it is seen to share with us. Imaging-consciousness, however, poses its object as absent, elsewhere, non-existent, or with its 'position' undecided.[6] It is crucial to note, says Sartre, that the unreflective acts of posing the object in one of these ways is not *added* to the image, but is an essential part of the imaging-consciousness. To suppose otherwise is to fall for the 'illusion of immanence',[7] the view that in imagining Pierre I have a picture-like simulacrum of him in mind which is only externally related to the real Pierre.

(4) Finally, Sartre distinguishes the passivity which is a feature of consciousness in perception from the spontaneity characterizing imaging-consciousness.[8] Each of these features is a transparent property of the respective consciousness. Therefore there is no question, for example, of imaging-consciousness having to recognize what mode of consciousness it is. We never have to infer that we are imaging. In terms of the distinctions we have noted earlier, there is some sense in which we know that we are imaging, or perceiving—even if this knowledge is not constituted in a judgment. Where it is so constituted, it is not an inferential judgment; the sole and sufficient basis for making it is an immediate awareness of what we have just been

[1] *L'Imaginaire*, p. 19. [2] Ibid., p. 22. [3] Ibid., pp. 20–1.
[4] Ibid., p. 21. [5] Ibid., p. 22. [6] Ibid., p. 24.
[7] Ibid., p. 24. [8] Ibid., p. 26.

doing.[1] 'Consciousness appears to itself as a creator', says Sartre, 'but without posing this creative character as an object.'[2]

Now, many difficulties emerge from this account, not least of which relate to internal consistency; for example it is unclear how Sartre can (e.g. in explicating what he means by an object outside consciousness) or does (e.g. regarding the characteristic of 'spontaneity') confine himself to the deliverances of reflection. Other problems relate to the general applicability of the account to all cases of the consciousness of something in imagination. But we shall leave these questions aside and examine in detail two other main sets of problems: first, as a preliminary, the question of what Sartre means by an object of imaging-consciousness, and secondly, our main question, how the four general features noted justify a conclusion expressed as 'the image is an act and not a thing',[3] or, alternatively, as 'an image is nothing but a relation'.[4]

4. OBJECTS AND APPEARANCES

Sartre says that the object of the imaging-consciousness is to be understood as that which is imagined, that is, Pierre or the chair. It is the same thing that could also be perceived; it is Pierre who is in Berlin that I imagine, or the chair that I was looking at just a moment ago. As Sartre says later,

'The two worlds, imaginary and real, are constituted by the same objects; only the grouping and the interpretation of the objects vary. What distinguishes the imaginary world from the real world is an attitude of consciousness.[5]

And yet, on the other hand, it appears that the object in imaging is a creation of consciousness, bounded by the moment of consciousness, nothing more than the consciousness of it. But obviously Pierre and the chair are themselves not creatures of consciousness. They are the same things which, when I perceive

[1] Cf. p. 94 above.   [2] *L'Imaginaire*, p. 26.   [3] *L'Imagination*, p. 162.
[4] *L'Imaginaire*, p. 17.   [5] Ibid., p. 34.

them, 'overflow' my consciousness of them. But is Sartre not then
involved in a fundamental inconsistency? The object of an
imaging-consciousness which the illuded immanentist regards as
being the image-object *in* consciousness and which Sartre is at
pains to stress is the intentional object and, by its nature, outside consciousness,[1] turns out to be a product of consciousness. But since Sartre also claims that consciousness can only
act upon itself,[2] this creature can presumably only exist inside
consciousness. Moreover, it looks as if Sartre was in a dilemma.
If he chooses to identify the object of imaging with what exists
only by leave of consciousness, then there seems still to be a
question of how this object is related to the possible object
of perception outside consciousness, and it would be natural to
regard the relation of immanent to transcendent here as an external one in the sense he criticizes. If, on the other hand, he
prefers to say that the object of imaging is identical with a
possible object of perception, the latter being 'outside' consciousness, the image will surely appear to reflection as something which *mediates* the peculiar imaging-consciousness of this
absent object.

I believe, however, that although the resolution of this
problem raises further difficulties for Sartre, it can be resolved
and is indeed no more than prima facie; for the following reasons.
If we confine ourselves to the deliverances of introspection, or
rather of immediate reflection upon unreflective consciousness,[3]
all we can say about the object we imagine is in terms of the object
as we imagined it. A description of what we imagine that is confined to our imagining of it, is of a purely intentional object; if the
descriptions were to prove inapplicable to anything in the world
this would not count as an objection to the claim that I imagined
what I claimed to. But this does not mean that such a description
may not be true or false of something that is in the world, and be
intended as such; that is, there is no reason in principle why the

---

[1] *L'Imaginaire*, p. 23.   [2] *L'Imagination*, p. 126.

[3] Sartre himself does not regard 'introspection' as a synonym for 'phenomenological reflection'. He reserves the former for a special mode of reflection that
tries to grasp empirical facts, not essences. See *L'Imagination*, p. 140.

object of such a description and that of a description purporting to apply to something in the world should not be identical. This point may be clarified by noting Miss Anscombe's distinction between an intentional and a material use of 'see'. She claims:

'While there must be an intentional object of seeing, there need not always be a material object. That is to say "*X* saw *A*" where "saw" is used materially, implies some proposition "*X* saw—" where "saw" is used intentionally; but the converse does not hold.'[1]

The basis of this claim is, first, that there is, for every visual sensation, a description of what it is of, and secondly, that there are two senses of 'see' in which, on the strength of a visual sensation, we say that we see something. The first of these senses is what Miss Anscombe terms the 'material' use of 'see', a use which demands a *material* object of the verb'. Here we withdraw the claim to see the thing if there is no object before us answering the description; in this sense 'the verb "to see" is not allowed to take a *merely* intentional object; non-existence of the object (absolutely, or in the situation) is an objection to the truth of the sentence'.[2] In the other sense of 'see', however, we do not withdraw the claim; in this sense the non-existence is not an objection.[3]

Criticisms have been made of this distinction, and we shall discuss them in the next chapter. However, nothing that is tenable in the criticisms affects the distinction's applicability here, which is to show how seeing Pierre in imagination can still be seeing Pierre. We begin by applying it to the case of seeing a picture of Pierre. Thus when, for example, we mistakenly believe we see Pierre when what we really see is a skilfully placed *trompe l'oeil* painting of him, it is only in the material sense of 'see' that we should withdraw the claim to be seeing

[1] G. E. M. Anscombe, 'The Intentionality of Sensation: a Grammatical Feature', in R. J. Butler (ed.), *Analytical Philosophy*, 2nd Series (Blackwell, Oxford, 1965), p. 176.

[2] Ibid., pp. 171 and 172, Miss Anscombe's emphasis.

[3] Cf. Ryle's corresponding distinction between post-perceptual and primary uses of the verbs 'feel', 'look', 'sound', etc., referred to on p. 31 above.

him. In this case we should replace the withdrawn claim by a new one, that what we are seeing is a *picture* of Pierre. And in the slightly different case where what we mistakenly take for Pierre is someone else very like him, we should replace the claim to have seen Pierre with a claim to have seen someone else. But in neither case do we have to give up the claim to be seeing, or to have seen, Pierre in the second sense. Nor does this mean that what we see in this sense is something other than Pierre, for example a visual impression or appearance. To argue that it did would be to transfer to this sense what applies only to the second: namely, that if nothing perceptually present answers the description under which we claim to see Pierre, then something else must. It is this illicit transference that makes us want to substitute the impression for the object in the perceptual absence of the latter.[1]

To apply this to visualizing: in visualizing Pierre we know we do not see him in the sense of 'see' which demands a material object of the verb. But this does not mean that we do not see him at all, for we can be seeing him in the second sense—or if that is not acceptable, perhaps on the grounds that visualizing provides nothing sufficiently analogous to a visual sensation and cannot be seeing in any literal sense—at least in some sense that is a metaphorical extension of the second sense. And the absence of the material Pierre does not require us, in this sense of 'see', to substitute an image as the object of our imaging.

Now for the supposed dilemma facing Sartre: that either the object of imaging is something immanent that must be related externally to its transcendent intentional object, or it is the transcendent intentional object itself and must therefore be mediated by an immanent image. The sense in which Pierre is immanent, because a creature of consciousness, is simply that in which Pierre figures as an intentional object in the description under which I imagine him. He is the Pierre I could be seeing in the first sense. To see him in the second sense involves reference to nothing beyond the content of my image, my imaging; yet 'he' is clearly the same Pierre in both cases. Anscombe points to a parallel between the incorrectness of saying

---

[1] Taking 'perceive' here as synonymous with 'see' in its 'material' use.

things like 'He cannot have seen Pierre, because Pierre was not there' and that of saying: 'They cannot have worshipped unicorns, because there are no such things.'[1] But it can only be incorrect if the unicorns worshipped and the unicorns whose existence is denied are the same; what one is allowing is that unicorns which never existed were nevertheless worshipped. Similarly one is allowing that the Pierre who conceivably does not exist and who is not, in any case, seen there, is nevertheless seen.

We can see also how it can be misleading, then, when we form an image of Pierre, to say that instead of having Pierre appear, what really appears is something else, the image that is the immediate object of consciousness and which itself mediates the thought of Pierre. It could be misleading in suggesting that we should not think of the imaginary appearance of Pierre as a genuine member of the class of appearances constituting the ways in which Pierre himself can appear to us. The case is similar to seeing a portrait or photograph of Pierre. In an important sense a pictorial appearance is as real as any. In order to be recognizably of Pierre, to depict him for us, a representing medium must mediate a genuine member of the class of appearances of Pierre. That a medium represents him is not the same, for example, as its being able to *resemble* him. One can observe resemblances between things without seeing them as pictures of one another.[2] Far from mediating Pierre by resembling him, a representing medium conjures Pierre before us. Only visually, of course; it does not conjure him before us in person. But this is enough to show that in *re*-presenting Pierre, the representing medium in effect presents *him*, not a representation of him. To say that it only presented a representation of him would not only be phenomenologically incorrect, it would imply that in seeing a picture of Pierre I could not be seeing him even in the intentional sense. So in this Sartre is undoubtedly correct. We should not think that if Pierre is for the time being unperceivable, he is

---

[1] 'The Intentionality of Sensation', p. 172.
[2] Cf. Alastair Hannay, 'Wollheim and Seeing Black on White as a Picture', *British Journal of Aesthetics*, 10 (1970), No. 2, p. 112, and pp. 156 ff. below.

simply not available on the *terrain de l'intuition sensible*.[1] Seeing pictures of him is one of the ways in which he is still available to sensory intuition. Imagining him is another.

However, there is still an apparent difficulty. In insisting that the way in which I have Pierre 'in mind' in imagining him is not one in which I refer an image to the real Pierre, Sartre seems to be saying also that what I have of Pierre 'in mind' is contained wholly in the image, or rather, the imaging-consciousness I have of him. He seems to assimilate the object imagined with the *way* in which it is imagined. Thus in criticizing Berkeley for prescribing for the image conditions that apply only to perception, he asserts that although a hare that is vaguely perceived is in itself a determinate hare, a hare that is an object of a vague image is an indeterminate hare.[2] In one way this seems correct. As suggested earlier, in perceiving something we apprehend it incompletely but not as incomplete,[3] for we see it as having the property of being capable of further determinations. But in imaging we are not prepared for further determinations and so, in this sense, what is present in imagination is not seen as having this property. This could be expressed by saying that in imagining something, to apprehend it incompletely is to apprehend it as incomplete. But does this not mean that not only must the range of an object's genuine appearances be extended to include imaginary ones, but the very identity of the object must be stretched to allow it to instantiate descriptions that it would be *contradictory* to apply to real objects? If it does, we seem to be faced once more with the difficulty we have just attempted to resolve. How can the imagined hare be identical with the real hare, if the latter is by definition determinate and the former not?

What we want to say, of course, is that '*A* imagines a vague hare' can be replaced by '*A* imagines a hare incompletely'; for this latter presents vagueness as a property ascribed not to the hare but to the manner in which it is imagined. What we must ask here is whether Sartre, too, can say this, and indeed whether he wants to. As for the first question, although the

[1] *L'Imaginaire*, p. 25.   [2] Ibid., p. 28.   [3] See p. 91 above.

point is not altogether clear, I think he can. For it is certainly possible to distinguish properties ascribed to something on the basis of our knowledge of it (e.g. that it is a material object and therefore determinate) and properties ascribed to it on the basis of our present experience of it, and there seems nothing in Sartre that would make him deny this possibility. On the other hand, the second question, of whether he wants to say this, arises precisely because he sometimes suggests that a description of what we imagine as we imagine it is the only source there is of descriptions of what the imager has 'in mind' or 'intends'. Indeed the suggestion accords with a central part of Sartre's thesis on imagination, namely that in imagining something we are aware of that thing as something that it is not. But since it is just as important a part of his thesis that the imager be aware of the thing *as* that which it is not, and hence that he *believes* that what he imagines is not as he imagines it, he cannot mean that in imagining a hare vaguely the imager altogether loses sight of the fact that hares are determinate objects. In fact he talks of imaging in terms of a visual knowledge of things 'filling', not *replacing*, an 'empty' intention, where the empty intention is itself a function of our ordinary beliefs or knowledge;[1] and we may assume that he means that the imager knows while he imagines a hare that the properties he imagines it as having are only some of those that he could imagine it as having, and that he could never imagine a hare as having more determinations than it is imagined as having. So however much Sartre stresses a weakening of the hold of our ordinary beliefs in imaging, a stress that may perhaps be phenomenologically justified, he does not mean that these beliefs do not remain to some extent intact and in play.

In saying that the hare which is the object of a vague image is a vague hare Sartre is at least stressing that the determinacy of a hare is not an imagined property of it, which far from implying the impossibility of distinguishing what appears from how it appears would seem to show it was just as possible in the case of imagination as in that of perception. Sartre's point is surely that we must not take this to imply for the *imager* a distinction

[1] See, e.g. *L'Imaginaire*, pp. 79–92, esp. p. 88.

in identity between object imagined and object *as* it is imagined. Phenomenologically this is no doubt correct; in the experience of imaging *qua* imaging there is no object that is the object we imagine distinct from the object *as* we imagine it. For there to be another object 'in mind', it would have to be as the correlate of another act of consciousness. We cannot, for instance, distinguish *in the moment of imaging* between the imaginary appearance of the object and the object itself (in Berlin, or in the next room). Nor does the success of the performance of imagining something that we believe exists or did exist depend on an implicit judgment that there is or was such an object distinct from its imagined appearance; the distinction between real and imagined has no place here. As we have noted, the appearances in imaging are in an important sense still genuine appearances. Although it might, in some ways, seem less misleading to say that in imagining Pierre, what we have is *as good as* an appearance of him, what is wrong with this, as we saw, is that it implies a distinction between what we do get and ways in which Pierre could 'really' be an object of consciousness. We could only 'reach' Pierre really, then, by performing another act of consciousness, say by the appearance bringing the thought of the real Pierre to mind, or by our 'referring' the appearance to the real Pierre. This would be to put him well and truly outside the imaging-consciousness, as Sartre insists it is his nature to be; but if Sartre's insistence that an act of imaging is, so to speak, referentially self-sufficient is correct, so far outside that nothing could count as an unreflective imaging-consciousness of Pierre. Thus to bring out the full force of Sartre's remark that the imaginary and real worlds are constituted by the same objects,[1] we must see that in an intentional sense of 'appear' the same objects *literally* appear to both modes of consciousness.

In the material sense, of course, they do not; and it is this that gives Sartre's apparent equivocation about whether the object transcends or is created by consciousness the appearance of an internal inconsistency. But in order to see the sense of

[1] *L'Imaginaire*, p. 34. See p. 101 above.

affirming the phenomenological identity of the object imagined and the object as it is imagined, we need only consider how we do not require to explain my experience of seeing a portrait as a portrait of Pierre (as opposed to recognizing on some basis other than the visual experience that it is intended to be of Pierre) in terms of my having to *refer* the picture to Pierre. The seeing-as is a basic and irreducible experience. For me to refer, on the basis of visual experience, to a picture as of Pierre, it is not even necessary, surely, that I have an individuating description of Pierre in mind, as that which explains my ability to use the term in this context to refer to Pierre. There seems no reason, either, that I should be able to produce such a description, or call it 'to mind', on request. To produce or call such a thing to mind would simply be to intend the same object in some way other than on the *terrain de l'intuition sensible*. And if, as seems the case, each is possible without the other, there is no reason to regard them as logically necessary for one another, or to think of one of them as logically basic. Indeed, if any priorities are to be assigned it would seem that sensory intuition was to be preferred, as the field in which we first exercise our knowledge of the things around us.

But, as we have said, this interpretation brings its own difficulties. Indeed in some respects it appears to defeat Sartre's own purposes. We recall that his general criticism of an immanentist view of imaging-consciousness is that it misconceives the relation of the imaging mind to its object; it sees it as a perceptual kind of relation to a special object (the image), instead of as a *sui generis* relation to an ordinary, publicly observable object. But according to the above account, there is a sense in which the object of this special relation (Pierre) actually appears. This is because, phenomenologically, the range of genuine appearances of X is wider than that of logically real or 'personal' appearances of X. But by allowing this, we have introduced into the analysis of the relation something, namely an appearance, that might well be regarded as an image. Moreover, the argument that phenomenologically it is the imagined object and not an image that the mind intends in imaging-consciousness no longer seems to have the desired force, since according to the advocated interpretation the mind is directly related to its object *as* an image.[1] Much of the initial attraction of the argument derives from the idea that an analysis of imaging need mention only the act of imaging and the object intended by the act; if we can think of the latter as being identical with the object that we could, in principle, perceive, there seems as little reason here to introduce a third item, the image, as there does in the case where we simply refer to the object by name, or by some individuating description. But the phenomenological account requires that we do introduce something, namely an imaginary appearance of the object itself, it being precisely this that distinguishes cases of simple reference from those of imaging reference.

Thus the claim that imaging-consciousness is not a perceptual kind of relation to a special object but a *sui generis* relation to an ordinary object lacks the full disjunctive force that its form at first suggests. For in admitting the second part of the claim we seem to have created a special kind of object, whatever the peculiarity of the mind's relationship to it, which could lead us to deny at least half of the first part of the claim. That is, in admitting we are not seeing an image that is externally related to the imagined object, but imagining the object directly, we still find a use for the notion of a special object for an imaging-consciousness. The question arises, Why not call it an 'image'? But as we have seen, this is the wrong question, for Sartre does talk of imaging-consciousness as consciousness of an image, only not an image that is not in some sense identical with its object. So the question we really have to ask is, Why is this image not a special kind of object?

5. WHY IS AN IMAGE NOT AN OBJECT?

To answer this we must see what Sartre means more generally by an object. And to do that we can formulate a series of arguments

---

[1] Indeed Sartre frequently expresses himself in this way. He talks, for example, of imaging-consciousness as 'the consciousness of an image', of 'the object in the image' (ibid., p. 27); cf. also ibid., p. 21: 'The very act which gives me the

which Sartre uses, or implies, in support of a conclusion expressed as 'Images are not objects'. The arguments can be arranged in ascending order of their capacity to generate conclusions having the generality and significance, or non-triviality, that we may assume Sartre attaches to his claim that images are not objects. They are as follows:

It is wrong to describe an image as an object because:

(1) In so far as imagining X is consciousness of X, it is not consciousness of an image of X.
(2) To do so is to place images in the category of things that are the aim, not the content of consciousness.
(3) As creations of the mind their content is no more than that of which consciousness is aware in the image-experience.
(4) If they were object-like they would infringe the rule that consciousness is always transparent to itself.
(5) The only transaction an object can have with consciousness is as its object.

(1) Obviously this is not sufficient as an argument against images being objects, since the fact, for example, that when we recognize a portrait as of someone, we attend to the representational theme and not to the representing object, does not lead us to conclude that the latter is not an object. But the argument may seem, in Sartre's case, to be irrelevant anyhow, since by allowing a phenomenologically direct relationship of the imaging mind to its object he treats what we might be tempted to regard as the image, as *identical with* the (imaginarily) appearing object.

However, this may lead us to distinguish two separate claims that may be expressed by (1). The sentence can be interpreted as a denial that the intentional object is an image; and interpreted in this way it would be equally correct to deny that the intentional object was an imaginary appearance, or even an appearance, of X, and not X itself. For when I imagine X what I *mean* to imagine is precisely X and nothing else. For just as when I see X I do not

object in (an) image', and p. 23: 'The transcendent consciousness of a tree in image.' Also *L'Imagination*, p. 138: 'I constituted Pierre in (an) image', and p. 146.

say that I see an appearance of X, so in imagining X I should not say that I imagine an appearance (and certainly not an imaginary appearance) of X, for that would be to perceive or to imagine something else. Or, secondly, the sentence can be interpreted as a claim that in so far as we are intending X, and not an image or an appearance of X, there is *no* sense in which that of which we are conscious in imagining X is an image. Now where the first claim amounts to an analytic truth, explicating the sense of the notion of an intentional object, the second certainly involves a claim that could be denied without contradiction; if only because we can think of senses in which what is phenomenologically present to a mind that is imagining X *can* be described as an image, for example as *only* an image of X, as opposed to X itself. On Sartre's analysis, indeed, this would be the logical description to give, in that what the mind creates, in his sense, is not X, but only an image of X. And furthermore, he claims that this is what the mind should know, even unreflectively, that it has before it, inasmuch as the imaging mind knows immediately and non-inferentially that the appearances of X are not appearances of X in person, but only, as it were, its own home-made substitutes for X.

(2) In saying that to describe an image as an object is to categorize it wrongly under 'aim' instead of 'content' of consciousness, the second argument, as it stands, is also clearly insufficient. For in the broad sense of 'object' images may just as well be 'aimed' at, or intended, by consciousness as any other topic of discourse, as Sartre's own treatise on the subject clearly demonstrates. The broad sense of 'object' is that implied in the characteristic phenomenologist's division of the world into subjective states, or (as Sartre prefers)[1] acts of consciousness, on the one hand, and objects on the other, where by the latter are meant no more than the necessary correlates of the former, and not, at least in principle, exclusively physical objects or objects in the world. The argument is in fact deficient in two respects, for

[1] Cf. *The Transcendence of the Ego*, p. 109: 'The expression "state of consciousness" seems to me inaccurate owing to the passivity which it introduces into consciousness.'

not only are images not excluded as objects in this sense, but nothing is said as to why what is an object in this sense can only be correlative to, and not part of the analysis of, subjective states or acts of consciousness. 'Aim' and 'content' are not self-evidently disjuncts.

However, there is reason to suppose that Sartre adopts the argument in a more restricted form which would eliminate both these deficiencies. What he denies is not that images can be referred to, but—at least by implication—that they can be objects of thought in any sense in which to think of them (or of the consciousnesses they really are) is to form in one's mind an adequate idea of what they are (one could say: in which to think of them is to have them as possible objects *for* consciousness); and furthermore, it is only in the sense in which a correlate of consciousness is something such that we *can* form in our minds an adequate idea of it that he denies that whatever can be correlative to consciousness can be used in the analysis of consciousness. Let us consider this in more detail.

By 'object' in the most general sense one would expect Sartre to mean the formal notion of 'correlate to an act of consciousness'. In fact he does treat the two as equivalent. Except for the consciousness that consciousness has of itself,[1] which is 'non-positional', all other acts of consciousness intend, or pose, an object in this sense. Even when we think of, or in terms of, abstract ideas or relationships of ideas, our consciousness poses something as its object; Sartre calls it, in this kind of case, a 'nature' (or *essence universelle*).[2] If a nature is affirmed we get a judgment. But in some modes of consciousness objects are posed in such a way that a relationship (*sur le terrain de l'intuition*)[3] to the conscious subject is ascribed to them. The typical case of this is where the objective correlate to consciousness is a thing belonging to the world. In perceiving, consciousness posits its object positively as existent.[4] In imagining, however, consciousness posits its object negatively, as absent, existent else-where, non-existent, or with an indeterminate 'position' (Sartre

---

[1] See p. 94 above.   [2] *L'Imaginaire*, p. 25.   [3] Ibid., p. 24.
[4] Ibid., p. 24.

says that this suspension of belief still remains *un acte positionnel*).[1]

And yet in claiming, as he does, that the objects of consciousness are '*by nature* outside consciousness'[2] Sartre seems to deny that images could be objects even in this broadest sense. For clearly he does not want to say that *images* are by nature outside consciousness. One solution would be if the claim referred only to objects in the world (*choses*), but although the example Sartre gives is that of a physical object (a tree) no such restriction is hinted at in the context. Another solution is that Sartre holds that objects in the broad sense can only be intended by consciousness under the category (or guise) of objects in the narrow sense. The claim would then be the interesting phenomenological one that for *consciousness* objects are posited as outside consciousness. And Sartre does say that 'even the attention we give a thought implies a kind of localization in space'.[3] But an object that is *by nature* outside consciousness is one that is genuinely 'heterogeneous' to consciousness, not merely treated as such.

A second difficulty is that an image is not something we can *posit* in any of the senses Sartre provides: it is not an essence, nor is it visible, and we cannot, at least in any clear sense, imagine an image. Indeed, it appears from what Sartre says, here and elsewhere, that it is indeed impossible to imagine an image, but that this follows from a more general impossibility, namely that of *conceiving* (as opposed to 'referring to') another consciousness. Thus, in *The Transcendence of the Ego*, he writes: 'Pierre's consciousness is radically impenetrable . . . [since] it is not only refractory to intuition, but to thought.' For 'I cannot *conceive* Pierre's consciousness without making an object of it (since I do not conceive it as being *my consciousness*). . . . A consciousness cannot conceive of a consciousness other than itself'.[4] It is clearly the impossibility of *forming an idea of* another consciousness that Sartre means, not that of conceiving the *existence* of other consciousnesses. And if an image is, as he claims, a con-

---

[1] *L'Imaginaire*, p. 24, fn. 1 Cf. p. 100 above.   [2] *L'Imaginaire*, p. 23, my emphasis.   [3] Ibid., p. 64

[4] *The Transcendence of the Ego*, p. 96. For consistency I have retained 'Pierre' in place of the translators' 'Peter'.

sciousness, it follows that one cannot form an idea of an image—at least not adequately, for all we can 'conceive' in this sense is something on the analogy of a visible object. We can only form an idea of an image, therefore, by conceiving of it under the wrong category, that of things belonging to the world, instead of that of consciousness.

We have established the (or a) sense in which Sartre thinks that images are not possible objects *for* consciousness, but the argument to this effect depends on the assumption that it *is* correct to classify 'images' as acts and not as things. Nothing has as yet been stated in defence of this claim. In fact something we said before may seem to undermine it. We argued earlier that Sartre seemed to accept that the imagined object, from consciousness's point of view, is an image. In this sense, and subject to the identification, one presumably can regard images (e.g. the image as Pierre, or, Sartre's expression, 'Pierre in an image')[1] as proper objects for consciousness. Why, then, can we not, by abstracting from the identification, regard images as mental objects in their own right? Why, we wonder, do they become possible objects of consciousness only in so far as they are intended by consciousness as the things they represent?

Now in one way this objection fails. As we noted earlier, the notion of X's determinateness in 'A imagined determinate X' does not enter by way of A's experience of his image. It is a property ascribed on the basis of A's knowledge of the kind of thing he means by 'X'. So when imaging-consciousness intends an image as what it represents, it does not see the image *as* a determinate object in the way that, on Sartre's account, a perceiving consciousness does, by apprehending X's capability of further determinations as itself a property of X. So the objection does not show that Sartre must accept that, for consciousness, images are as good as objects, in the sense in which, say, Pierre is an object.

On the other hand, this only shows that images are not analogous to objects in that sense. They do not present themselves as capable of further determinations. But in order to see why images are not to be regarded as objects in any sense, but as

[1] *L'Imagination*, p. 138.

acts, we certainly need another argument. We need to know what it is in virtue of which all things fall into two types ('of existence'): 'that of things belonging to the world and that of consciousness.'[1] Clearly it is insufficient to be told that images are not analogous to physical objects. We want to be told why images are not objects in any sense, and what it is about an object in any sense that makes 'object' an inappropriate expression for referring either to an image or to any component of consciousness. One suggestion is provided by the considerations Sartre mentions under the headings of 'quasi-observation' and 'spontaneity', and these bring us to the third argument, that images are not objects because their content is no more than that of which consciousness is aware in the image-experience.

(3) That the most fully determined object in an image 'possesses only a finite number of determinations, those precisely of which we are conscious' is what leads Sartre to call imaging 'quasi-observation'.[2] It is distinguished from perception, or real observation, by the object in the latter being 'constituted by an infinite multiplicity of determinations and possible relations'.[3]

So far this might seem just another way of putting Ryle's distinction between 'seeing' and seeing, or Shorter's between 'depicting' and depicting. Given | that we do apprehend a common world in perception, it follows that an object in that world, whether or not a representation, transcends our perception of it; not just in the sense that it is only partially perceptible to one person at one time, but also in the sense that it can be correctly described in an infinite number of ways—not all of them ways of describing how it appears—depending on one's selection from an infinite number of possible coordinates in the system of common things. The object in the image, in comparison, is a poor thing. A description of it is confined to how it appears to the imaginer on a single occasion of his imagining it. Thus in imagining a hare vaguely there is nothing one has failed to

---

[1] *L'Imagination*, p. 126.
[2] *L'Imaginaire*, p. 27; cf. also p. 22, and p. 100 above.
[3] *L'Imaginaire*, p. 28.

apprehend clearly, any more than when one imagines a hare clearly there is more to the hare than one's clear image of it. There is no basis even for saying that the clear image has clarified what was unclear in the vague one, for that would require a way of identifying the two image-hares as the same hare, and the only source of identity-descriptions here is the imager's intention, which relates not to image-hares but to real, that is transcendent, hares.

That mental images are no more than they seem, if true, would be a good argument for saying they were not objects. The point would be, roughly, that mental images are transparent, in the sense that they do not in fact have hidden depths, as do objects of perception. They are, in this respect, like the empiricist epistemologist's 'immediate objects of sensation'. But here we must note a very important divergence between Sartre and the other two philosophers we have examined. Both Ryle and Shorter accept that imaging may be mistaken for perceiving, without detriment to the claim that mental images are not objects. However closely one's imaging experience duplicates that of really seeing— for instance, by presenting image-things as capable of more determinations than those they appear to have, or by 'revealing' their further properties—this in itself would not give one an excuse to refer to images as objects. Even the bizarre experiences Shorter requires of our seeing a mental image would be no warrant for the claim that images had in fact an infinite multiplicity of determinations and possible relations. For that one would need to give meaning to the idea of identifying and reidentifying the same mental object. Failure to give it meaning means that mental images are not objects in this sense. Sartre, however, adds a crucial specification to the requirement that mental images are no more than they seem, namely that the image be not merely transparent, but also transparently an image. That is, Sartre argues that the fact that an image possesses only those determinations of which the imager is conscious must itself be part of what the imager is conscious. A mental image should never even seem to have hidden depth. Unlike Ryle and Shorter, therefore, Sartre would take the phenomenological duplication of perceiving in imaging as *disconfirmation of an essential part of his thesis that mental images are not objects*. It is this part that he expresses by saying they are acts. And clearly the argument that images are only *in fact* transparent is insufficient for that conclusion. An image whose content was transparent but which was not transparently an image would be no different in kind from a sense-datum, and no one has suggested that sense-data should be called acts.

(4) Sartre says that the illusion of immanence must have remained at the implicit level since

' . . . otherwise we would have seen that it was impossible to slip these material portraits into a synthetic conscious structure without destroying it, turning off the switches, stopping the flow, breaking the continuity. Consciousness would cease to be transparent to itself; above all, its unity would be broken by the opaque, inassimilable screens.'[1]

It is important to see just what he takes this obvious impossibility to be. On the basis of the arguments of stages (1) and (2), one might think it was the impossibility of transcendent objects being in, rather than for consciousness. This, if not contradictory, as would be the notion of a transcendent *common* object in consciousness, may well be 'incoherent' in the Strawsonian sense, given the conceptual scheme that we ordinarily employ. But it is clear that Sartre has another impossibility in mind, and a full-fledged impossibility at that, not an inconsistency internal to a given way of speaking. The impossibility is that mental images should impose themselves upon the mind, like objects, as though from outside consciousness.

Now clearly in ordinary visualizing the image does not appear as a piece of intractable mental matter, or 'linen', breaking in upon the smooth flow of consciousness. Sartre is claiming, however, that this not only never happens, it never could. And the counter-example that he thinks he must avoid is one where, for consciousness, there is no difference between seeing something in an image and seeing it in fact. He wants to avoid it not because

[1] *L'Imaginaire*, p. 16.

he thinks that if an image-object appeared as having amongst its apparent properties the property of being capable of disclosing more determinations than those that it appeared to have then it would indeed have more determinations, and thus be a transcendent object in the mind, but because he thinks that if it appeared in that way, the mind's own acts could no longer be described as transparent to itself; and this is what he finds impossible.

Perhaps an analogy will help to convey what Sartre means. What a sentence means to someone writing it down in order to express what he means is transparent to that person. It is not transparent to him in the same way if he comes upon that sentence again and asks himself what he meant by it. He must try to remember what he meant, or how he meant it. And something similar would apply if he wrote down a sentence without knowing that he wrote it, or if he wrote it without guiding his own hand. Here he may, and usually will, see a meaning in the words, but what meaning he is meant to see in them, or whether he is meant to see any, is something he cannot tell simply by consulting his own intentions. Sartre's view, then, is that all mental contents are transparent in the way that the meaning of a sentence can be as it is being written, and are not at all opaque in the sense that one has to infer the meaning, either from the sentence itself, or from circumstances attending its production.

Now it is clear that mental images are not normally like other people's sentences, or even like our own sentences written on previous occasions. But it is not clear that an image necessarily conforms to this paradigm of transparency. Consider the following case. I imagine myself delivering an eloquent speech to an enthralled audience in a packed hall. Then, or subsequently, it dawns on me that the description of the hall as imagined fits that of the scene of my first humiliating failure as an orator. Do I not then come, in fact, to realize a further determination of what it was I was imagining? Now we could not say, I think, that this further determination had been part of *how* I imagined what I imagined. I may come to realize how something once did look to me, but not how it looks to me now. We are left, then, with these alternatives: either (i) the additional property was an unimagined property of what I imagined—like 'capable of further determinations', but not, as with the latter, known or realized as such—or (ii) it is simply an imagined property of a new and richer, imagining. Since it seems clear that for Sartre the only way in which the *mise en scène* could figure in a description of *what* I imagine is either in a description of what I know about what I imagine or in one of *how* I imagine it, his natural preference would seem to be for the latter. But is he not then crippling himself from making a potentially important distinction between this and another kind of case? Suppose I imagine, randomly, a seaside pier. After picturing a pier to myself I realize the description of the pier as imagined fits that of Brighton Pier. Furthermore, I then recall that, perhaps not all that recently, I had a photograph of Brighton Pier from the same view, and I conjecture that repeated optical exposure to this photograph has induced in me the tendency to picture piers of this description when thinking of piers in general or of a particular but unspecific pier. Now here I think that, even without Sartre's reasons, we would not be tempted to say that the realized determination, that it was Brighton Pier, was a determination of what I imagined at all. I might well say, upon realizing the similarity, that what I pictured was in some way *caused* by my earlier visual history, but an adequate explanation of this would be that as a result of that history I now had a tendency to picture piers of this description when not consciously trying to picture piers of another description; it would not be necessary to say that a description of the causal circumstance, my seeing a photograph of the pier, was in anyway *internally* related to the caused circumstance, my imagining what I did.

In the former case, however, we might well want to say just that; it might occur to me, for example, that what I really imagined was what I would like to have happened on that painful occasion. But then should we not want to allow that, as in (i), this was something I imagined without realizing it? Or if not this, might not the hypothesis that the past event had a lingering significance for me give some point to the proposition that the particular *mise en scène* was part of what I had been imagining though without me realizing it? Sartre's own examples do not help us to decide whether he would accept this possibility or not. The kind of case he mentions is an attempt to recall in visual memory a detail of a no longer familiar object.[1] Here it is fairly clear that, in the way he must favour, the recalled determinations are *added* to the content of the image, or the imaging, as in the familiar case of serial recall, for example recalling a tune by trying to whistle it, or remembering how the road is about to go by driving down it. Sartre's special preoccupation here is twofold: on the one hand, a rather Rylean interest in showing that serial recall happens without recourse to a purely verbal stage, that is, in this instance, that it is an exercise, or recovery of *visual* knowledge as such, and, on the other, a rather un-Rylean interest in showing that the added determinations do not emerge as ready-made memory, but require the affirmation of a 'free and spontaneous decision' to the effect that they are indeed memory. However, a question that should really occupy him apart from whether visual memory imposes its content upon a mind without benefit of the mind's *imprimatur*, is whether such content can be constituted in an image without the mind's knowledge.

Be this as it may, the examples serve to stress that it is the transparency of the imaging mode, or, in Husserlian terminology, of the 'thetic character' of an act of imaging, that is the crucial issue for Sartre, as that which distinguishes mind from matter and, equally for him, subject from object. The correspondingly crucial counter-examples to his thesis, therefore, are those which would show that there was a structural similarity between the world of common objects, which the mind 'intends', and the mind which intends that world. I have suggested that such a similarity would obtain in two kinds of case: first, if imaging was sometimes phenomenologically indistinguishable from perceiving, and secondly, if it was necessary to infer the content or meaning of one's images from facts outside the moment of one's imaging-consciousness.

Now if this is the whole of Sartre's thesis that mental images are not objects it is evidently a very different thesis from those of

[1] *L'Imaginaire*, p. 127.

Ryle or Shorter. Furthermore, the immanentism it rejects is a much more special one than Sartre himself suggests. The sense of 'object' in which the argument at stage (4) denies that images are objects might be applied equally to any aspect or product of mental activity, from the agent's point of view. A sentence uttered in quotation or imitation would have some of the opacity that Sartre denies of the mental image, so it, too, could be described as an object, even, we should note, if the sentence is, in Rylean terminology, pregnantly non-said, uttered 'in the head'. A sentence uttered aloud, on the other hand, so long as it was intended to express something, but again only while it was being so intended, would not be an object to the utterer in this sense, nor presumably would a painting or poem to the painter or poet as he painted or poetized.

If Sartre's denial that mental images are objects were based only on the 'transparency of mode' argument; that is, if he would take his thesis to be established if no images were mistaken for perceptions, he would be saying nothing of consequence in support of the claim that ordinary, 'tractable' images, the normal ones which he mostly discusses, cannot be described as objects, or as object-like. But without an argument to support this, the general conclusion that images are not objects becomes extremely weak, saying no more than that we would never *mistake* a mental image for a real object. And it would surely be odd if Sartre's phenomenological description of images as acts rather than objects were founded on no more than the—in any case rather dubious—claim that images can always be distinguished from perceptions, a foundation, we should note, that would lead him to conclude that if Ryle's and Shorter's accounts were true then at least some mental images would be objects.

(5) I suggest that there are two ways of understanding Sartre's argument in our reconstruction of it. The first is as a series of four steps leading towards the conclusion that there are no images in consciousness. Understood in this way the arguments are quite clearly inadequate. They show only: (1) that in imaging we are thinking of common objects, not private ones; (2) that when we think of mental images we inevitably misrepresent them

by abstracting from their total structure as acts of thinking about common objects; (3) that all true descriptions of how we imagine what we imagine are transparent to consciousness; and (4) that the fact that we are only imagining is transparent to consciousness. Nothing here compels us to dispose of the image altogether.

The second way of understanding the arguments, however, is as a series of independent theses all necessary to establish a quite different conclusion, namely that all things fall into one of two mutually exclusive categories: 'that of things belonging to the world and that of consciousness.'[1] From this latter conclusion we can then derive a conclusion about mental images as a special case: namely that they belong to consciousness rather than to the world, a much weaker conclusion than that there are no images in consciousness.

Understood in this way, the role of the arguments is to refute individual theses, any one of which would suffice to rebut the general thesis that objects and minds are mutually exclusive kinds of entity. Thus if (1) were false, our references to a world would be exclusively to a private world, in which case the categories of mind and world merge into one; if (2) were false mental images would be of a kind with physical representations, and could therefore exist even in the absence of an intentional act; if (3) were false the objects we 'see' in an image would have the transcendence we ordinarily attribute only to things in the world, outside consciousness; and if (4) were false we would have to attribute to the mind some of the opacity that belongs, in Sartre's view, exclusively to the world of common things.

Sartre tends to confuse the two roles of his arguments. He is inclined to speak as if the conclusion he can legitimately draw from them could be expressed by saying that there are no images, as if the notion of images as things evaporates altogether once one sees that they occur exclusively in act contexts. A number of factors make this confusion possible.

First, Sartre is pointing in two directions at once. Negatively, he is showing that, contrary to some traditional assumptions, we have no need to understand imaging in terms of specific physical

[1] See p. 116 above.

analogies, in particular of physical replicas or representations. Here the arguments noted under (1)–(3) apply: they can be interpreted as showing that we are not forced to conceive images as a kind of material object; that it is wrong to argue, for example, that when we do not see a thing but imagine it, there must be something *of the same kind as the thing itself* present to the mind. Positively, on the other hand, Sartre also holds the extreme dualist view that objects belonging to the world and consciousness are radically different kinds of thing, and that physical analogies *cannot* be used to explain the structure of mind. Mind is composed of a succession of transparent acts of consciousness, of intendings, and cannot be conceived as a function of the influence of discrete things upon one another. Sartre is arguing, then, not merely that we do not have to bring specific object-analogues into our account of consciousness, though this is a necessary part of his argument, but that object-analogues are wholly inappropriate for such an account; objects come into the analysis of the intentional complex exclusively as the *termini* of acts of consciousness.

The special significance Sartre attaches to 'object' in this connection is also responsible for some of the ambiguity in his thesis. This significance derives mainly from his negative thesis, that is from his insistence that physical objects are directly accessible termini of consciousness. Empiricist epistemology sees consciousness as directly related only to modifications of its own states, the physical world being at best, as with Hume, something whose existence these states suggest but never conclusively establish, and at worst, as with Berkeley, nothing but collections of these states themselves. Sartre's view, on the contrary, is the realist one that the physical world is both distinct from our states (or as he prefers, 'acts') of consciousness and directly accessible to these. The physical world presents itself as such to consciousness, its objects being identical with the things that consciousness *means* by objects. The 'content' that empiricist (and Husserlian)[1] epistemology sees as a modification of its own

---

[1] Husserl analysed the relationship of consciousness to the world as containing an 'I' distinct from, or 'behind', consciousness. To solve the problem of how

states, logically separated, bracketed from the real world, Sartre sees as the way in which consciousness directly apprehends that world. The 'immanentism' that he opposes is the classification of what is experienced as an object as simply content of consciousness, the viewing of what we *intend* as an object as no more than an object-like thing in our mind. Sartre's view is that the objects of experience are the objects themselves outside our minds. They form the class of things we perceive or imagine, or otherwise 'posit'. When we imagine an object, therefore, we are relating ourselves to something that could in principle be directly perceived if it were present, and not to something whose reference is necessarily externally related to it as something different in kind. The image is a way the *perceptible* object has of appearing, or in Sartre's terminology, of being posited on the level of sensory intuition. It is not impressions of chairs we imagine when we imagine chairs, but the chairs themselves.

And yet, as we saw, Sartre seems to regard imaging as not just a relation to an object that we *could* be directly related to on the level of sensory intuition, but as a way of actually being directly related to it. That is, he is not content with claiming that the object of the description under which I imagine something can be a real chair in the world, but that when I imagine it the thing answering the description actually puts in an appearance, though not, as we noted, a 'personal' one.

But how is it, we also wondered, that a non-personal appearance can occur without there being precisely some *thing*, the image, to effect it? Having rejected the perceptual object's candidature to be an object in consciousness, is there not this further item at least to dispose of before consciousness can be seen to be rid of mental objects altogether?

to conceive the relation between the I, or Ego, consciousness and the world in a way that allows the Ego to 'intend' the world, Husserl introduced the notion of *hylé*, a 'content' of consciousness which can represent or resemble the object that the Ego intends. In perception, for instance, a certain coloured shape, comprising a directly given content of consciousness will be 'meant' as an object by the Ego. In *The Transcendence of the Ego*, the substance of Sartre's criticism of Husserl is that there is neither an Ego nor a *hylé*. What Husserl regards as content of consciousness is the transcendent object itself in the various ways it can be *for* consciousness.

Sartre's view of the nature of this residual item appears to be as follows.[1] There is indeed something that mediates imaging-consciousness. As Sartre puts it, in imaging-consciousness an intention aims at (*vise*) its objects on some kind of medium.[2] He mentions five distinct kinds of case: first, those where a physical object, a portrait, say, or a caricature, is that *on* which the imagined object appears, without our willing it to do so; secondly, cases similar to these except in so far as there is a distinct contribution on the part of the imaginer, as where even very incomplete sketches are 'filled out' or 'read' in certain, typically stereotyped ways, either from convention or the application of a gestalt; thirdly, the kind of free invention that can happen when our minds, free from the inhibition of any fixed intention, see shapes in clouds, faces on the wallpaper design, in the flames, and the like, that is where the medium minimally determines the description under which an imagined object appears on it; fourthly, cases similar to this except in so far as the medium is psychical and the imagined object is even more freely invented, since the 'stuff' accommodates itself to the intention rather than vice versa, as in hypnagogic imagery;[3] and then fifthly, the mental image subject to a fully spontaneous act, where the medium is again psychical and its determinations are exhausted by those constituting the description under which the imagined object appears.

Now we may grant that arguments (1)–(4) give good reasons for not regarding mental images as objects in the sense implied by these arguments. If they are products of an intention and neither survive the intention nor contain properties that are not functions of the description under which the imagined object appears, then they are clearly very different from the kinds of things we perceive, depict, and picture. And if Sartre is correct in saying

[1] *L'Imaginaire*, pp. 30–76.

[2] This looks like the *hylé* again. But Sartre would reject the idea that the medium is itself a *mental* content.

[3] 'Imagery of any sense mode, of a strongly autonomous kind and sometimes of almost hallucinatory vividness occurring in the drowsy state prior to sleeping . . . and while waking in the case of hypnapompic images.' Peter McKellar, *Imagination and Thinking* (Cohen & West, London, 1957), p. 201; cf. Richardson, op. cit., pp. 95–100.

that images are always transparently images, then to describe them as acts is not altogether inappropriate; they would be more like 'things' I do when I am doing them, that is *activities*, than things that I might properly call the *product* of my activity. But when all this has been said, and granting the anti-immanentist point that when I imagine Pierre it is Pierre himself I imagine and not a thing of another epistemological order, are we not still inclined to say that there is a copy of Pierre in my mind? Or more perspicuously, can't we call the appearance as of a real thing in the world that consciousness knows to be its own product when I imagine Pierre, a copy of him? Isn't it very misleading to say there isn't a 'something' in my mind that looks like Pierre?

We may consider this point in conclusion of our discussion of Sartre's denial that images are objects. For if it remains an open question as to whether the imaginary appearance is to be described as something distinct from what appears imaginarily, Sartre's precise differences with immanentism become less clear-cut than he no doubt intends them to be. So let us examine his opponent more closely.

6. HUME AND THE ILLUSION OF IMMANENCE

Sartre summarizes the incorrect view as claiming that the image is *in* consciousness, and the object of the image *in* the image.[1] In saying that to imagine a chair is to be conscious of a copy chair, empiricist philosophers and all those they have misled, have fallen for the 'illusion of immanence'. Correctly noting that to imagine something differs from perceiving it in so far as only in the latter case must the thing itself put in an appearance, they incorrectly conclude that what makes imaging possible is the appearance in imagination of a mental substitute for the thing.

What precisely does Sartre take to be the nature of their mistake? He singles out Hume's account as a typical case in point, taking a passage from the *Treatise*:[2]

[1] *L'Imaginaire*, p. 14. Cf. p. 27 above.
[2] David Hume, *A Treatise of Human Nature*, Bk. I (Meridian Books, New York, 1962), pp. 63–4, quoted (in French) by Sartre, *L'Imaginaire*, p. 15.

'... to form the idea of an object, and to form an idea simply, is the same thing; the reference of the idea to an object being an extraneous denomination, of which in itself it bears no mark or character. Now as it is impossible to form an idea of an object that is possessed of quantity and quality, and yet is possessed of no precise degree of either it follows, that there is an equal impossibility of forming an idea, that is not limited and confined in both these particulars.'

Sartre interprets the passage as follows:

'Thus my actual idea of chair is only related externally to an existing chair. It is not the chair in the outside world, the chair that I have just perceived; it is not this chair of straw and wood which will allow the distinction between my idea and ideas of table or inkwell. And yet, my actual idea is certainly an idea *of* chair. What can this mean except that for Hume, the idea of chair and the chair in idea are one and the same thing. To have an idea of chair, is to have a chair in consciousness. What proves this, is that what goes for the object goes for the idea. If the object must have a determinate quantity and quality, the idea must also possess these determinations.[1]

We can examine this reconstruction of Hume's argument in two phases. First, the sentence: 'Thus my actual idea of chair is only related externally to an existing chair.' Now if 'idea of' is understood as 'idea intentionally of' then Sartre attributes to Hume the view that in imagining X the fact that it is X that I mean is something I do to the image, make *it* mean—where this is not a property of the image. It seems fairly clear that this is indeed the kind of thing Hume would say. The image I have in any particular case is 'referred to' something in the world, at least in some cases, and may be at least in some sense in all cases. However, there is little doubt that empiricist philosophers, due to the very nature of their preoccupations, tend to confuse, even to fail to notice, different senses in which an image can be said to

[1] Ibid., p. 15.

be 'of' something. Not unnaturally their focus rests chiefly on the relationship between images and their perceptual origins. Berkeley, for example, stresses:

'Ideas of Sense are the Real things or Archetypes. Ideas of Imagination, Dreams etc. are copies, images of these.'[1]

But he also says that

'. . . properly speaking Idea is the picture of the Imagination's making, this is the likeness of and *referred to* the real Idea or (if you will) thing'.[2]

Let us consider possible senses of 'referring an image to its perceptual archetype'. One possibility, that for any X that we imagine, X must be a past perceptual event of ours, must certainly be rejected. Berkeley cannot have meant that we can never imagine what *might* happen, or has happened though not to us. For similar reasons we must reject as a possibility that the general description under which we imagine X must be, and be recognized to be, a description under which we have perceived something. For what about the creations of fancy? Now if in general we reject the idea that Berkeley meant the reference to be to some particular perception, a third possibility would be that the description under which we imagine X must simply be, and be recognized to be, a description of what *could* be perceived, though only in so far as parts of the description apply to what *has* been perceived. In one place he says:

The having Ideas is not the same thing with Perception, a Man may have Ideas when he only Imagines. But then this Imagination presupposeth Perception.'[3]

So perhaps all Berkeley means by reference to an archetype is that we only imagine the kinds of things we perceive, that images are 'post-perceptual'; in which case he would be in essential agreement so far with Sartre's claim that 'the two worlds, imaginary and real, are constituted by the same objects'.[4]

---

[1] *Commentaries*, op. cit., p. 365, Entry 823.
[2] Ibid., op. cit., pp. 364–5, Entry 657a, my emphasis.
[3] Ibid., p. 364, Entry 582. [4] See p. 101 above.

A fourth possibility is that Berkeley means that the description of an image is only general and that its reference to a particular real thing, where applicable, is made by an act of relating the image to the particular. But against this it is extremely unlikely that Berkeley, or Hume, thought of images as a kind of general descriptions; Hume at least referred to them as particular ideas, and not to ideas themselves as general descriptions that could be instantiated by other particulars. And furthermore, as we shall indicate below, there is nothing in the empiricist epistemology that precludes a particular idea being intended as an image of some other particular.

But let us now turn to Hume's claim that the reference of the idea to an object is 'an extraneous denomination, of which in itself it bears no mark or character', and see in what senses one might say that 'An actual idea of chair is only related externally to an existing chair'. Apart perhaps from the fourth of the possibilities mentioned above, this might be taken as expressing two quite distinct claims. First, it could be stating that there are such things as mental images and that in imagining (typically, in visualizing) something, the description under which we imagine is not determined by properties of the image itself. Now if we allow that there is an image, this latter observation could be saying no more than that, in imagining, the image does not come into consciousness without a specific meaning attached to it. Sartre of course would again agree, but uses this as an argument for saying there is no such thing as the image.

A second claim that could be expressed by saying that an actual idea of chair is only related externally to an existing chair could be formulated otherwise by saying that images have identities independent of the meaning attached to them on any one occasion (though not necessarily independent of such occasions themselves). This Sartre would apparently deny, though in the absence of any account of the criteria of identity he might set for images as acts, it is not clear that he would not allow there was some sense in which an image could be the same image on two occasions which were not, in another sense, the same act. Would he not allow, for example, that in imagining Peter, whom I have never seen, I might be having an image that was, whether or not intentionally, of his twin brother Paul, whom I met for the first time yesterday?

The fact is, however, that Sartre considers none of these distinctions. Rather he sees Hume as being forced directly into the illusion of immanence by failing to accept that the meanings images have are internal properties, that is, by failing to accept that images are no *more* than acts of intention. This is clear from the second part of his interpretation, where he construes Hume as saying: 'It is not the chair in the outside world, the chair I have just perceived, it is not this chair of straw and wood which will allow the distinction between my idea and ideas of table or inkwell. And yet, my actual idea is certainly an idea of chair.' It is obvious here that Sartre means by 'idea', a specific intentional act. He argues in effect that by speaking of an idea which does not have an intrinsic relationship to its intentional object (the chair that I have just perceived), Hume is forced to explain the fact that the idea is of a chair (rather than of a table or an inkwell) by taking the chair in the image to be the sole and sufficient source of the description under which I am said to be imagining something. It is as if Hume, by making the intentional reference of the image external to it, had put it beyond the pale of possible objects of thought and was forced to make do with the stay-at-home image, but that in doing so he had to confer on the image all the properties that should belong to a fully-fledged thing in the world. 'What proves ... that, for Hume, the idea of a chair and the chair in idea are one and the same thing,' continues Sartre, ' ... is that what goes for the object goes for the idea. If the object must have a determinate quantity and quality, the idea must also possess these determinations.' Thus the two errors of the 'illusion of immanence' follow one another in neat succession: first we have an image without its meaning, and then, because its genuine intentional reference is excluded, we have to elevate the image to the status of an object proper to serve as a substitute reference, thus generating the heresy of an object in consciousness. In other words, Sartre maintains that Hume is forced into accepting a fully determinate surrogate chair as a reference for the mind because he excludes the reference to the real chair imagined from the structure of the imaging consciousness. Hume, according to Sartre, has failed to see that imagining and perceiving are two ways of referring to the same X, and that the reference to X is contained in the image.

But it can be argued that this turns Hume's reasoning on its head. In the first place it was, for Hume, a premiss, not a conclusion, that the image must be fully determinate. He accepted 'a principle generally received in philosophy that everything in nature is individual', and no individual in its 'real existence' can be conceived (thought), let alone seen, to have 'no particular degree . . . of quantity and quality'.[1] Berkeley too, and as a corollary to his view that ideas of imagination (and sense) have all and only those properties they are perceived to have,[2] held that the properties they do have are perfectly determinate. Berkeley accepted that anything that exists is particular, where 'particular' means 'numerically one and completely determinate'.[3] The 'conclusion' that images (ideas of imagination) are fully determinate is entailed, for both Hume and Berkeley, by the fact that they exist.

Furthermore, the context of Hume's remarks is such as to make it very unclear what conclusions should be drawn as to his views about intentionality. They occur in the course of his refutation of the notion of abstract ideas. We can digress briefly to recount the argument.

It is in three steps. First he states that 'the mind cannot form any notion of quantity or quality without forming a precise notion of degrees of each';[4] secondly (a) 'that no object can appear to the senses; or in other words, that no impression can become present to the mind, without being determined in its degrees both of quantity and quality', and (b) 'since all ideas are

[1] *Treatise*, p. 63.

[2] Berkeley argued that 'since [ideas of sense and imagination] and every part of them exist only in the mind, it follows that there is nothing in them but what is perceived'. *Principles*, ibid., p. 71.

[3] Cf. Julius R. Weinberg, *Abstraction, Relation and Induction* (University of Wisconsin Press, Madison and Milwaukee, 1965), p. 21.

[4] *Treatise*, p. 62.

derived from impressions, and are nothing but copies and representations of them, whatever is true of the one must be acknowledged concerning the other . . . its copy or representative'; and thirdly that (*a*) since 'everything in nature is individual' and hence it is 'utterly absurd to suppose a triangle really existent, which has no precise proportion of sides and angles . . . it must also be absurd *in ideas*; since nothing of which we can form a clear and distinct idea is absurd and impossible', and (*b*) 'to form the idea of an object, and to form an idea simply, is the same thing'.[1]

Hume's somewhat vague terminology here makes it difficult to identify exactly what propositions he intends, but the following seems a plausible reconstruction of the argument:

(1) To think of quantity or quality (not: to acquire a notion of them) is to think of an individual instantiation of some precise degree of quantity or quality.

(2) (*a*) An object (or equivalently, an impression) must be determined in degrees of quantity and quality. (*b*) When a given object is present only in idea (or thought) there must be a copy or representative of it before the mind ('since all ideas [or thoughts in absence] are derived from impressions'). A copy of an object must itself be an object, and therefore likewise determined in these respects. (As distinct from the *non-sequitur* that because the thing must be determined in this way, therefore the copy of it must also be so determined.)

(3) (*a*) Any actual triangle must be determinate in respect of its size and the properties of its sides and angles; to *think* of a triangle must be to think of something about which it would be contradictory to say it was indeterminate in these respects.[2] (*b*) To have an idea, acquire the concept, of triangle is the same as to have some specific triangle in mind.

---

[1] *Treatise*, p. 63.

[2] The principle that all existents are individual (Hume) or particular (Berkeley) also applies to what we think of *by means* of an image. This follows from a further principle that Berkeley and Hume both subscribe to, that it is impossible to separate in *conception* what cannot exist so separated in *fact*. Hume maintains that what is 'absurd in *fact and reality* . . . must also be absurd in idea' (ibid., p. 63). For Berkeley and Hume, therefore, the following three cases are impossible: (i) imagining an indeterminate thing by a determinate image, (ii) imagining

Hume's statement that it is the same thing to form the idea of an object and to form an idea simply, is a consequence of his confusion of the notion of having a concept with the power to form mental images, or perhaps more basically and more generally, of his assumption that ideas, conceptions, etc., must be objects present to a mind.

This confusion enters at stage (3b) where Hume assumes that all we can mean by an abstract idea is an idea of some triangle about which, contradictorily, we would have to say that it was indeterminate in the respects mentioned. We would have to be able to visualize a triangle that was neither equilateral nor scalenon, etc., and for Hume the impossibility of this was the same as that of there being such a triangle. Which is to say that for Hume the question, How could one picture in one's mind what it would be impossible to draw on a sheet of paper? is a rhetorical one.

Thus, as we suggested, the statement quoted by Sartre, 'to form the idea of an object, and to form an idea simply, is the same thing', tends to show not that Hume thought that the object had to appear itself or by proxy as the determinate thing it necessarily is, but that to have an idea of any particular when one has no impression of it, or—to take the kind of case Hume is discussing—to exercise a concept of a kind of particular, must necessarily be understood in terms of having a particular *literally* in mind. It is true that Hume thought the image had to be as determinate as the impression, but this, as in (2b), was only because he assumed that a mental image of a triangle must present a particular triangle-shape to the mind in just the way that a perceived drawing of a triangle does; because he assumed, one might say, that a triangle in an image is nevertheless an existing triangle. It is unclear, however, that he thought that whenever I try to visualize a triangle, say the triangle I drew yesterday, the triangle existing in idea is necessarily the intentional object of

a determinate thing by an indeterminate image, and (iii) imagining an indeterminate thing by an indeterminate image. Sartre, however, by taking an object of a vague image to be a vague object (see pp. 106 ff. above), would deny that it was impossible to imagine a vague object (as in [iii]); but, as we suggested, his view might also be expressed as a denial of the impossibility of (ii).

the act of imagining, that my intention must stop at, rather than proceed via, the image-triangle—that for Hume to give any possible account of intentionality in these terms, he would have to say that what goes for the triangle in image also goes for the object I imagine, that the two would have to be equivalent.

The reason why it is unclear what Hume would say about intentionality in Sartre's sense is that this question was not clearly separated in his mind from that of the relation between the contents of mind (for Hume, possible objects of thought) and preceding sense impressions. It was clearly this latter question that preoccupied him, as amply testified by his own identification of the purpose of his treatise as the 'full examination of [the] question [of] how [simple ideas and impressions] stand with regard to their existence and which of the impressions are causes, and which effects'.[1] So when Hume considers an image (or idea) to be *of* something he naturally tends to construe this relation in causal language and to treat 'image of' as equivalent to 'copy of'. Its *of*-ness in this sense would indeed be a property the image possessed in virtue of circumstances external to itself.[2]

It seems obvious that we cannot in general make sense of the notion of what we intend by an image by referring to an impression from which it is derived. One kind of instance where this cannot be done is where I imagine something whose appearance I know only through someone else's description of it. Another might be where I have only seen a representation of the thing. And a third may be where, though I know I have seen the thing, I have no reason to associate the image I have of it with any previous visual experience.[3] (We may think of the case where I intend to visualize a thing which I know to be visually indistinguishable from another thing in my visual experience, say one

[1] *Treatise*, p. 48.

[2] Hume's tendency to confuse causal and intentional relations is evidenced in his using 'copy' and 'representation' in apposition, as when he says, all ideas are derived from impressions, and are nothing but copies and representations of them. . . .' Ibid., p. 63.

[3] That Hume mentions only the example of a person who has never seen a particular shade of colour but who could scarcely be thought on that account to be unable to imagine such a shade (ibid., p. 50), indicates his special interest in the sources of what we might today term our recognitional capacities.

of two identical twins.) In none of these cases can any equivalence be claimed between what I intend by means of an image, and what I have at one time or another perceived. All that could reasonably be claimed is that having the image, or the general description under which there is, in imagining, something I seem to perceive, there must have been at least some previous occasion on which the description, at least in its 'simple' elements, applied to something I saw. This says nothing of how I can imagine precisely the thing that I intend to imagine.

How Hume would account for this factor is hard to say. However he does refer to one kind of case where the sense of the image is not equivalent to that of the description ascribable to the image itself, where he talks of a particular idea becoming general by being annexed to a general term.[1] And although this has no direct bearing on the case in question, it at least suggests that an account of intentionality in terms of general descriptions is not to be excluded in Hume's terms. If so, then the converse process of annexing a general description to a particular reference, to explain the possibility of imagining something under a definite description could perhaps be understood in terms of the feeling I have that the present idea (image), which serves as a representative of an impression, is really the thing I mean. This would be an illusional account of the intentionality of the idea. Another way of putting it would be to say that I tend to treat the image not just as a particular image, but as the particular it is an image of. In that case, my intending it as such would be the same as to tend to feel that the particular I have literally in my mind is something answering to a general description to which nothing *literally* in my mind can answer. That is, I would have an *illusion of transcendence*. In the case of the chair that I have just seen, the illusion would be induced by the force of recent memory. 'When we remember any past event,' says Hume, 'the idea of it flows in upon the mind in a forcible manner.'[2] But no doubt in other cases the feeling could be associated spuriously with (come to 'enliven') images which are 'referred' to particular things we have never seen. This, incidentally, suggests one possible way of

[1] *Treatise*, p. 66. [2] Ibid., p. 52.

understanding a rather enigmatic remark of Berkeley's, quoted earlier, that the image is a likeness of the real thing and also *referred* to it.[1] We could, not unreasonably, take him to mean that when we imagine something, we know it is *only* an image we have, a 'picture of the Imagination's making', as Berkeley puts it in the same entry, but the fact that it is not just the *image* we address ourselves to, but reality by means of it, is to be explained by our *referring* the image to reality.

But then is this so very different from Sartre's account? Superficially the main difference appears to be that empiricists assume what Sartre denies, that one can talk of images as things apart from the intentional complexes in which we refer in imagination to reality. But the empiricists could conceivably be right in this assumption without being committed to the view that the meanings that images have within these complexes are external properties of the images in any sense that Sartre denies. And even if the assumption was incorrect, and the image was only to be identified by the description of the way in which the imagined object appears on one occasion, the way empiricists have of saying that images are *referred* to reality may be understood as no more than their manner of describing the way in which we contrive, by an image, to have an object appear in imagination.[2]

The issue may be clarified by reverting to the terminology of intentional and material objects, and the corresponding uses of 'see'. When I see X in imagination I see X in the sense of 'see' that does not require a material object of the verb. And (in the supposed case) I know I do not see X in the sense that does require a material object of the verb. Now the ability to refer to reality here is no more than that in which an image-experience, or

---

[1] *Philosophical Commentaries*, op. cit., pp. 364–5. See p. 129 above.

[2] My points in mitigation of Sartre's critique of Hume in this section apply equally to Fraser Cowley's somewhat uncritical rehearsal of it in Chapter 4 of his *A Critique of British Empiricism* (Macmillan, London, 1968). Like Sartre, Cowley claims that if an image is of something, and is no more than it seems, then it is not an 'entity' (p. 27), and that to treat it as an entity is to accept it as the proper terminus of imaging-consciousness. 'On [Hume's] theory, you could not imagine the buildings of Paris, for your present lively ideas, enlivened by

if you like, imaging, or imagining (in this sense), always implies a description of an intentional object. This means that the fact that we do not see X in the material sense of 'see' does not itself require us to substitute an image of X for X as an object of the image-experience, for we are seeing X in the intentional sense of 'see'.

The above is an argument, therefore, against the assumption that seeing X in imagination has to be regarded as a kind of material seeing, in which an image of X substitutes for X. However, nothing has been said thereby as to whether or not seeing X in the intentional sense requires that I see an image in *some material* sense; not of course as the object of imagining, which is the intentional object, but as the picture which enables me *to* picture X in its material absence. And indeed must we not *assume* of an image-*experience* that it entails a use for a verb of experience demanding an object in just the same sense in which, in one sense, 'see' requires a *material* object? The object here would be the image, and whether or not a material object, or a material object in the same sense, formally it would be an object of the same kind, since its non-existence would be an objection to the claim that there was an image-experience.[1]

If this is correct, then the claim that there is only one object in imaging, the transcendent object which is imagined, is wrong. The transcendent object is what we think of, or 'intend', but in order to think of it as we do when we see it in imagination there must be some immanent object as well; namely, the imagined object's imaginary appearance. So there is still this one

---

belief, would *be* the buildings of Paris' (p. 27). Thus he argues: (i) that Hume cannot therefore distinguish imagining the buildings from seeing them; (ii) that to make the distinction Hume must postulate 'the thesis of the world' (p. 33); and (iii) that to postulate this thesis is to dispense with the mental image. However, (i) if, as I suspect, Hume meant the enlivening of an idea of the buildings to lead to the belief in the *existence* of the buildings, and not also to the belief in their presence, the distinction can be preserved; (ii) as far as the distinction itself is concerned it is indifferent whether one postulates the existence of the world or merely acquires a belief in it, as Hume allowed; and (iii) surely the fact that what I imagine is not 'internal and perishing' like an impression or an idea but an absent thing (p. 24), far from rendering the image superfluous, makes its indispensability even more apparent.

[1] Though see p. 189 fn., below.

sense of 'object' in which the imager is aware of an object immanent in his own consciousness. And he would discount this
object only to the extent that he took the imaginary appearance
for a real one. That is, he would escape this appearance of
illusion only by succumbing to an illusion of transcendence.

Sartre's foisting of the 'illusion of immanence' on to empiricist
accounts of imaging is premature on two counts. Not only does
he not show that empiricists are restricted to immanent ideas as
determinants of intentional objects (Hume, significantly, talks of
images as incidental to thought, in that they are 'excited' by
'discourse', and that they occur *in* thinking and reasoning',[1]
rather than thinking and reasoning in them), he fails to convince
us that, as far as the image-experience goes, he is not still restricted
to such ideas himself. Indeed, if only an illusion of transcendence
can cause these items to drop out, his failure to convince will be
complete. For on his own account this illusion should be impossible on principle, as betokening a blindness of the mind to its
own transactions with the world. The point of course is that the
imaginary appearance is not *illusorily* immanent. It is there, and
what makes imaging possible. And the criticism applies even if
we accept that these items are not objects of the order of the
objects that appear directly to consciousness in perception and
imaginarily in imaging. For the only conclusion we can draw
from the relevant considerations here, as we saw, is that images
are not the same kind of thing as the objects we directly perceive.
And although this seems to be a point on which Sartre and, for
example, Hume genuinely differ, it does not explain why Sartre
should see images and physical objects as being absolutely
distinct types of thing; that is, it does not explain why images
should not be conceived as a species of object at all, but as acts.

7. SARTRE ON IMAGING AND THE MIND ACTIVE

The required explanation is found in Sartre's postulation of a
radical distinction between mind and matter. To understand his
conclusion that mental images are acts not objects, therefore,

[1] *Treatise*, ibid., p. 45, my emphasis.

I propose that we take the terms 'act' and 'object' throughout as putative references to the two basic, mutually exclusive categories upon which Sartre's analysis of human reality is based. Obviously this analysis incorporates a good deal of traditional dualistic metaphysics. Thus Sartre's distinction in *L'Être et le néant* between two fundamental modes of being, 'being for itself' and 'being in itself', corresponds in an important way to the Cartesian distinction between mind and matter. Mind, or consciousness, is 'transparent'; that is, it is always pre-reflectively aware of its operations. In a certain sense, *we* always know what we are doing—though one must again note that Sartre is content to make this presupposition without going on to analyse it or to mark distinctions in this kind of self-knowledge. Matter, on the other hand, or the world of which we are conscious, is opaque; that is, its existence does not depend on consciousness; and since it lacks activity or consciousness itself, it is inert.

But it is in its radical departures from the tradition that the force of Sartre's terminology emerges. One such departure is in regard to the notion of mental activity itself, and it can be presented quite clearly by contrasting it with that implied by Berkeley's claim that (some) imaging properly denominates the mind active. Berkeley, too, regards mind as 'active being' or 'that which acts',[1] but refers to the 'mind' as something 'entirely distinct' from its ideas.[2] There is, he says, something which 'knows or perceives' the ideas, and 'exercises divers operations, as willing, imagining, remembering, about them'.[3] Imagination is significant for Berkeley in providing immediate evidence of this activity. What struck him as significant and confirmatory was that we *can* consciously frame ideas, make and unmake them. However, he saw nothing of this activity in the ideas themselves. 'The ideas are effects impotent things.'[4] And: 'A little attention will discover to us that the very being of an idea implies passiveness and inertness in it, insomuch that it is impossible for an idea to do anything, or strictly speaking, to be the cause of anything. . . .'[5] Images are not active, therefore, they are the mere

---

[1] *Principles*, op. cit., p. 72.   [2] Ibid., p. 72.   [3] Ibid., p. 61.
[4] *Commentaries*, ibid., p. 369, Entry 712.   [5] *Principles*, ibid., p. 71.

materials and products of imagination. They are precisely that *about* which the knowing and perceiving mind exercises its 'divers operations'. Because he sees the mind's activity as the activity of willing (not willed activity), Berkeley comes to regard ideas as a kind of object to which the mind stands in a relation not unlike that of the practising gymnast to his dumbells; or perhaps more perspicuously, and as Berkeley himself suggests, of God to his creation.

For Sartre, however, it is not ideas that display inertness, but the things of the outside world. Particulars are not in, or reducible to, but outside consciousness; and consciousness itself is active. Now it is tempting here to invoke a further Berkeleyan principle in support of Sartre's description of mental images as 'acts' and his reservation of the term 'object' for things in the outside world. Berkeley held that: 'Such is the nature of Spirit, or that which acts, that it cannot be of itself perceived, but only by the effects which it produceth.'[1] What 'properly denominates' the mind active, in the sense which Berkeley clearly implies of what provides the content of our notion of mental activity, is only the effect of that activity. Now, what Berkeley regarded as inert Sartre sees as just such an effect. Where Berkeley found the content of the notion of 'activity' in the 'divers operations' exercised 'about' ideas, it being the manipulations *with* ideas rather than properties *of* them that provide us with the 'notion' of activity, Sartre sees ideas, or in general contents of acts of consciousness, as themselves products of such acts, and hence as the source of our knowledge of mental activity. Consequently, just as allowing an external world shifts the 'proper' denotation of 'object' to the things comprising that world, so the reclassification of ideas as products, in default of direct access to their producer, makes an image, among other of mind's 'effects', a proper denotation of 'act'.

Unhappily, Sartre's views on the mind-matter distinction prohibit this handy justification of his description of mental images as acts. On his own version of *esse est percipi*,[2] there is

[1] *Principles*, ibid., p. 71.

[2] See the Introduction to Sartre's *L'Être et le néant*, (Gallimard, Paris, 1943).

nothing to mind or its activity outside the range of consciousness's non-positional consciousness of itself. Mind is thus *truly* transparent. Its images, as also its qualifications of the world in perception, are not just the visible evidence of its activity, they *are* its activity. No inner processes give rise to these images or qualifications. There is just what we are conscious of, that is, pre-reflectively, the world as qualified in a certain way, either in perception or in imagination, and, reflectively, the qualifyings themselves. So in the final analysis, perhaps the closest grammatical justification that can be found for Sartre's acceptance of the notion of images as acts is that they are indeed qualif*yings* of the world in imagination.

At the beginning of this chapter I claimed that Sartre provided something essential to an account of imaging which Shorter failed to provide. This claim can now be substantiated. We noted that Shorter offered no explanation of how it might be proper to describe *imagining*, in a sense that involves some element of pretence or deception, as a *doing*, nor any indication of how to describe the hallucinator's or anyone else's *experience* of imaging. Sartre offers illumination in both areas. Regarding the nature of the activity of imagination he has two proposals: first, that imaging of any kind, deliberate or otherwise, is in any case an act of consciousness with something in the world qualified in a certain way as its 'aim' or 'object', and the qualification of that object in that way as its product, together with awareness of the fact that the qualification is *altogether* its own product, and owes nothing to the influence of perceived structures or configurations; secondly, that the qualifying is something that unfolds spontaneously at the level of visual knowledge, and not as the result of deliberate intention. As we suggested earlier, this can reasonably be claimed to be a feature of even the most deliberate visualizing, in so far as to visualize a boat, for example, is not to *use* one's visual knowledge of boats, but to realize or invoke that knowledge.

As for the hallucinator. To say that he is not seeing anything because he is not seeing what he thinks he sees, in the way he thinks he sees it, would of course be totally to ignore the phenomenon of hallucination from the hallucinator's point of view. No account of the kind of imagining the drunkard does can omit to say what the drunkard really is doing, as opposed to what he mistakenly thinks he is doing. In fact Sartre would disagree with Shorter that what the drunkard (or the psychotic) does can be described as thinking that he really sees snakes, if 'thinking' here means 'genuinely believing'. But whether or not we follow him in this, we must surely admit that Sartre's account at least has the merit of trying to say what imaging positively is, as opposed to what it falls short of being. I would add further that in allowing the hallucinator's 'snakes' to put in genuine snake-appearances, Sartre has provided the basis of a correct analysis of imaging as a visual experience. For as I shall argue in the next chapter, having a mental image of something *is* a way of seeing that thing.

V

TO BE A MENTAL IMAGE

I. THE UNEXPLORED PARALLEL

To understand a phenomenon is at least in part to find the appropriate language with which to describe it. And to do that is at least in part to place it in a conceptual relation to other phenomena. When we are unclear how to describe something, the proper initial procedure is the Wittgensteinian—though not only Wittgensteinian—one we saw demonstrated by Shorter, namely to see how far we can use in regard to it a way of talking we would find natural or 'literal' in another context, to see where parallels begin and where they end. Because visual imaging is at least some kind of visual, incipiently visual, or quasi-visual experience, then, one would think that the obvious first step in this case was to find out how far ways in which it is natural to talk about *seeing* can be applied, without strain or loss of point, to this phenomenon.

Why is it, then, that all three philosophers whose accounts we have examined, including Shorter himself, omit this first step? Why indeed do they all argue as if it was unnecessary, as if it was a foregone conclusion that none of the ways in which it is natural to talk about seeing could be applied to imaging? Why, in particular, has it seemed so obvious to Ryle, Shorter, and Sartre that the only thing that imaging has in common with perceiving is that it addresses itself to the same set of objects?

A trivial answer would be that the philosophers in question are weak imagers, that for them what is called 'imaging' just fails to give rise to anything that could be properly called a 'visual', or even an incipiently or quasi-visual, experience. Certainly not everyone has good mind's-eye sight. Witness Galton's report that many would-be respondents to his questionnaire about the visual characteristics and strength of their imagery thought he was joking. Galton's data even suggest that lack of mind's-eye sight is no obstacle to vivid visual imagining. He tells of people who 'declare themselves entirely deficient in the power of seeing mental pictures' but 'nevertheless can give lifelike descriptions of what they have seen, and . . . otherwise express themselves as if they were gifted with a vivid visual imagination'.[1]

But our philosophers don't give any evidence of lacking mind's-eye sight. Indeed Sartre gives detailed descriptions of imaging-consciousness that suggest he himself is a strong imager. Even Shorter allows that there is something which in certain circumstances we may call the 'image'. And if Ryle, in saying that picturing something is, in a certain way, like seeing it, isn't *only* saying that the picturer and the perceiver both address themselves to the same set of objects, perhaps his remark indicates that he too is familiar with the visual aspect of imaging. No, what I believe to be the correct answer is far from trivial. It is not that these philosophers do not acknowledge the phenomenon of imaging (even Ryle says 'imaging occurs'), or even that for them there is nothing visual about it, but rather that however much the phenomenon *visually* resembles perceiving it will be incorrect, or at least misleading, to apply to it the visual terminology of 'picture' and 'to see'. That is, it is not that the phenomenon of imaging is somehow less impressive or vivid than imagers sometimes suggest in their informal ways of reporting what they see in their minds' eyes, but rather that the terminology of seeing is too fixed and unbending, committed to too many implications, to lend itself to this, as it were, *merely* visual phenomenon, or to a visual phenomenon which arises in such special circumstances.

This may seem an unduly conciliatory interpretation of the arguments examined. Why not say simply that they just fail to show why we shouldn't retain the ordinary belief in mental pictures and seeing in the mind's eye? Indeed why not be downright unconciliatory and say that the arguments are nothing but

---

[1] Francis Galton, *Inquiries into Human Faculty and Development* (London, 1883), quoted, e.g., in William James, *Principles of Psychology*, I (Dover edn, New York, 1950), p. 53.

unsuccessful attempts to eliminate a painfully obtrusive counter-instance to certain favoured theories of mental reference?

This would be an appropriate attitude to take if we could safely interpret the conclusions argued for as simple denials of natural fact—which is admittedly how they look at least in the cases of Ryle and Sartre—and not rather as linguistic claims about the inability of certain terms in a natural language to apply to such widely differing kinds of case. But I think there is both internal and circumstantial justification for taking the conclusions, of all three philosophers, in the formal rather than the material mode. For one thing, taking them in this way makes them at least plausible and therefore interesting, as we are entitled to expect their supporters intended. But also it enables us to read the arguments as expressions of fundamental views on the nature of philosophical discussion of mind, views which I think it not unreasonable to assume are indeed implicit in at least two of the accounts we have examined—and that adds a further dimension of interest to their conclusions. So I shall adopt as both realistic and rewarding the interpretation of these denials that I have suggested: namely that they are claims to the effect that the terms 'picture' and 'to see', when correctly used, are not appropriate for describing the phenomenon, or phenomena, of imaging.

We can elicit two main, and potentially conflicting, kinds of reason in the arguments examined, each corresponding to a different interpretation of what it is for the terms 'picture' and 'to see' to be *correctly* used. The first is implied in Shorter's procedure. It is, roughly, that words like 'see' and 'picture' have established ordinary uses, and the contexts in which they acquire these provide, as it were, their natural linguistic roots. A picture is something about which it is convenient to ask and say certain things, and being able to ask and say those things is essential to the word 'picture' retaining its point. The ordinary picture—a portrait or a photograph—is the exemplar, so to speak, and it is the ability of the aspiring *mental* picture to measure up to it which decides whether, or to what extent, we give it 'picture' status. We have seen how in Shorter's application of this principle the mental image emerges as a kind of twilight entity, not so much a picture as a way of talking, a *façon de parler* for the imager when describing his bosh shots—the blurs he gets instead of the mind's-eye view he tried for—or the view itself—how the 'whole thing' looked—in fact, and oddly, for the precise respects in which the mental image *fails* to be, or to be spoken of as, something pictorial. This anomalous consequence of Shorter's application of the principle does not, of course, invalidate the principle. It may be an acceptable principle, and there may be a way of drawing a less paradoxical conclusion from it. In order to invalidate the principle itself one must attack its core—the idea that words are rooted in their ordinary contexts, and that this makes them resistant to our attempts to make them mean what *we* want them to mean.

There is the threat of such an attack in the second reason for withholding the terminology of 'to see' and 'picture' from imaging. This other reason we elicit from Sartre. As we saw, Sartre's denial that there are mental images is to be understood within his own special frame of reference. In saying that mental images are not things, objects, pictures, etc., what he is denying is not that the corresponding words in their established usages cannot be extended to cover anything in the phenomenon of imaging, but that the *things themselves* ordinarily designated by the words have a certain structure that, in his view, makes it impossible that *they* should have analogues in the mind's eye. There is nothing here about the words 'properly' designating only what they ordinarily designate. Accordingly, the counter-instances Sartre is interested in are not the bizarre occurrences required by Shorter for the terminology to apply 'correctly' to imaging (though these would perhaps be counter-instances to Sartre's claim too), but occurrences which Shorter, and Ryle, as well as most people, already take for granted, namely our mistaking a mental image for a perception (e.g. in dreaming and hallucinating). Indeed one might say that in Sartre's case it is the *denial* of the image that is the *façon de parler,* not its acceptance. It is his 'official' way of talking in the terms of his dualistic scheme. The usage is 'correct' here because 'object' is reserved for one of the two irreducible categories of entities—consciousness and *its* objects—and because the things we ordinarily call 'pictures' or 'images' belong to the latter category. In fact, as we noted, Sartre himself freely adopts the normal way of talking about images, and there seems no reason to suppose that the correctness of this way of talking would be an objection to his main thesis—as it clearly would be in the cases of Ryle and Shorter. Even if the image-appearance were properly referred to as an 'image' and there was a sense in which this image could be said to be 'in' the mind, Sartre's principal claim would still stand. For what he denies is not that mental images are correctly *called* 'images', 'things', 'objects', but that it is correct to say that images are sometimes not transparently images. And the threat in this to the principle inherent in the former reason is, as I shall argue later, that claims like *this* can only be asserted if the words we use to describe the mind are not *too* firmly rooted in their ordinary contexts.

If we embed our philosophers' arguments in the context of this wider and deeper issue it becomes unrealistic to see the philosophers themselves as contributing to a definitive and shareable pool of 'facts' about imaging; more realistic to see them as, to the philosophical manner born, grinding the axes of special theories—whether a speculative theory of mind or an anti-speculative theory of language about mind, or, as perhaps in the case of Ryle, both, where the axe is two-bladed and the special doctrine of mind delivered on the same haft as a special doctrine of meaning about mind. Just how much more realistic we see when we note that Ryle's own account of imagination comes as the eighth chapter in a book on 'mind', and not as the first chapter in a book on imagination, or when we see that Shorter's conclusion so obviously requires the support of a premiss stating a special theory of meaning, or realize that Sartre's book, though ostensibly and in fact about imagination, is also a sustained attempt to vindicate a radical dualism in the neo-Platonic *creator spiritus* vein.

But to return to our original question. Even if this wider and deeper issue is a source of assumptions that might justify the conclusion that none of the ways in which it is natural to talk about seeing can be correctly applied to imaging, whatever justifications these assumptions may provide cannot be justifications for cancelling the search for parallels that is the *first* step towards understanding the phenomenon. We should look to the phenomenon before settling for a theory that merely deprives us of one way of describing it. So before we get involved in these larger issues there remains the question which our theorists—for reasons not necessarily best known to themselves—have omitted to ask: How far do ways in which it is natural to talk about *seeing* apply, without strain or loss of point, to imaging?

The answer I propose is that there is no linguistic strain or loss of point whatever in calling imaging a kind of seeing. Indeed I shall argue that imaging is simultaneously two kinds of seeing: seeing the imagined and seeing the image.[1] There are two main points I shall try to establish in furtherance of this claim: (1) that seeing something in imagination, or 'in the mind's eye', is a way of really seeing it, and (2) that it is unintelligible to suppose that one could see something in imagination without also seeing something *not* in imagination. Both points are made in amplification of Anscombe's distinction, noted earlier, between a material and an intentional use of the verb 'to see'. The first point claims in effect that imaging is a case of the merely intentional seeing of something, and the second that one cannot see something merely intentionally without at the same time seeing something else materially.

2. SEEING THE SECOND OBJECT

(1) The thing that must be seen materially whenever something is seen *merely* intentionally is one visible that Anscombe's distinction doesn't cater for. Her claim, we recall, is that for every visual sensation there is a description of what it is of, and that there are two senses of 'see' in which, on the strength of the sensation, we say that we see something. The first sense, corres-

[1] Cf. my 'To See a Mental Image', forthcoming in *Mind*, in which I argue for the same conclusion, but in rebuttal of specific arguments for its rejection.

ponding to the material use, 'demands a material object of the verb'.[1] The claim to see the thing is withdrawn if there is no object visually before us answering the description; in this sense 'the verb "to see" is not allowed to take a *merely* intentional object; non-existence of the object (absolutely, or in the situation) is an objection to the truth of the sentence'. But in the other sense of 'see' we do not withdraw the claim; in this sense the non-existence of the object is not an objection. Anscombe claims the distinction applies to (proper) uses of all verbs of sense perception; beyond being verbs of sense *perception* 'these verbs are [also] intentional or essentially have an intentional aspect'.[2] Thus for 'see':

'While there must be an intentional object of seeing, there need not always be a material object. That is to say "X saw A" where "saw" is used materially, implies some proposition "X saw —" where "saw' is used intentionally; but the converse does not hold.'[3]

But there is a sense, though not one which Anscombe's concern with the intentionality of sensations requires her specifically to note, in which the converse does hold. When I withdraw a claim to have been seeing Pierre because I discover he is not there, I am usually able to replace the false description 'Pierre' with a correct one, namely of whatever I mistook for Pierre. If I am not able to do that, it is only because in practice I am not always in a position to identify the object in question. We assume, however, that some identifying description is true of whatever it was. Furthermore, there is both precedent and reason for saying that what that description describes is something I *saw* even when I mistakenly thought it was Pierre.

Suppose that on my first meeting Pierre he is introduced to me as someone I have already seen. 'Oh?' I say, and my host says: 'Yes, he was the bartender in Act Three.' 'Ah yes, of course,' I say. I *was* awake during that act and noted the antics of the 'bartender'. I say 'Yes' here because I can have seen Pierre even

---

[1] Anscombe, op. cit., pp. 171–2; cf. pp. 103 ff. above.
[2] Ibid., p. 169.　　　　　　　　　　　　　　　　　　　[3] Ibid., p. 176.

before he was, so to speak, part of my visual repertoire, before I could be said either to have realized or have failed to realize that *he* was the bartender. I might have said 'Yes' even if he had been heavily made up for the part and now looked quite another man, or, to stretch it further, if, instead of the bartender in Act Three, he had been the hind-legs of the horse in Act One. My affirmations here are acknowledgments of what might be called 'inadvertent achievement' senses of 'see', derivatives of the 'spotter's' sense in which one sees what one can pick out before one's eyes, except that here one is said to have seen something under descriptions which far exceed the amount of visual and other information one had at the time for saying that *that* is what one saw, or even to be able to recognize that thing as the same thing on another occasion. In such a sense of 'see' I may be said to have seen a picture that I actually thought was Pierre in person, even before I discovered that it was only a picture, indeed even if I never discovered that. Clearly it is a material use of 'see'; a material object is demanded of the verb. It is just that at least some of the descriptions that go into the object phrase correspond to nothing noted, or even noticeable, in the visual experience itself—e.g. the two-dimensionality of the coloured surface which I saw as three-dimensional Pierre, the canvas, the paint (as opposed to the colours), and so on.

So although there is of course the best of all reasons, namely Pierre's perceptual absence, for saying that I did not see Pierre when I only saw a painting of him, there is no corresponding reason for saying that up to the time of discovering my mistake I did not see the painting. That is, although, on Anscombe's definition of material seeing, a claim to see Pierre is falsified by the absence of Pierre, a claim to *have* seen the painting is not falsified by the fact that 'Pierre' rather than 'painting of Pierre' is the object-phrase corresponding to what I had thought I was seeing. That claim would be falsified only by the absence of the painting at the time for which the claim is made. It is tempting to conjecture that this is why in defining the distinction between material and intentional seeing, Anscombe leaves a blank, instead of putting an '*A*', for the object phrase following the intentional use of 'saw' which she says is implied by its material use in 'X saw A'. If X saw the painting materially when he thought it was Pierre and not the painting that he saw, then 'painting of Pierre' could not be part of an intentional description of what he saw at that time, nor therefore could a description including *this* object phrase be implied by X's claim, at the time, that it was Pierre that he saw materially. The trouble with the conjecture is that it presupposes that Anscombe *is* catering for the kind of visible in question, in which case, because the converse does hold here, the definition she gives would be false.

Be that as it may, according to her definition I should now be credited with two objects of vision, the painting and Pierre. And this, it will be objected, is needless reduplication. For aren't the facts of the case, where I only seem to see Pierre and Pierre is not there before me, adequately covered by postulating just one object of vision, namely the thing that *is* there before me and about which we can say, in simple but satisfactory explanation of the kind of mistake I have made, that it possesses the property of looking (at least to me) like Pierre? Indeed isn't that precise visible that Anscombe's distinction doesn't cater for the *only* one we need in an analysis of the facts of visual experience here?

This recalls Ryle's reason for denying that sensations have properties: in our present terminology, that where an object is materially seen, all descriptions of visual content are descriptions of how the materially seen object appears. This kind of claim is much in vogue nowadays, and has come particularly to the fore in recent criticisms of Anscombe's proposed intentional use of 'see'. Alan R. White, for example, maintains against Anscombe that when a descriptive phrase like 'I see two pennies' is used in contexts where it is not true of what is seen materially it is to be understood as an elliptical expression. For instance, the experience of seeing the double image of a penny, or a penny and its mirror image, is to be described as 'seeing what looks like two pennies'.[1] White concludes that because all descriptions of visual content

---

[1] Alan R. White, 'Seeing What is Not There', *Proceedings of the Aristotelian Society*, 1969–70, p. 62; cf. 'To See a Mental Image', where I attempt to refute White's criticism of Anscombe.

are descriptions of how a materially seen object appears when a materially present object is appearing, they are not intentional descriptions; that is, 'two pennies' in 'I see two pennies' is not an intentional object phrase, nor is 'see' used intentionally. In other words, 'two pennies' refers here only to something that we would have been seeing *if* there had been two pennies there. It is, as it were, an oblique reference to something outside the visual experience, not a direct reference to something within it. Recalling the conclusions of Ryle and Shorter, all we can positively say about the experience in terms of seeing two pennies is that this is what we *seem* to see, or what it is *as though* we saw.

There are a number of reasons why this 'one object' analysis is totally misguided. The main reason, as I shall presently argue, is that the 'two object' analysis is the correct one. But it is misguided, too, to the extent that its proponents offer it in any precautionary Occamist spirit, to curb an unruly proliferation of entities in the analysis of visual experience; Occam's razor draws blood here. Moreover, if the idea of the one-object analysis is to keep a more faithful record of quantificational needs, then on any plausible reading of those needs it is mistaken; the objects denied by the analysis simply don't generate any ontological pressure that doesn't already strain the belt of an ontology which allows talk of the ways in which materially seen objects appear. If, on the other hand, the analysis is an ontologist's pre-emptive strike against talk of mental images, then it is both misleading and unsuccessful. To get rid of this bulge, his ontology must put on weight all round.

Earlier we saw the strategy of such a strike in one of Ryle's arguments. 'Seeming to perceive' is a genus, he says, and of this genus one species is seeming to see when looking at a snapshot of what one seems to see, while the other is where there is no physical likeness before the nose.[1] Likenesses, we are then invited to conclude, drop out of the account of imaging as a peculiarity of their congener. We don't have to look for likenesses behind the nose. A similar attempt to drive a wedge between imaging and the seeing of pictures and likenesses is found in analyses

---

[1] See p. 43 above.

which offer 'imagine that I see' as the most perspicuous rendering of the way in which seeing enters into picturing, hallucinating, dreaming, and the rest. Thus, corresponding to his analysis of 'seeing two pennies' as 'seeing what looks like two pennies' in the case where descriptions of visual content can be construed as ways in which some perceptibly present object appears, White offers for cases where they cannot be so construed the unelliptical forms, 'seeming to see two pennies' (as in pure hallucination) or 'dreaming or imagining that we see two pennies'. Again we are to conclude that the only reference to two pennies is oblique, to what two pennies would be looking like *if* they were there.[1] And because there is no materially seen peg on which to hang the obliquely used description, the only way 'seeing' can be introduced here is by saying, again like Ryle and Shorter, that there is no seeing at all, only *seeming* to see, or imagining or dreaming *that* one sees. We are not, of course, to draw the fateful conclusion that there is something directly seen corresponding to the materially seen peg. Whatever basis there is for adopting Ryle's genus 'seeming to perceive' for both kinds of case, no similar generic tie covers the presence of likenesses, pictures, or images. In the one kind of case there is an object that we see and in seeing which we see a property of it that makes it look like two pennies, and in the other there is simply nothing there to have that property, there is only our as-it-were seeing of absent things.

Disclaimers can never provide acceptable rock-bottom analyses. For the only real function of a disclaimer is to delimit a proposed analysans by saying that it should be rejected, and that does nothing at all to explicate the analysandum. What is wrong with this 'analysis', then, is that it doesn't even begin to say what imaging is. I shall now try to show that the further analysis of 'as-it-were seeing' reveals it as a term denoting a species of intentional seeing, and that this, counter to the conclusion we are invited to draw from the unanalysed form, brings this species under the generic rule of intentional seeing, that whenever one

[1] White, op. cit., p. 62; cf. Roger Scruton, 'Intensional and Intentional Objects', *Proceedings of the Aristotelian Society*, 1970–1, p. 202.

sees something merely intentionally then one must be seeing something, its likeness even, materially.

(2) I am looking at a portrait of Pierre. A very good likeness. So good, in fact, that on this occasion I mistake what I see for Pierre himself. But then I discover my mistake, and of course no longer believe I have been seeing Pierre there in front of me. As philosophers would have it, I withdraw my original material-seeing claim, and replace it with another in which 'Pierre' does not occur in the object phrase. I have argued that the new claim can be retrospective. But it would be quite wrong to assume that 'Pierre' has now become a false description altogether, either of what I saw then or of what I see now. For, in the first place, it was Pierre that appeared, and perhaps still does. My mistake is not a visual one; I may have failed to pick out a material object on the strength of what I saw, but I have not failed to find the right description for what I saw in the sense of what appeared to me. I have simply made an incorrect identification of the object whose appearance it is—or less ambiguously, of the object which has put in the appearance—and many objects can put in the same appearance. And secondly, as we noted in defending Sartre, it is wrong to regard an appearance of something that is not an appearance of it 'in person' as not being a genuine member of the class of appearances of that thing.[1] In a sense which is important for capturing our ability to individuate things and types of thing on the basis of visual experience alone, a pictorial appearance is as real as any. In order to be recognizably of Pierre, to depict him for us, a perceptibly present object must mediate a genuine member of the class of appearances of Pierre. This I take to be the real justification for Anscombe's intentional use of 'see'. We need intentional object-phrases for 'see' corresponding to our material ones because in giving accurate descriptions of things that are perceptibly present, hence seen materially, we may have to include in them descriptions of what is not perceptibly present. There is no multiplication of entities here. The only 'existences' guaranteed by the descriptions are the references of their material object-phrases, and the object phrases in the enclosed descrip-

[1] See p. 105 above.

tions are not guaranteed a reference simply by being mentioned in the enclosing descriptions. The fact that what the former description describes *appears* is still to be construed as just a 'way' in which the objects designated by the latter descriptions appear. All the introduction of an intentional use of 'see' amounts to is that if what I see materially is only, say, a speaking likeness of Pierre in person, and not Pierre in person, then a description that does justice to what I see, in a sense of 'what I see' that does justice to the facts of visual experience, will include a description of Pierre in person.

Note also that it isn't because one was *mistaken*, only *thought* one saw Pierre, or only *seemed* to see him, that 'see' is used intentionally here; the disclaimers here pertain only to 'see' in its material use; rather it is because the visual experience in itself, at least in part, answered, and possibly still answers, to the description 'appearance as of Pierre', whether one believes Pierre to be there in person or not. And it is for this, philosophically perfectly innocuous, reason that when I discover that what I see is, say, Pierre's double or a cunningly placed *trompe l'oeil*, it could very well be wrong to say that what I see, subsequent to the discovery, is not Pierre but only something that looks like, or resembles him. Of course, if it is wrong, and I do see Pierre intentionally, the thing that looks like him continues to be something that I see. But I see that only in a kind of extended 'inadvertent achievement' sense of 'see'—extended because, unlike the cases of this kind noted earlier, I should say here that I *know* I am seeing it in that sense. It is the kind of inadvertent seeing I do when I concentrate on the pictorial theme of a painting, seeing its three-dimensionality, but know all the time that I am looking at a two-dimensional surface. Or when I concentrate on the surface and see the pictorial theme, as it were, only out of the corner of my eye.[1]

It is because we can make the distinction between seeing a mere resemblance and intentional seeing that it is wrong to say that 'seeing' enters only obliquely into a description of picturing, hallucinating, dreaming, etc. For the distinction corresponds to

[1] Cf. Hannay, 'Wollheim and Seeing Black on White as a Picture', p. 117.

that between an oblique and a direct reference to some perceptually absent object in a visual report. Let me illustrate this by means of one of Anscombe's examples, namely 'blurred print'.

When I see a pattern of black marks under a microscope, I may be reminded of blurred print. In fact the unfamiliarity of scenes under the microscope often calls for and provokes visual similes of this kind for conveying what we see, and the basis for the simile may be quite tenuous. Thus the similarity between what one sees and blurred print may consist in no more than is conveyed by a description like 'a linear sequence of not quite discrete but uniformly high black marks'. And the scene under the microscope can instantiate this description in a quite straightforward way; indeed in just the same way as it does the component properties 'linear', 'sequence', 'black', and 'uniformly high', etc. Consequently the scene's sharing of this description with blurred print no more needs an explanation in terms of its being *seen as* (or to be) blurred print than does its sharing these component descriptions with blurred print. In noting this amount of visual similarity between the black marks under the microscope and blurred print I do not have to see the former as the latter. All the explanation requires is knowledge of the kind which forms the basis of all our recognitional powers, namely that a property seen to be exemplified is, or can be, exemplified by other things than those that are presently seen. In this case 'blurred print' occurs only obliquely in a description of what I see.

In order for 'blurred print' to occur directly, there must be something *in my experience* answering to the description 'appearance of blurred print'. It is not easy to specify criteria for something one sees answering to descriptions of the form 'appearance of X'. But at least they must not be so narrow as to include only what could be (mis)taken for X. Cartoon-sketches and caricatures could never be mistaken for their subject-matters, yet they present their *appearances*. Indeed a person may be seen by those who know him well in representations that depart so far from the illusion of his being present in person that some people unacquainted with him may find it difficult to see a visual similarity between what they see materially and any human being at all.

In another respect, however, the formula 'what could be (mis)-taken for X' is too liberal. A dark shadow by the edge of the forest may be taken for an animal, but its being precisely an appearance of an *animal* may be something we determine on purely circumstantial grounds: for example by having been warned to expect one there. Even if it is correct to say that that is how an animal on the edge of the forest is in fact appearing, something more would be needed to make it qualify as an animal-appearance—perhaps a distinctively stealthy and neither human nor merely wind-imparted movement would be enough. To exclude appearances identified other than on a visual or con-figurational basis, some qualification such as 'visually char-acteristic' would have to be prefixed to 'appearance'. In fact the notion we need is something like 'visually characteristic appear-ance of X' where what is characteristic is what serves for an individual perceiver to sort visual appearances according to what is, to him, recognizably X-like, and where what is X-like is what looks *to be X*, and not what merely bears some degree of simi-larity to X. The important point here is that the range of appear-ances of X is wider than the range of appearances of X in person (where X *is* a person); and the domain of the use of 'X' as an intentional object-phrase of the verb 'to see' is precisely at least that part of the wider range not comprised of appearances of X in person.

In presenting an appearance of Pierre, then, a portrait offers an experience quite properly described as one of seeing Pierre. To say that it is one of seeing what looks like Pierre is not sufficiently specific. For the 'looks like' here has to mean the same as 'looks to be', and the analysis of that calls for an inten-tional use of 'see'. I have argued that it would be quite wrong to say that in seeing Pierre in a portrait I only 'see' him, or that it is only *as if* I saw him. In fact the only contexts in which such disclaimers can ever be in order are ones in which the intentional use of 'see' is already required.[1] For to say that one doesn't see

---

[1] Scruton (op. cit., p. 204) says: 'When someone describing a dream says "And then I saw a tiger", we do not suppose that he is using "see" in a special sense, such that it does not entail the existence of what he claims to have seen.

something only has a point when there is some question, in one's own mind or in someone else's, of whether one does see it. In this case, for example, I might say that it was 'as if' I saw Pierre, with a positive, appreciatory ring to express the vividness with which the portrait presents him to me—just as one might say 'It's almost as if I could reach out and touch him'—or I might say it with a negative, repudiatory ring to reassure my neighbour that in saying 'I see Pierre' I didn't mean Pierre in person, but only a picture of him (perhaps not even necessarily a portrait of him—I might be seeing him in a portrait of someone else, and of course seeing a portrait of Pierre is no guarantee that I see *him* in it). But for the 'almost as if' and the 'not in person' to be in place here the experience has already to be one in which the criteria of 'visually characteristic appearance of Pierre' are satisfied, and hence, if I am right, also the criteria of an intentional use of 'see'.[1]

(3) Given an intentional use of 'see' which does not require the existence, absolutely or in the situation, of an object corresponding to its object phrase, what now stands in the way of describing imaging as intentional seeing? It certainly seems a natural description, and if proper, throws at least one conceptual bridge across the deep divide that some philosophers seem so intent on preserving between imaging and seeing pictures. Short of a reason which I cannot find for the confinement of the word 'see' to its 'spotter's' uses (descrying, sighting, glimpsing, discerning, making out, perceiving, and the like), I can think of no genuine

For why not a special sense of "tiger", in which tigers do not exist?' My argument is that if the dreamer had an experience describable as one in which he saw a tiger, in the sense of 'saw' employed in ordinary judgments of perception, then 'tiger' *must* be used in its ordinary sense, of a tiger that exists, and that therefore the 'saw' must be intentional. Cf. 'To See a Mental Image'.

[1] This use of 'see' has been recognized by other philosophers. Cf., e.g., A. J. Ayer, *The Problem of Knowledge* (Penguin Books, Harmondsworth, 1956), p. 90: 'In general, we do use words like "see" in such a way that from the fact that something is seen it follows that it exists. For this reason, if one does not believe in ghosts, one will be more inclined, in reporting a ghost story, to say that the victim thought he saw a ghost than that he did see one. But the other usage is not incorrect. One can describe someone as having seen a ghost without being committed to asserting that there was a ghost which he saw.'

objection to the proposal, unless perhaps it be that one cannot be said to see a thing merely intentionally unless one is also seeing something in a spotter's sense—or in a related 'inadvertent achievement' sense—*as* what one sees merely intentionally. But since we do seem to see things even when our eyes are shut, we might just as well take this principle to show, not that imaging isn't seeing, but, anomalously, that even when our eyes are shut there must be something *perceptibly* present.

The justification for saying that imaging is intentional seeing is one that I think at least Ryle really wants to accept. To justify his claim that 'a person picturing his nursery is, in a certain way, like that person seeing his nursery' he has to show that there is something of the same kind that the person does in each case. And since this, surely, should be more than just having the same object in mind, what better candidate than seeing the nursery? A sense of 'see' which does not demand a material object is a minimal condition of this amount of resemblance, and the condition is fulfilled if we allow, as it seems we can, that in perceiving his nursery the person can have a visual experience similar to that which he has when picturing it. Similar in that the content of the experience in perceiving would be a sufficient basis for his retaining the claim to have been seeing it even if he had found out that it was not his nursery that he perceived but only something that presented the same appearance. Sufficient basis, too, for our rejecting his denial in that event that he had seen it at all.

We saw how Ryle's 'type' arguments effectively prevent him from having this reason for his claim. That need not mean that he would reject the proffered respect of resemblance; he may just have chosen his arguments badly. But we did find in his analysis of sensation reasons why he should positively deny the resemblance. We must be careful, however, in saying what these reasons are. It is not that if there is a kind of seeing that one can do both as picturer and perceiver, then there must be some species of object that is seen in the same way in both cases, hence not a *common* object inasmuch as common objects can be seen only by a perceiver. In fact far from offending Rylean scruples at just this point, Anscombe's distinction nicely accommodates them. Descriptions of what is seen merely intentionally are still descriptions which in their 'primary application enter into the object phrase for the appropriate verbs of sense',[1] that is, object phrases referring to common objects. What the picturer and a perceiver both see is the nursery, not some intermediate thing that comes between the *perceiver* and the nursery. But then what do they have in common? Precisely a visual experience of the nursery. As Anscombe says: 'The sense in which ["He who sees must be seeing something"] is true is that if someone is seeing, there is some content of his visual experience.'[2] But this content is, or is referable to, a visual sensation, and if this means the sensation can be described must one not allow, contrary to Ryle's view, that sensations possess properties that make them discriminable things in their own right, and therefore sensing an 'exercise of a quality of intellect'?[3] Well, they still do not have these properties in their own right in the sense that one can describe sensations independently of 'how common objects regularly look, sound and feel'. And sensations are not objects in the sense that *they* are things we can see; reports of sensations are still only ways of referring to things like 'haystacks, things that hum, and pepper'. But here, nevertheless, is the Rylean sticking-place. Reports of sensations, for Ryle, are exclusively reports of how objects appear when they are perceptibly present. As we saw earlier, Ryle argues as if, to be a species of sensory experience, imaging would have to be a way in which some *mental* object was being *inwardly* perceived. However, that what appears be perceptibly present seems a quite unnecessary requirement. Remove it and require only that the object be one that *could* be materially seen, and we have the basis of an account of visual sensation that can apply equally to perceiving and picturing.

(4) But now it seems both natural and logical to throw another bridge across the official divide between imaging and seeing pictures. Recall that when I am mistaken about its being Pierre that I see before me, I can be said (by others) to be seeing

---

[1] Anscombe, op. cit., p. 172.   [2] Ibid., pp. 173-4.
[3] See p. 32 above.

or (by myself subsequently) to have been seeing whatever it was I mistook for Pierre. I saw Pierre, because that is what I seemed to be seeing, and I also saw whatever it was I mistook for him, because that is what was before my eyes. These are the two objects of vision proper to the analysis. Now what it seems both natural and logical to say is that there must be some corresponding object before my mind's eye when I see Pierre in imagination. For if there were no corresponding object, that would be as much an objection to a claim to be seeing Pierre in imagination as it admittedly is to a claim to be seeing Pierre in a physical depiction.

The word 'corresponding' may be an obstacle to progress here. Quite clearly there can be no complete correspondence between a physical likeness and whatever we might have reason to identify as the second object. The question is rather whether anything that is essential to some physical object's depicting, or being seen as, something else is also part of seeming to see or picturing something when no physical object is being seen as that thing.

It is an advantage to ask the question in this way, because it involves no prior commitment to a definition of 'image' or 'picture'. It would merely hamper an examination of the descriptive needs of the case to be unwilling beforehand, for example, to call anything an image unless it was 'convenient to ask questions . . . [like] "Is that mental picture you produced yesterday still in existence, or have you rubbed it out?" [or] "Where is it?"' [1] For the result of the examination should be precisely to show us whether it is reasonable to *extend* the use of the terms 'picture' and 'image' to cover cases where by the very nature of the facts it will not be convenient to ask the *old* questions (e.g. 'Have you rubbed it out?') or if to ask them, to give the words in them just the same sense (e.g. '*Where* is it?').

Now I propose that the only thing essential to some physical object's being a picture is its possessing pictorial properties. If so, our answer will be in terms of what is essential to that. I will not attempt any exhaustive account of what it is to be a pictorial

[1] Shorter, op. cit., p. 531; cf. p. 63 above.

property. Some preliminary suggestions will suffice for present purposes, the main thing being to indicate what is not necessary for something's being a pictorial property.

First, then, let us begin fairly safely by saying that a pictorial property is a relation between something seen materially and something seen merely intentionally. What relation then? There seems no reason to suppose, as I propose elsewhere,[1] that it is not that of a one-to-one correspondence in respect of visual similarity. This seems at least an intuitively correct basis of an analysis of pictorial representation. Its niceties would have to account, for instance, for the fact that properties in the pictorial relation are not always just the same property ascribed to different objects. Thus although the part of a picture that depicts a crimson cloth must be in part crimson, a picture of something looming need not be a looming picture. If not, then looming-ness seen intentionally must be a function of some pictorial property that has the look of how looming things appear, without being an instantiation of the property of loomingness itself.

This leads to further points. First, pictorial properties are seen materially, not intentionally. Secondly, it is the function of pictorial properties, and a peculiarity they share with grammatical and syntactical properties, to be ignored, though obviously in some sense recognized or seen, though seen only inadvertently in the process of seeing something else. But thirdly, and unlike grammatical and syntactical properties, to be a pictorial property is at least to be seen as part of a picture, as having a certain representational value—not, for example, just to have the function of giving rise to such a value. Fourthly, although it is not necessary in order to be recognizably of representational *intent* that there be the presentation of illusion—visual similarity and certain conventional indicators may suffice to convey that something was *meant* pictorially—a pictorial property *seen as such* is itself typically illusional (as I have argued elsewhere).[2] Conse-

---

[1] 'To See a Mental Image', from which this synoptic account of pictorial properties is extracted.

[2] 'Wollheim and Seeing Black on White as a Picture', pp. 113 ff.

quently our visual attention is directed away from the instantiation of the property in question to that of the object represented. And finally, although pictorial properties form the basic content of what we see materially when we see something represented, they are still properties of something seen materially; and it is reasonable to suppose that pictorial properties must be composed of elements that are not pictorial—for example particles of colour pigment in the case of physical representations—and that pictorial properties therefore also stand in the non-pictorial relation of 'being composed of' to these elements, as well as in other non-pictorial relations to such elements of other pictorial properties, and that they even possess the non-pictorial property of having a determinate, if not necessarily determinable, magnitude.[1] In sum, a pictorial property is distinguished from other visible properties of a present object Y by being, usually by virtue of its configuration, that peculiar instantiation of a property that presents the appearance of its instantiation by an absent object X.

Now if this is an essentially correct account of what it is to be a pictorial property, there should be nothing to prevent our ascribing such properties to visual sensations before the mind's eye. Granted, of course, that there are any such sensations to host them.[2] In particular there is nothing in the account which would confine the possession of pictorial properties to things with continuing identities. So we don't have to say that a pictorial property is identical with the pictorial *aspect* of something. We can distinguish between, on the one hand, a physical object like a snapshot as the host of its pictorial aspect (among others), a role for which it needs a continuing identity in space as well as time, and which therefore cannot be performed before the mind's eye, and the properties of the snapshot by virtue of which it has its pictorial aspect. In other words, that a pictorial property is an aspect of something is not essential to its being a pictorial

---

[1] The absolute size of a pictorial property has no pictorial function in itself, only its comparative size in relation to other pictorial properties.

[2] This is a psychological question, not a conceptual one. Cf. James, op. cit., pp. 72 ff.

property.[1] So there is nothing in principle against allowing pictorial properties to be instantiated by things that have only those properties, including the pictorial ones, that they are seen to have at the time of showing, and have them for only as long as they show. No reason, in short, to require that some re-identifiable thing should be the picture, and so nothing in principle against saying that the materially seen thing that is the picture is a *mental* picture.

(5) But not a very good example of the *genre*, you might say. You can't rub it out, store it away, measure it, step back to admire its theme, or ignore its theme to inspect its surface texture. And indeed, in order to find this conceptual connection between imaging and seeing pictures, haven't we had to attenuate the notion of a picture so much—had to make 'being a picture' something that can be in principle so intangible, short-lived, and feeble—that no really significant conceptual point has been established? Philosophically, too, isn't it a rather disappointing outcome of the hunt, for all the hue and cry of the chase, to return with a trophy so obviously incapable of being hung on the wall?

Just how important it is for what we call a 'picture' that it can hang on a wall depends on a number of things, in particular the correctness of the view outlined earlier in this chapter: that the context in which a word like 'picture' first acquires its meaning provides its 'natural' linguistic root. We shall examine this view in subsequent chapters. As for the question of philosophical interest, that too is a complicated matter upon which the correctness of that same view has a direct bearing. We will come to this later, but note in the meantime that we may yet find that in our

---

[1] Cf. my criticism of Ishiguro ('Imagination', *Proceedings of the Aristotelian Society*, Supp. Vol. XLI [1967]) in 'To See a Mental Image'. Ishiguro applies the 'see Y as X' model to imaging and concludes that in the case of mental images 'the Y's disappear' and we are 'left with activities of seeing as X' (p. 50). For criticisms of the idea of a 'second object' see Ishiguro, ibid., J. E. R. Squires, 'Visualising', *Mind*, LXXVII (1968), No. 305, pp. 65 ff., and Douglas Odegard, 'Images', *Mind*, LXXX (1971), No. 318. For a defence see Reynold Lawrie, 'The Existence of Mental Images', *Philosophical Quarterly*, Vol. 20 (1970), No. 80.

mental image we have a more significant *kind* of object than we think. Even if not, however, and the mental image remains a philosophically rather dull sort of thing, we haven't done as badly as some philosophers would have predicted. The mental image—if we still want to call it that—isn't a snark. And that might disturb philosophers with a vested interest in supposing that it is.

Still, the complaint that our trophy isn't much of a *picture* is one we must take seriously. We *do* want to call it that, for it is, after all, a picture or an image that we should be said to see, in a material sense of 'see', if the parallel which philosophers have denied is to be established. In conclusion of this chapter, therefore, I shall defend this description of our trophy against a recent argument that claims that imaging involves nothing 'pictorial', an argument we should take up here because it does not depend on the assumption that if something is properly called a picture then one must be able to rub it out, store it away, measure it, etc.

3. PASSING DENNETT'S ACID TEST

D. C. Dennett argues that even the 'visual' element in picturing is not properly called pictorial. It fails to pass what he calls 'an acid test for images'.[1] The peculiarity of an image as a type of representation, he says, is that it

' . . . represents something else always in virtue of having at least one quality or characteristic of shape, form or colour in common with what it represents. Images can be in two or three dimensions, can be manufactured or natural, permanent or fleeting, but they must *resemble* what they represent. . . . Now I take the important question about mental images to be: are there elements in perception [and imagination] that represent in virtue of resembling what they represent and hence deserve to be called images?'[2]

---

[1] D. C. Dennett, *Content and Consciousness* (Routledge & Kegan Paul, London, 1969), p. 133.

[2] Ibid., p. 133. Dennett also applies his acid test to the content of perception. In the passage quoted he surely means to include imagination with, possibly under, perception.

Dennett's argument that there are not takes account of two 'levels' at which he thinks the question of there being mental images must be taken up. One, which he calls the sub-personal level, is that at which the phenomenon of visual experience in general is a physical process; the other, the personal level, is that at which a person or person-analogue (since Dennett is concerned to show the possibility of mechanical duplication of all essential capacities at this level) *sees* things—veridically or otherwise. We shall confine the discussion to the personal level.

Dennett's own presentation of his argument lacks something in clarity and rigour, but a plausible reconstruction of its main steps might go as follows:

(1) Something is an image of X only if it resembles X in respect of at least one quality or characteristic of shape, form, or colour.

(2) I can imagine X without imagining X as determinate in respect of some perceptual quality or characteristic.

(3) X is not itself indeterminate in respect of the quality in question. Therefore:

(4) X is not represented by an image in my imagining X.

On one reading, even if we grant the truth of (1), (2), and (3), the argument as it stands is clearly invalid. Because (1) requires only that *some* quality be shared by the image and what it represents it is quite compatible with (2) — that is, my imagining X indeterminately in respect of *some* quality or characteristic—that I imagine him determinately in respect of some other quality or characteristic, thereby satisfying (1), and invalidating (4). The problem is how to interpret (2). As it stands it is ambiguous. It can mean (to take one of Dennett's examples) that I can imagine a man indeterminately as to whether he is wearing a hat or not, though without thereby imagining a man who stops short where headgear begins. Or it can mean (to take another of his examples) that I can imagine a striped tiger though without imagining the tiger as showing a definite number of stripes. In the former case one's imagining the man to the extent that one does, as having *some* shape, form or colour, should permit the minimal resemblance required by (1). Presumably Dennett means by (2), therefore, that *all qualities as imagined* are indeterminate and that this is sufficient to establish that the minimal resemblance does not obtain. If so, then the reason why the acid test does not admit mental images is simply that the particular quality cannot be pinned down as it can in perception; though in practice it cannot always be pinned down there either. The argument then is that although, say, 'stripiness' can still be a quality which the tiger is represented as having, it is not a quality that can be said to be represented in an image, because an image, like the tiger itself and (according to Dennett at least) a snapshot of the tiger must show or reveal a definite number of stripes,[1] and also presumably stripes of a definite shape and shade. If this is what Dennett means, then we should understand (1) to 'express the Berkeleyan requirement that an image must resemble what it represents in respect of being perfectly determinate in regard to its *own* qualities or characteristics.[2]

This may seem an unduly potent acid to submit the aspiring image to. Not everyone would be so demanding. Armstrong, for example, claims against Berkeley that it is 'perfectly possible . . . to have a mental image of a piece of crimson cloth *of no particular shade of crimson*'.[3] However, I have two reasons for preferring the stronger test. First, there seems something needlessly puzzling about the notion of a person imagining something as crimson but without there being something crimson before his mind's eye— and so, one would think, a determinate shade of crimson—if only because the latter looks very like a condition of the success of the former. Secondly, in view of the fact that I am claiming not only that there *are* mental images, but also that mental images are seen, in the material sense, it would be to my advantage to be able to show that mental images are as determinate as the material objects they represent. Indeterminacy seems to belong to the realm of the intentional. So I shall argue on the basis of this stronger requirement. That is, I shall assume it to be a condition

---

[1] D. C. Dennett, *Content and Consciousness* (Routledge & Kegan Paul, London, 1969), p. 136.

[2] See p. 132 above.

[3] David M. Armstrong (ed.), *Berkeley's Philosophical Writings*, op. cit., p. 28.

of there being mental images that they are determinate (though not necessarily determinable) in respect of their *pictorial* properties (these being the only ones that matter).

Accordingly, and because I accept (2) and (3), my argument must be that (2) does not in fact show that what we want to call mental images are not determinate in respect of their pictorial properties.

The simplest explanation of why we cannot 'pin down' the number of stripes with such questions as 'more than ten?', 'less than twenty?'[1] would be one that Dennett has already equipped himself to accept in allowing that an image may be 'fleeting'. Might it not be that the image is just too short-lived for the imager to count its stripes? To this one may object in at least two ways. First, by pointing out that often the indeterminacy of mental imagery is not of the kind that could be resolved merely by retaining it for a longer period; it just *does* present a vague picture. This I think is a valid objection, and I shall come to it in a moment. Let us look first briefly, however, at the second objection. This is the argument that no meaning can be attached to the notion of *discovering* more about imagery than what the single, often fleeting glimpse one has of it affords. Discounting verificationism,[2] whose adequacy I would in any case consider to come under test here, there are two most likely sources of this objection, both inadequate. One is the view that statements about so-called immediate objects of perception are incorrigible because such objects cannot be other than they seem.[3] Then because such statements are incorrigible it is logically impossible that one should both be aware of such objects and also be able to make discoveries about them, for that would imply that *predictive* statements about them could be falsified. However, this objection wrongly assumes that we are aware of everything that is visually 'immediate' in this sense in just *one* sense of 'aware', that being the sense in which we are aware of, and hence know, what we

---

[1] Dennett, op. cit., p. 136.

[2] Cf. Shorter, op. cit., p. 538: 'if we did decide to apply [the expression 'notice a feature of my mental image'] . . . we would still be unable to give criteria establishing what the overlooked feature was like, what the colour really was.'

[3] Cf. Berkeley's 'there is nothing in them but what is perceived'.

seem to see. This is a mistake which Dennett himself points out in regard to the *ordinary* objects of perception, as we shall see. The second likely source of the objection is the mistaken belief that from the fact that the imager does not have to discover what he is imagining one can infer that there is nothing for him to discover about the pictorial properties of his image. The invalidity of the inference is evident in the case of such an 'exemplary' (Dennett's word)[1] image as the snapshot of a tiger. I can *see* it as a snapshot of a tiger—and so know in that sense what it depicts—and yet not notice, and perhaps not even be able to make out, the precise number of picture-stripes. Why then should we not say that imaging is just that special case where the impossibility of pinning down such precise degrees of quantity and quality is precluded by the picture's evanescence?

Dennett's own reason is to be found in the wider context of his discussion. He wants to give an account of 'awareness' that, while omitting 'no important residue in the ordinary concept',[2] could be applied as much to a 'perceiving machine' as to a person; and it seems that a necessary part of the success of this project is that the only content of *visual* awareness be that provided directly by the outside world. There must be no mental imagery, either in perception or in imagination, for that would form a specifically *mental* visual content. Now the belief in such a content in the case of perception may arise from supposing that because a tiger can be seen as having 'numerous' stripes but without being seen as having a definite number of stripes, there must be some only partially scanned but momentary and irretrievable visual content, an impression, which *is* determinate in this respect. On the contrary, says Dennett, what we scan in perception is the outside world,[3] that is, the tiger itself—which may or may not be retrievable. The fact that not everything in the available vista is noticed is to be explained by our selective focusing on only certain items in the vista. 'When we perceive something in the environment we are not aware of every fleck of colour all at once, but rather of the highlights of the scene, an edited commentary on the things of interest.'[4] Now Dennett's

---

[1] Dennett, op. cit., p. 133.   [2] Ibid., p. 121.   [3] Ibid., p. 139.   [4] Ibid., p. 136.

point about imagining a tiger is that what we have here is analogous to the edited commentary, except that there is no vista out of which it can be said to have been edited. In short, there is nothing determinately striped that the image-report of a 'numerously striped tiger' passes over.

But is that at all obvious? One might as readily suppose imagining to be the special case of visual experience in which there *is* a mental vista, a pictorial vista of fluttering, febrile, vanishing images complete with stripes, and that Dennett's analysis of *perceptual* awareness could as well be applied to *picturing* awareness as an explanation of the possibility of imagining striped tigers without imagining tigers with any definite number of stripes. That is, why should we not say that we simply fail to note the definite number of stripes that are nevertheless, though all too momentarily, revealed by our images? The answer is that there is no *logical* reason why we should not. There can be empirical reasons, but we shall come to that in a moment. Dennett is also wrong, however, to require of someone seeing a *picture* that he be presented with a vista of which his present seeing extracts but one 'commentary'. This is wrong because it suggests that a necessary condition of his experience being properly called 'seeing something as a picture' is that it be possible for him to have further experiences of the same thing. Not only is this requirement manifestly gratuitous, it would exclude even some fairly exemplary, fleeting and not easily reproducible (e.g. television) images from being seen as images. That the requirement is unnecessary can be seen from Dennett's own illustration of the 'descriptional' character of perception. He points out how the filmed version of *War and Peace* cannot but go into immensely greater detail than is provided by Tolstoy's book, for example the colour of the eyes of each filmed soldier,[1] and says that the 'end product of perception, what we are aware of when we perceive something, is more like the written Tolstoy than the film'. Yes, but *seeing* the film is again more like reading Tolstoy than, say, describing everything that the film offers to perception. And it is the end product of my perception here that *is*

[1] Dennett, p. 136.

my seeing a picture, not the visual presence of the screen vista. Dennett's mistake is to have equated seeing a picture with seeing a piece of unedited vista, for what a picture reproduces is the seeing of something rather than the thing itself.

We may grasp this point and the mistake more clearly when we come back now to the first, empirical objection to my suggestion that an inability to pin down the number of stripes on an imagined tiger may be due to the fleetingness, not the absence, of the image. The objection was that mental imagery often seems to be inherently vague, not simply too rich in quality to be grasped in one exposure. I said that I believed that to be a valid objection, at least for some, and perhaps most, visual imagery; but now it may be clear that it is not an objection to there being a determinate image. For if an image is what presents the *appearance* of something—that is the 'end product' of seeing it—then just as the end product of seeing a tiger may be expressible as 'numerously but numerically indeterminately striped tiger', so a *picture* of a tiger may have as its determinate *pictorial* property no definite number of stripes, but only some impressionistic agglomeration of incompletely individuated bands and spots of colour. Add to this that the inherent instability of much visual imagery may be shared by some kinds of exemplary image—for example a tiger may be represented by a changing assortment of dots and streaks—the numerical indeterminacy of the imagined tiger's stripes should seem no reason at all for denying that we see an image of it before the mind's eye. Our inability to pick out the number of stripes may be due to there being an image with no definite number of stripes to pick out.

Note that this does not mean that I have watered the acid test down. In the form in which I have accepted it, the image must resemble X in respect of being perfectly determinate in regard to its *own* qualities or characteristics. The question of whether there is an image is not, as Dennett suggests, a question of whether there is something that is determinate in some respect in which it resembles some *thing* represented, but of whether there is something with determinate properties of its own which, in virtue of some of those properties, presents the appearance of that thing.

Given this reading of the 'acid test' there is no straightforward reason why the answer to Dennett's important question may not be answered affirmatively in the case of mental images.[1]

4. CONCLUSION

The simplest and best argument for mental images is that if in picturing, hallucinating and dreaming one is seeing something intentionally, it would seem wholly inexplicable that one saw nothing at all materially. Without a 'mental' analogue of the pictorial property that allows us to see something when it is perceptually absent one could no more picture or imagine something to oneself than one could see something represented without seeing a representation. 'Imaging' and 'seeing things represented' denote analogous visual experiences, and both require a 'material' object. If there were no mental images there would be no imaging.

A person who had never seen anything in his mind's eye might well be suspicious of talk of 'mental imagery', but one who does see things there knows that the suspicion in his own case would be unfounded. We should not, of course, reject out of hand Galton's evidence of people who can 'give lifelike descriptions of what they have seen' and behave as if they had 'vivid visual imagination' yet report that they see no mental images. But a number of

---

[1] Dennett has another argument against imaging being 'pictorial'. Citing Shorter (op. cit. though misattributing to him the view that 'imagining is more like depicting—in words—than like painting a picture' [p. 136]—Shorter, it will be recalled, says that it is a metaphorical depicting [p. 530] and that mental images are half-way between pictures and descriptions [p. 542]), Dennett says that 'If I imagine a tall man with a wooden leg I need not also have imagined him as having hair of a certain colour, dressed in any particular clothes, having or not having a hat. If, on the other hand, I were to draw a picture of this man, I would have to go into details . . . unless something positive is drawn in where the hat should be, obscuring that area, the man in the picture must either have a hat on or not' (p. 135). But Shorter does not say this, nor is it relevantly true. An uncompleted picture is no less a picture, so far as it goes, and the artist no more than the imaginer need say that he has *depicted* something unfinished. Of course the artist, like others, might say it looks like a man who has been scalped, but if we had more stable mental images we might make the same kind of appraisals about them.

interpretations of the evidence are possible. What the people in question reported doing might have been something like describing what they had seen or re-enacting their responses to it, activities that would seem no more to require the presence, or seeing, of an image of what they had seen than would drawing a picture of what they had seen. Some may even have been describing what they seemed to see in their mind's eye but truthfully reporting that what they seemed to see was not a picture, because—not having succumbed to the illusion of immanence—they would say it was, for instance, their friend, and not a picture of their friend, that they saw. If asked, 'Do you see *anything?*', they might have said 'Of course, my friend so-and-so'. They would then have been seeing mental images.

I said there was a campaign against mental images. Dennett I am sure speaks for many philosophers when he admits that to be able to dispose of them would be 'a clear case of good riddance'. He says, 'We can all do without the dimensionlessness of mental images (that strange quality that prevents us from putting any kind of ruler, physical or mental, along the boundaries of mental images), and their penchant for inhabiting a special space of their own, distinct from physical space'.[1] A little presuming, perhaps, this observation *ad hominem*. Not everyone finds it so strange that the mental resists being forced into the Procrustean bed of the physical, or is so convinced of the power of the ruler to determine what exists. But if anyone really does find the image's unmeasureableness and its 'penchant' disturbing I suggest he must find a better way out of his discomfort than trying to convince himself that the image does not exist, or as Dennett puts it, that '"mental image" is valueless as a referring expression in *any* circumstances'.[2] It needs more than a nudge and a wink to make good what a poor remedy lacks.

[1] Dennett, op. cit., p. 141.
[2] Ibid., p. 141. The vital conclusion is tucked away in a footnote.

VI

WITTGENSTEIN ON THE NATURE OF THINGS

I. INTRODUCTION

Imaging occurs, there are mental images, and we see them. I am inclined to say that any valid argument which contradicts this conclusion must contain a false premiss, simply because it requires us to deny a 'well-known fact about the mental life of human beings'.[1] But of course it would be the height of philosophical *naïveté* to suppose that a well-known fact was a well understood one. And our conclusion gives rise to many perplexing questions. Where, for instance, do these images exist?

This seems to be a genuine question, and not one to be passed off as an unnecessary puzzlement, a philosophical headache, as Wittgenstein would say, or a bump that the understanding gets by running its head up against the limits of language.[2] On the other hand there are unnecessary puzzlements to which our conclusion may give rise. In speaking of *mental* images, and of seeing them, and also in arguing in the way in which we have for this way of speaking, we might seem to be hinting that a mental image was no more than a weaker brother of the 'exemplary' image. In fact our very willingness to follow Dennett in calling physical representations 'exemplary' implies that in accounting for the place of imaging in mental life, all we can do is measure the extent to which imaging conforms to this paradigm, as if *it* was the measure of all things representational. We then come, as he does, to think that the respects in which the mental image fails to conform to the paradigm, are deficiencies on its part. We would need mental rulers to measure them, mental magazines to store them in, special receptors to see them with. Finally, be-

---

[1] Cf. Ryle, *The Concept of Mind*, p. 16, and p. 28 above.
[2] Ludwig Wittgenstein, *Philosophical Investigations*, trans. G. E. M. Anscombe (Blackwell, Oxford, 1958), Pt. I, § 119.

cause the facts of mental life offer no foothold for *these* exemplary notions, we are forced to conclude, like Dennett, that our 'use of the word "image" is systematically misleading, regardless of how well entrenched it is in our ordinary way of speaking'.[1]

Wittgenstein himself warned against this blind alley. We approach the mental as if it *ought* to conform to the physical and then find ourselves in the position of having to deny the obvious. Not that ordinary modes of speech are sacrosanct, but when a denial of the aptness of a common expression brings with it an abnegation of the familiar fact which it is used to describe, we may well suspect we have approached the mental in the wrong way. Wittgenstein offers two correctives. First, he suggests that we treat the mind as *sui generis*, allowing for a radical dualism close to that of Sartre, in which it would be wrong to think of the mental in terms of physical analogies. Secondly, he points out certain features, or preconditions, of our understanding of mental phenomena which show that it is wrong in any case to regard the inner as an autonomous sphere of mental life, as if, for example, what distinguished a *mental* image from a so-called exemplary one was its privacy, unmeasurableness, and so on.

Having tested our *naïve* assumption that mental images exist and are seen against arguments that deny it, we may now try to divest it further of its *naïveté* by exposing it to some of the sophistication of the New Enlightenment.

2. UNDERSTANDING MENTAL PHENOMENA

In the *Investigations* Wittgenstein says: 'One ought to ask, not what images are or what happens when one imagines anything, but how the word "imagination" is used.'[2] He realizes this looks as if he were saying that we should give up hopeless inquiries into the essence or *nature* of imagining and take up instead the more

---

[1] Dennett, op. cit., p. 133.

[2] *Investigations*, Pt. I, § 370. The German original has: '*wie das Wort "Vorstellung" gebraucht wird*'. In rendering 'Vorstellung' by 'imagination' we should think of its use in expressions like 'in imagination' and not expressions like 'with imagination'. Wittgenstein could just as well have said that we should ask how words like 'imagine', or 'see in the mind's eye' are used.

fruitful investigation of language habits, but he is not saying that. He continues: 'the question as to the nature of the image is as much about the word "imagination" as my question is.' So he is not denying that there is a question of what we may properly refer to as the 'nature' of the image, only that 'this question is not to be decided—neither for the person who does the imagining, nor for anyone else—by pointing; nor yet by a description of any process'.

What is it, we might ask, that connects the use of a word to the nature of something it is used to refer to but does not connect the description of a process to that nature? The answer is to be found in Wittgenstein's view on the 'nature' of our understanding of mental phenomena. According to this view the content of our understanding of the mind has two necessary components: distinctions in experience and what, for want of a better label, we may term 'contexts of importance'.

The distinctions Wittgenstein particularly has in mind are those that lead to obviously unacceptable answers.

'Think of the expression: "I heard a plaintive melody". And now the question is: "Does he hear the plaint?" And if I reply: "No, he doesn't hear it, he merely has a sense of it"—where does that get us? One cannot mention a sense-organ for this "sense".'[1]

To help arrive at the right answer Wittgenstein makes much of the notion of seeing-as, or aspect-seeing, where a drawn figure can be seen alternately as a representation of different things. This helps by showing how we can hear things like 'plaints' in a way that is different in kind from having sense impressions:

'The colour of the visual impression corresponds to the colour of the object (this blotting paper looks pink to me, and is pink)—the shape of the visual impression to the shape of the object (it looks rectangular to me, and is rectangular) —but what I perceive in the dawning of an aspect is not a property of the object, but an internal relation between it and other objects'.[2]

---

[1] *Investigations*, p. 209.　　　　[2] *Investigations*, p. 212.

Instead of postulating a mind's ear sensitive to plaints, there-fore, we look for a similarity between detecting the plaint in the melody and the case of seeing an aspect of something in which the sense-organ explanation seems quite unfitting because one does not regard the aspect as a property of the thing that appears. Such an aspect can be the object's depicting for me my friend. Because, as Ishiguro points out, this aspect 'can be said to have an internal relation to my friend since one would not be able to identify the aspect without reference to my friend',[1] the explana-tion must lie in what one contributes to the object, not in another kind of impression that one may receive from it.

However, this too is liable to be given the wrong kind of explanation. The question of whether the aspect is seen in the same way as the thing that it is seen as an aspect of is not to be settled by drawing *theoretical* conclusions from the fact that one can see something in two different ways. Instead of thinking that it *follows* in some way from this fact that 'I *see* something different in the two cases', the fact must stand on its own as that which 'gives us a reason to use this expression here'.[2] The kind of thing that can give us a reason to say that we see something in a new way is that we can 'give a new kind of description of it'.[3]

'"And is it really a different impression?"—In order to answer this I should like to ask myself whether there is really something different there in me. But how can I find out?—I *describe* what I am seeing differently.'[4]

The concept of an aspect is *fixed*[5] in terms of the importance the expressions referring to aspects acquire for us in ordinary contexts.[6] This is what gives us the right to say such things as 'I am now seeing it as . . .', not some story about a personal contri-bution.

Take another example: the difference between seeing that an animal in a picture is transfixed by an arrow and seeing the same representational theme merely in silhouette. Now this distinction

---

[1] Ishiguro, 'Imagination', *Proceedings*, p. 42. [2] *Investigations*, p. 195.
[3] Ibid., p. 199. [4] *Investigations*, p. 202.
[5] Ibid., p. 204. [6] Ibid., pp. 202 and 205.

assumes an importance because we want to ask in respect of the latter, 'Do you *see* the arrow—or do you merely *know* that these two bits are supposed to represent part of an arrow?'[1]

But it would be wrong to take this question to be answerable in terms of a physiological explanation, in terms of a description of what *actually* happens. The problem is 'not a causal but a conceptual one'.[2] That is, it has to do with the extent to which the conditions we have fixed for the use of the word 'see' can accommodate the new case, or be amended so as to do so without blurring the distinctions which the conditions were fixed in order to mark. Ultimately it is a question of the extent to which the empirical distinctions which we use the term 'see' to discriminate are reproduced in the problematic case. The task is one of accommodating the new distinction into an existing context of importance, a framework of distinctions that are already 'important for us'. When we ask whether the problem case is a *genuine* visual experience, the question is: 'In what sense is it one?'[3]

Suppose there *was* a causal or physiological explanation of this particular distinction. Even so, that would add nothing to the kind of explanation of the phenomenon that comprises our understanding of it. For to understand a phenomenon is always to seek a *conceptual* justification for it. If we said, for example, that in the case of the silhouette we genuinely see to the extent that the 'content' of the impression 'corresponds' to the 'publicly visible configuration', and that whatever has no correlate in the 'public object' is not genuinely seen, we introduce notions that have no obvious bearing on our understanding of 'seeing' at all. Whether we 'see' something or not, Wittgenstein suggests, has to do with our attitude, or the way we treat it.[4]

'Seeing' *Y* as *X* is distinguished from 'knowing that *Y* is meant to represent *X*' in terms not of physiological processes but of the different kinds of activity, and the consequences important in

---

[1] *Investigations*, p. 203.　　[2] Ibid., p. 203.　　[3] Cf. ibid., p. 204.

[4] Cf. *Investigations*, p. 204. 'For when should I call it a mere case of knowing, not seeing?—Perhaps when someone treats the picture as a working drawing, *reads* it like a blueprint. (Fine shades of behaviour.—Why are they *important?* They have important consequences.)'

respect of *them*, we wish to discriminate. In this respect looking for physiological explanations, of course, can itself be an activity supplying its own terms of reference. But as such it cannot have consequences important for our understanding of seeing in Wittgenstein's sense; if the result of such investigations is that some of the visual impression corresponds to what is 'literally' seen and the rest added in such a way as to be only 'metaphorically' seen, in the form either of a quasi-visual 'addition' to the impression or of a merely 'intellective' interpretation, this conclusion in no way affects the features of the original distinction that makes it important for us. It is a conclusion that is totally irrelevant to what *roles* pictures have in our lives,[1] and which ignores differences in attitudes,[2] expectations, and the relevance of different kinds of mistake.[3] Certainly it would supply one context of importance for the distinction, but not one that affected the place of 'seeing' in our conceptual scheme. Rather than supplying an autonomous context of significance, such an investigation would indeed presuppose the kind of understanding that forms the only genuinely autonomous context of importance, namely the context of practical needs and consequences that our psychological vocabulary is inextricably bound up with.

If this is the gist of Wittgenstein's remarks both in the passages referred to and in others, notably those concerned with 'language-games' and 'forms of life',[4] their viewpoint could be expressed in the following proposition:

(1) Accounts of mental processes are neither necessary nor sufficient for our understanding of psychological phenomena.

They are not sufficient because our understanding of psychological phenomena is necessarily evinced in part by our non-theoretical application of psychological terms, and they are not necessary because our non-theoretical application of psycholo-

---

[1] Cf. *Investigations*, p. 205.

[2] *Investigations*, p. 205.

[3] Ibid., p. 204.

[4] Ibid., Pt. I, § 23, but also *passim*. Cf. also ibid., p. 200 where Wittgenstein talks of having to '*accept* the everyday language-game. . . .'

gical terms constitutes an autonomous understanding of the phenomena.[1]

However, that accounts of mental processes are neither necessary nor sufficient for our understanding of psychological phenomena in no way implies that psychological terms cannot be found to designate inner objects (e.g. mental images) or inner processes (e.g. imaging). It only shows that whether they do or not is irrelevant for our understanding of the phenomena. It implies, one might say, that for the purposes of explaining the content of this understanding a search for mental objects or an investigation into mental processes would be misguided, but it does not imply that they would be altogether fruitless.

Yet Wittgenstein often speaks as if they *would* be fruitless, indeed that to the philosophically unprejudiced they obviously are; so the point is not quite clear. For example, in answering the question 'How does the philosophical problem about mental processes and states and about behaviourism arise?' he says:

'The first step is the one that altogether escapes notice. We talk of processes and states and leave their nature undecided. Sometime perhaps we shall know more about them—we think. But that is just what commits us to a particular way of looking at the matter. For we have a definite concept of what it means to learn to know a process better. . . . And now the analogy which was to make us understand our thought falls to pieces. So we have to deny the yet uncomprehended process in the yet unexplored medium. And now it looks as if we had denied mental processes. And naturally we don't want to deny them.'[2]

The point here seems to be not *just* that an exploration of the medium of the mind affords nothing corresponding to 'learning to know a process better', but that the very expedition, with its goal thus predetermined, is destined to produce the perplexing, unwanted result of behaviourism. The denial that there are pro-

---

[1] 'Autonomous' is deliberately vague, since I am not clear to what extent, if at all, Wittgenstein would allow psychological theory to affect our uses of terms, or on what basis.

[2] *Investigations*, Pt. I, § 308.

cesses is a direct product of the search for a process; but as such it is misleading, because one should not even *expect* to find such things. What is wrong is the idea that the mind should follow patterns laid down in a quite different medium.[1]

Wittgenstein seems to be making two points: first, we should not expect the mental to mirror the physical; and secondly, we should restrict ourselves to the phenomena, that is, we should not persist in assuming a process even if we cannot discern one. The dispute between behaviourists and advocates of mental states and processes arises, thinks Wittgenstein, because *we* speak for the facts rather than let them speak for themselves. Thus in stipulating processes and states even where there is nothing identifiable to which to attach the labels, the 'mentalist' becomes an easy target for the behaviourist, who then, in his turn, seems to deny not only the natural and, to non-philosophers, harmless assumption, of a *mind* at work,[2] but also, as in the case of pains and images, an obvious empirical fact, namely that there are private mental occurrences and objects. The fault common to both is to project the physical on to the mental. The prejudice of the mentalist gives way, when tested, to the misleading denials of the behaviourist.

For Wittgenstein the dispute should presumably be settled by finding 'conceptual' justifications for the expressions of either viewpoint. This would mean, in his case, that it is to be settled by appealing, first, to experience to see whether there is anything to be distinguished, and secondly, to the kinds of consideration

---

[1] Cf. Wittgenstein's remarks (610 and 611) in *Zettel* (trans. G. E. M. Anscombe [Blackwell, Oxford, 1967]): 'I saw this man years ago: now I have seen him again, I recognize him, I remember his name. And why does there have to be a cause of this remembering in my nervous system? Why must something or other, whatever it may be, be stored up there *in any form*? Why *must* a trace have been left behind? Why should there not be a psychological regularity to which *no* physiological regularity corresponds? If this upsets our concept of causality, then it is high time it was upset.' And: 'The prejudice in favour of psychological parallelism is a fruit of primitive interpretations of our concepts. For if one allows a causality between psychological phenomena which is not mediated physiologically, one thinks one is professing belief in a gaseous mental entity.'

[2] Cf. Ryle, *The Concept of Mind*, p. 34.

that he takes to determine the importance of a distinction. The question of whether there are mental states, mental processes, or mental objects is to be settled by a 'grammatical investigation,'[1] the results of which are determined by the uses that have already been given to words in everyday situations.

However, there is a curious, though concealed, hiatus in Wittgenstein's thought here. The everyday situations in which we learn our psychological vocabulary are those in which the unexplored medium plays no explicit role; the situations provide the self-sufficient foundation of the language. This explains why we do not need to consult the medium to describe what, in practice, we mean by 'mind'. But why should we not ask about the medium itself? Now there is a problem here. If Wittgenstein means to say that the descriptive force of our mental terminology extends no further than the needs of the contexts in which we learn the ordinary meanings of the words, and that this renders them incapable of describing whatever the unexplored medium may disclose, should he not conclude that the medium itself is indescribable, or even that as far as any explanation of 'mind' is concerned it does not exist? Wittgenstein, however, seems to regard this as misleading. But it can only be misleading to one who does *not* think that in denying inner processes one is denying an inner medium. If, however, the medium is not to be denied, what can be said of it? We might agree that questions of the grammar, or use,[2] of psychological terms are properly construed as questions about the nature of what they refer to; even

---

[1] It is difficult to find concrete results of such investigations in the *Investigations*. In some cases Wittgenstein denies that a specific non-behaviouristic expression could ever acquire a particular importance: he says, e.g., that 'no *process* could ever have the consequences of meaning'. (Ibid., p. 218; his emphasis.) But perhaps 'mental process' can acquire importance in other contexts, e.g. 'learning is a mental process'. He seems to allow there are mental states (e.g. of depression, excitement, pain), but that to call something a mental state is to accept certain 'grammatical' consequences which legislate against other mental phenomena being described as states. Cf. ibid., p. 59 n. However, 'mental (or inner, or private) *object*' is an expression that Wittgenstein consistently urges us to avoid. Cf. ibid., p. 196 ('The concept of the "inner picture" is misleading, for this concept uses the "outer picture" as a model . . .'), and, e.g., pp. 199 and 207.

[2] Wittgenstein uses the terms 'grammar' and 'use' interchangeably.

concede for the sake of argument that exploration of the medium itself can contribute nothing in the way of answers to such questions; but if the medium so much as exists, we want to know why the search in it would be so fruitless.

We could understand Wittgenstein as follows. To give the nature of something is to give a description of it;[1] and there is nothing to explore here simply because there is nothing to describe. The best we can do when invoking the medium is to talk of something 'gaseous' and 'aethereal' (as when we try to explain what must be added to a sign to give it meaning by postulating something that envelops it, gives it life),[2] a kind of non-body that is the missing but vital factor; or to point to genuine experiences, for example feelings, images, etc., which may *seem* to be typical accompaniments of acts, say, of remembering, day-dreaming, dreaming, expecting etc.,[3] but which nevertheless do not necessarily accompany them and so do not serve to distinguish them. In other words there is nothing specifically mental to point to as the mind at work, or if there is something specifically mental it isn't an explanation of the mental works differentiated by our psychological vocabulary. Similarly when I talk of aspect-seeing in terms of a personal contribution to a basic impression received from outside, nothing in the experience corresponds to this; to see something as a portrait of a friend is not to see one thing superimposed upon another.

What cannot be described may nevertheless exist. One may think of this possibility in either of two ways. Both are ways of interpreting Berkeley's claim that the nature of mind is such that it 'cannot be of itself perceived, but only by the effects which it produceth'.[4] According to Berkeley, the describer of the mind can only record effects of mental operations, he can never 'represent' the medium itself. Now Berkeley certainly believed the medium existed, and even allowed that we can have 'some *notion*' of its operations, for example of willing, loving, and

[1] Not to give an explanation of it. He calls his own method 'purely descriptive' and says the descriptions he gives are not 'hints of explanations' (*Blue and Brown Books* [Blackwell, Oxford, 1958], p. 125).

[2] Cf. *Investigations*, p. 183, also p. 47.   [3] Cf. ibid., pp. 182 and 183.

[4] Berkeley, *Principles*, p. 71, cf. p. 141 above.

hating, in so far as we 'know or understand' the meanings of the words we use to refer to them.[1] The difficulty as he saw it was to form an *idea* of the operations themselves: we can only *experience* the activity of mind. Now his putting this by saying that the mind cannot be 'perceived' suggests that we should really have to get out of our mental lives to be in a position from which we can see our own mind's at work, a very difficult notion indeed, and its sheer oddity might lead one to conclude that if the only medium that can be conceived of is this one that lies beyond all *our* possible experience it would be as well to say there was no such thing. But the mind's unperceivability might be taken rather differently, as meaning that the mind is not something *distinguishable* in experience. To be distinguished in experience the mind would have to be identified with something *in* experience, but to deny that it can be identified with anything in experience does not mean that it cannot be experienced, or that it cannot be seen, or shown—to oneself—in experience. It only means that it cannot be described, 'represented', or as the epigrammatic Wittgenstein of the *Tractatus* would say, that it cannot be *said*. Now since the distinction between what can be said and what can only be shown is so fundamental in Wittgenstein, it might not be too rash to suggest that in this latter interpretation of Berkeley's claim we can find a remedy that Wittgenstein himself would accept to behaviourism, and one that would explain why behaviourism was an unwanted result. Behaviourism would be a consequence of assuming that a mental operation would have to be something distinguishable in experience *among* accredited mental phenomena, or in theory apart from all accredited mental phenomena, which it clearly is not. But why not take the phenomena as they stand as the content of our notion of mental operations and processes. The mental life, after all, is the one we live, and to suppose that something distinguishable in that life could be identical with, or with a part of, the continuing life itself would be to make a bad category mistake. To say that all we can describe here is what a living being does, in the sense in which the pronouncement 'This is your life?' does *not* involve a category

[1] *Principles*, p. 72.

mistake, does not mean that there is no element of *life* in what we describe. Similarly, the fact that we can only describe the language-games that minded beings participate in does not mean that there is no mind at work in their pursuance of these games—that in a perfectly appropriate manner of speaking the language-games themselves may not properly denominate the mind active.

What characterization of *imaging* then can we give that does not play into the hands of the behaviourist? As for processes, if all we mean by a process is the kind of thing Wittgenstein himself discusses as 'the dawning of an aspect', there would be nothing very misleading about the label. But it would help just as little as if all that was meant by saying that this was a mental process was that it was something mental. Whether, or what about, imaging might be called a process in any unmisleading sense is not a question Wittgenstein goes into. In fact it is clear that he regards the explanation of mental phenomena in terms of processes, indeed the very idea of an *explanation* of mental phenomena, as disastrous for an understanding of our understanding of these phenomena—as leaving too much to what is inessential and leading us to ignore what is essential to the basis of our *actual* understanding.[1] In other words it leads us to misrepresent the basis we actually adopt for accepting or rejecting statements involving psychological terms; it leads us to suppose that we could deny (1), that is deny that accounts of mental processes are neither necessary nor sufficient for our understanding of mental phenomena; or in other words to suppose that mental processes, happenings, objects, or whatever, can stand on their own and are what we really refer to as 'the mind'. But, in Wittgenstein's now celebrated expression: 'An "inner process" stands in need of outward criteria.'[2]

3. IMAGES AND OUTWARD CRITERIA

Wittgenstein first uses the term 'criterion' where he wants to disabuse us of the assumption that mental concepts are more or less straightforwardly analogous to physical concepts. It is this as-

[1] Cf. e.g., *Investigations*, Pt. I, § 363.   [2] Ibid., Pt. I, § 580.

sumption, as he sees it, that leads us into the terminology of inner processes, a terminology that he thinks leads us in turn to assume that mental phenomena correspond to publicly observable phenomena except for the fact that they are apprehended only by the person in whose mind they occur.

In a passage anticipating the one already quoted in connection with images, Wittgenstein says:

'"What happens when a man suddenly understands?" The question is badly framed. If it is a question about the meaning of the expression "sudden understanding", the answer is not to point to a process that we give this name to.—The question might mean "what are the tokens of sudden understanding; what are its characteristic psychical accompaniments? . . ."[1] The question what the expression means is not answered by such a description; and this misleads us into concluding that understanding is a specific undefinable experience. But we forget that what should interest us is the question: how do we *compare* these experiences; what criterion of identity do we fix for their occurrence?'[2]

As in the case of 'image', Wittgenstein seems to be suggesting that we should not look for a process that constitutes sudden understanding; what we need to look for is the use we have for the *expression* 'sudden understanding'. There are features of the situations where we use the expression which *determine* that we should use it in those situations. In fact *we* have determined that they should do so. We fix the features in question as the criteria of the expression, and they, not inner processes or inner events, form the substance of what we know as sudden understanding, of its *nature*. What, then, would such features be in the case of imagining? Mrs Wolgast suggests that to find the criteria[3] of

---

[1] *Investigations*, Pt. 1, § 321.

[2] Ibid. Pt. 1, § 322. Cf. *The Blue and Brown Books* (Blackwell, Oxford, 1958), pp. 24–5 for Wittgenstein's clearest explanation of what he means by 'criterion'.

[3] I am accepting Mrs Wolgast's interpretation of 'criteria' (Elizabeth Wolgast, 'Wittgenstein and Criteria', *Inquiry*, Vol. 7 [1964], No. 4), in preference to those of Norman Malcolm and Rogers Albritton. Malcolm thinks that for Wittgenstein 'The satisfaction of the criterion of *y* establishes the existence of *y* beyond

'imagining' we should follow Wittgenstein's advice that if one wants to define something 'at a *single* showing' one should *play-act* the thing.[1] She gives the following example:

'I close my eyes, lean my head back and say, "I am imagining that I am in Venice on a canal. It is evening. How beautiful the city looks in the dusk! How delightful the music I can hear from across the water!" After a bit I open my eyes and sit up and sigh that it's too bad I'm *not* in Venice.'[2]

This definition contains a number of ingredients—a narrative containing a description of an imaginary scene, prefixed by the words 'I am imagining'; the adopting of a certain posture; the closing of the eyes during the narration; and after finishing the

question; it repeats the kind of case in which we were taught to say *"y"* ' ('Wittgenstein's *Philosophical Investigations*', *Philosophical Review*, LXIII [1954], No. 368, p. 544). He then asks whether the *propositions describing* the criterion of someone's being in pain *logically imply* the proposition 'He is in pain', and says that Wittgenstein's answer is 'clearly in the negative'. So that pain-behaviour 'is a criterion of pain only in *certain circumstances*' (p. 545). Malcolm then shows that no entailment conditions showing that the circumstances themselves obtain can be formulated, and appears to conclude that we are still in the traditional epistemological position of doubt with regard to whether the criteria obtain: 'If it does not *follow* from [a man's] behavior and circumstances that he is in pain, then how can it ever be *certain* that he is in pain?' (p. 546). Albritton ('On Wittgenstein's Use of the Term "Criterion" ', *Journal of Philosophy*, LVI [1959], No. 22) argues that Wittgenstein's usage in the *Blue Book* is that 'to be a criterion of *X* is just to *be* (what is called *X*), or to be (what is called *X*) under certain circumstances, in case there is more than one criterion of *X*' (p. 853), and that in the *Investigations* (and *Remarks on the Foundations of Mathematics*) the idea of truth by definition here is applied to the justification for saying one knows things, as if it was a 'necessary truth' that 'a man who behaves in [a certain manner], under normal circumstances, always or almost always does have a toothache'. He denies it is a necessary truth. Wolgast (ibid., cf. also L. D. Houlgate, 'The Paradigm-Case Argument and "Possible Doubt" ', *Inquiry*, Vol. 5 [1962], No. 4) claims that the criteria establish the appropriateness of a description, not its truth, or, as Albritton suggests, the near certainty of its truth. This seems plausible to me. The criteria do not bridge the 'logical gap', they are on this side of it; except that Wittgenstein would not attribute to the gap the significance given it in traditional epistemology. The remaining doubts do not concern what is *essential*; the proper object of the description is not to be identified with the supplement that makes, e.g., a show of agony a case of real agony. The important thing is to see just how artificial the gap is.

[1] *Investigations*, p. 188.   [2] Wolgast, op. cit., p. 350.

narration, once again sitting up and taking notice of the surround-ings. Now there is a crucial consideration here. It is surely not the case that all these ingredients, or indeed any selection of them, form necessary conditions for imagining (i.e. picturing or visualizing) something. One can think of cases where any or all of them are absent, and yet one may still imagine; for example, when one is alone, lying down, and in the dark, or where one imagines fleetingly, and neither the imagining nor the imagined are relevant in the immediate context. And clearly the ingredients referred to do not form a set of sufficient conditions. This is shown by the fact that they can indeed be incorporated into the play-acting of such a definition. The conclusion one may be tempted to draw, then, is that the essential thing about imagining is what must occur even where the ingredients do not—what would have to be added to make the mock performance a real one. And what could this be but the image? For if the appropriate imagery did occur in the course of the enacted definition, would we not have to say for this reason alone that the definition was then not simply play-acted, but given by means of a genuine performance of imagining? And this seems to be confirmed by the possibility of imagining without betraying the fact to anyone by any characteristic posture, evident withdrawal of attention to one's immediate surroundings, or fictitious narration. Are we not then forced to conclude that imagining, in this sense, is essentially a private mental performance?

The core of Wittgenstein's doctrine of criteria is, I believe, to be found in the following arguments against this conclusion:

(2) Where at least enough of the characteristic behaviour is present to convey the definition of a typical case of imagining, the presence of imagery is redundant, and its absence does not detract from the value of the performance as a definition, even if it means that it is not an actual case of imagining.[1]

[1] To claim that the absence of imagery *entailed* that there was no imagining—in the sense of visualizing—might be to play earlier than need be into the hands of those who would impress one with Galton's report, mentioned earlier, of people who behave according to the paradigm, apparently without pretence, but yet 'declare themselves entirely deficient in the power of seeing mental pictures'. To warrant the entailment I think we should perhaps widen the notion of

(3) Where there is not enough of the characteristic behaviour to convey the definition the presence of imagery will not supplement the lack to make the situation a typical (paradigm) case of imagining, even if in the event we should say it is a case of imagining.

Wittgenstein's meaning may be further explicated by noting his comment that because a description of a process does not answer the question of what the expression 'sudden understanding' means, we are misled into supposing that it refers to some indefinable experience. 'But we forget that what should interest us is the question: how do we *compare* these experiences; what criterion of identity do we fix for their occurrence?'[1]

We can consider how we might, following Wittgenstein, show what the criteria of 'same' or 'different image' are.[2] Wolgast again provides the example.

'I sit here (in Zürich) and say to you, "I can just see the San Francisco Bay Bridge and how it looks from the east". You say: "Yes, I can too; it is very striking at night." I say: "Oh, you are thinking of it at night! Yes, it is pretty then, especially from a distance; I can see how it looks from the top of the Berkeley Hills." You reply, "Ah, yes—a wonderful sight!"'[3]

If we follow Wittgenstein and say that 'The mental picture is the picture which is described when someone describes what he imagines',[4] we may conclude that the above example illustrates a case of comparing images. Images differ or are the same according to whether the descriptions given by persons describing what they imagine differ. And Wittgenstein's point seems to be that we should not reject this as a case of comparing just because we find that it differs from cases of comparing, say, postcards of different views of the Bay Bridge; in particular we should not reject it as such on the grounds that we cannot, in imagining, set our images side by side for comparison. As Wolgast says: 'What imagery to include something like 'an evocation of a general orientation and response', a seeming to be (e.g. 'followed') rather than just a seeming to see, hear, smell, etc.

[1] *Investigations*, Pt. I, § 322.   [2] Cf. *Investigations*, Pt. I, §§ 378 and 382.
[3] Wolgast, op. cit., p. 350.   [4] *Investigations*, Pt. I, § 367; cf. p. 178 above.

"comparing" means is just what the example says: we are talking about the same object, giving descriptions, joining our feelings.' The criterion for saying that we are comparing images is that 'we talk together about the bridge and how we imagine it'. The criterion for saying that our images are alike is that 'we *agree* as we describe the bridge'.[1]

Similarly the criterion for saying that we have a mental picture is not that we can report the occurrence of an inner process or the existence of a private ('second') object, but, among other things that we can give a description of something of which anyone might have visual (or aural, etc.) knowledge. This indicates the kind of considerations that would count against the application of the description 'A imagines X'. They would include such factors as that A had never seen the thing he described himself as imagining, perhaps that he had never seen a picture of it either; or if he had (or had been given a vivid description of it), that he had lost the visual knowledge he once had of it (something we might test independently of his describing something to us). And whatever may be the criteria of retention of visual knowledge (of remembering what something looks like or what comes next by being able to recall what it looks like, or 'to go on from here'), it is clear that *they* do not include postulated occurrences of private objects, processes, or states.

The Cartesian view of mind makes acceptance and rejection of statements involving psychological terms turn ultimately on the inner observation of putatively discriminable mental states. According to Wittgenstein this view misrepresents our actual understanding of the mental phenomena in question, as shown in our grasp of the terms themselves. It would be incorrect to say that what makes us decide whether someone is imagining or not is whether or not he has an image. Looking at the matter more broadly, the kind of thing that would make us reject a description of someone as having imagined something is not that he experienced nothing private corresponding to a public representation, nor that he was unable to identify a process of some kind,

[1] Wolgast, op. cit., p. 351.

or even that there was no such process. The question of whether there is an image is really no more than a question of whether we can make use of the notion of an image in talking *about* imagining. Perhaps, in that context, we might find it expedient to explain the difference between describing what we see and describing what we seem to see in terms of the presence of an image. But the grasp we have of the 'imagining' terminology generally does not require us to postulate such a thing. Outside such special contexts what matters is whether or not the person who may be simply play-acting and not imagining at all goes on to fulfil the criteria we fix for saying that a person remembers something he has seen; and then if he does fulfil them, whether or not he also fulfils the criteria we set for saying that someone is not pretending something.

4. THE DENIAL OF INNER OBJECTS AND PROCESSES

We may now distinguish in respect of imaging two different senses in which Wittgenstein's view about how terms acquire meaning leads to a conclusion expressible as:

(4) 'Psychological terms do not designate inner objects or processes.'

In the first sense it is an empirical conclusion. It may or may not be the case that wherever a person describes what he seems to see we should say that there is an inner process or an inner object in the person's mind. It is in any case unclear what the terms 'process' and 'object' denote here. If we think of an image, for example, on the analogy of picture postcards and other public representational objects, we will find as a matter of fact that there are not, or need not be, or are not clearly, mental analogies of these. Thus even from the point of view of what can be discriminated in experience there is no basis for regarding imaging as parallel to perception except in that it involves sights that we cannot share with one another, and pictures which, consequently, we cannot compare with one another in the same way. And the same applies to processes, as we remarked earlier. So there is a sense in which the denial that 'imaging' designates either an inner object or a mental process expresses the empirical fact that in imaging there is nothing introspectible that fulfils the criteria we have fixed for the use of the terms 'object' and 'process'. But the facts might have been otherwise. We could express this as follows:

(4') The private references of psychological terms are not appropriately described in terms of 'processes' or 'objects'.

In the second sense, however, the denial expresses the claim that even had the facts been otherwise and a definite use found for the notions of a mental process and an inner object, nevertheless it would not be the reference to these that constituted our possession of the concepts of 'imagining' or 'imaging'. To have a concept, on the Wittgensteinian view,[1] is to have a use for a distinction and to be able to use an expression in accordance with the widely diversified sets of circumstances that form the criteria for applying or rejecting it. A blind man, as Geach points out, 'can use the word "red" with a considerable measure of intelligence; he can show a practical grasp of the logic of the word'.[2] Certainly we might say he had a different concept of 'red' from that of a man with sight and who could distinguish red from other colours, but not in the same way that the sighted man's concepts of 'colour' and 'shape' differ from one another. In having the practical grasp of the logic of 'red' that he does have, the concept he possesses is, so far, the same concept as that of the sighted man. Thus it is a mistake to say that to possess a concept of colour in general, or of one colour in particular, one must be able to make any specific empirical discrimination. If it is a mistake, then it cannot be the case that what we mean by '*A* imagines *X*' is that *A* is discriminating some inner analogue of a publicly identifiable object. We can express this by saying:

(4") The ability to pick out its private reference is not necessary for having a psychological concept.

If it is a mistake to think that in order to have a concept of imaging one must be able to recognize something as an image,

---

[1] 'Wittgensteinian' rather than 'Wittgenstein's' because in the published works it is hard to pin Wittgenstein down to an explicit thesis.

[2] Peter Geach, *Mental Acts* (Routledge & Kegan Paul, London, 1958), p. 35.

it is presumably an even worse mistake to think that to be able to do this is a sufficient condition of having the concept. And this brings us to a third sense of the denial that psychological terms designate mental processes or inner objects. It can be expressed as follows:

(4''') The ability to pick out its private reference is neither necessary nor sufficient for having a psychological concept.

In this sense the denial expresses the claim that in order to have a concept of a specific psychological phenomenon it could never be sufficient, let alone necessary, that one could refer to mental processes or inner objects alone.

It is in this latter sense of the denial that Wittgenstein's use of the notion of criterion acquires its specifically anti-Cartesian force. This aspect of it can be summarized in the propositions:

(5) It is by arguing that no amount of characteristic behaviour entails the occurrence of an actual case of imaging that the false conclusion has been drawn that no behaviour is truly characteristic of imaging.

(6) If it was the case that no behaviour was truly characteristic of imaging, then we could not know what other people mean by expressions like 'seeing in the mind's eye', 'visualizing', or 'imaging', and we would have no standard for determining the correct use of these terms—even in our own case.

Now it is important to see the interdependence of (5) and (6) in Wittgenstein's reasoning. Taking (5) by itself one might suppose that what makes it false that no behaviour is truly characteristic of imaging is the fact that behaviour does happen, but only happens, to play a part in our understanding of 'what it is for someone to see in his mind's eye'. It is a contingent fact that we do ascribe mental predicates in the way Wittgenstein indicates, and his doctrine of criteria is therefore a true description of our language habits, of the reasons we actually employ in accepting or rejecting statements involving psychological terms.

However, (6) offers an argument which, if valid, would seem to make the falsity of the conclusion mentioned in (5) a logical and not a contingent matter. The argument is that which purports to show the impossibility of there being private languages. In the early parts of the *Investigations* Wittgenstein argues that there cannot be purely mental events, observable only by introspection and merely contingently connected with their manifestations in behaviour. Any word purporting to refer to something observable only by introspection, and only causally linked to publicly observable phenomena, would have to acquire its meaning by a purely private performance. But no word could acquire a meaning in such a way; since a word only has meaning as part of a language; and a language is essentially public and shareable. If words like 'pain', for example, acquire their meaning for each of us in a ceremony which we attend alone, then none of us can have any idea what anyone else means by the word. Furthermore, no one can know what he means by it himself; since to know the meaning of a word is to know how to use it rightly; and where there can be no check on how a man uses a word there is no room for talk of a 'right' or 'wrong' use.

Now this argument seems to legislate quite generally against there being anything that we could both *call* a specifically mental occurrence and at the same time be able to *describe* as such. If so, then the denial (4), referred to above, would be entailed by an essential part of Wittgenstein's view of what it is to have a concept. That is, the truth of the claim that psychological terms do not refer to inner processes or objects would follow from the fact that to acquire a concept is to master the use of an expression. For to acquire a use of an expression, according to the above argument, one has to be able to point out to others an instance of what one means.

But then what about the mental image whose existence we are so blithely defending? It is one thing to grant that for purposes of what could be called our mental ascribings what we mean by a mental picture is what is described when someone imaging describes what he imagines—and even to grant that the image does not stand up very well to the criteria we set for 'object' in its normal use. But it is quite another to have to accept that 'mental picture' can be given no meaning.

5. SALVAGING THE MENTAL IMAGE

Wittgenstein, as we saw, suggests that the denial of mental processes is the result of our being committed to a 'particular way of looking at the matter'; we seem to have to deny processes when we naturally don't want to deny them.[1] But how, on Wittgenstein's terms, can we help but deny them? If it is his argument against 'pain' referring to a private experience that if this was so the word would have to acquire its meaning by a purely private performance, which is impossible since no word can acquire its meaning in this way, should not the same argument apply equally to all putative mental objects and processes, for example to imaging and the mental image? There would be difficulties whether it did or not. If the argument does apply then mental objects and processes go by the board along with private pains and the rest; if it does not apply, and mental objects and processes are not to be denied, then why should we deny this kind of privacy to elements in the concept of pain, for example to pain feelings (which we *may* wish to consider the quintessential pain), that are purely 'mental' in just that sense in which mental processes are supposedly purely mental in so far as they are observable only by introspection?

Some of Wittgenstein's remarks, however, suggest that he takes terms like 'pain', 'anger', 'remembering', 'imagining', and 'expecting' to belong to a special, or perhaps precisely non-special, i.e. unspecialized, type of discourse and that this effectively distinguishes them from the terms by which we refer to mental processes and objects. If so, perhaps the arguments against the existence of essentially private pains, etc. would not apply to mental objects and processes, inasmuch as the arguments concern the special feature of that type of discourse. The feature in question is that of 'telling', or 'giving information'.[2] Expressions like 'pain', 'anger', etc. play a part in the language-game of describing others as being in pain or anger and of

---

[1] *Investigations*, Pt. I, § 308; cf. p. 181 above.
[2] Ibid., Pt. I, §§ 296–8.

expressing one's own pain or anger—one might call it the language-game of mental ascribing. Mental processes, on the other hand, play no part in *this* game. At most they are but the necessary psychological foundation of the existence of such a language-game. Wittgenstein says, '"There has just taken place in me the mental process of remembering . . ." means nothing more than: "I have just remembered. . . ." To deny the mental process would mean to deny the remembering; to deny that anyone ever remembers anything.'[1]

Perhaps, then, Wittgenstein is saying only that processes furnish no more than the occasion for the construction of a concept. Processes exist, certainly, for remembering, expecting, and day-dreaming are all processes, but to say this is to say nothing about what people are doing, about the mental *activities*, one might say, of remembering, expecting, and day-dreaming. This means that the mental processes, simply as processes, happenings, play no part in the language-games where we describe our own and other people's doings to one another, or convey our feelings to one another. But this need not exclude them from a role in their own—though of course not auto-nomous—language-game, say the language-game of intro-spective psychology or of explanation.

However, once again we are faced with the principle that purely mental processes would have to be referents of a private language, and this should exclude them from figuring in language-games at all. To repeat the argument: if 'pain' designated some purely private experience, its meaning would have to be learnt in a private and uncheckable ceremony, and hence there would be no standard of the right or wrong use of the term. Because such standards are essential to language, the word 'pain' cannot designate a purely private experience. But then what about the terms 'mental process' and 'mental object'?

Geach, in *Mental Acts*, explains Wittgenstein's denial of private mental events (processes, objects, etc.) in terms of Frege's distinction between sense (*Sinn*) and reference (*Bedeut-ung*). Thus,

---

[1] *Investigations*, Pt. I, § 306; cf. p. 205 below.

' . . . what Wittgenstein wanted to deny was not the private reference [*Bedeutung*] of psychological expressions—e.g. that "pain" stands for a kind of experience that may be quite private— but the possibility of giving them a private *sense* [*Sinn*]—e.g. of giving sense to the word "pain" by just attending to one's own pain-experiences, a performance that would be private and uncheckable.'[1]

However, the requirements of public sense here are usually so interpreted as to close even this door to inner processes and objects. They are understood roughly as follows. For any term to have a use in which it could refer to, or be used to report, some inner occurrence, it must also be possible to use the term, in the same sense, to refer to something commonly observable. The implication is that in order to be able to refer to a private mental event at all we must use a word with a sense that it can only acquire in a public context. This means that words like 'remember', 'understand', 'anger', etc., when used to report outwardly invisible moments of remembering, coming to understand, and feelings of anger, must be understood in terms of the public contexts that provide the criteria for their correct use. The domain of private references of psychological terms is not autonomous. The privacy of the references is, as it were, contingent; it is dependent, moreover, upon *actual* occurrences of public references.[2]

But then if it is a necessary condition of a term's having a public sense, and thereby a meaning, that there be occasions on which it can be used, with the same sense, to refer to something publicly identifiable, a term referring to what was in principle not so identifiable could have no meaning. And in distinguishing remembering from the mental process without which no one would ever remember anything (and presumably which the Cartesian is supposed to confuse with the former), Wittgenstein cannot be thinking of something that is only contingently private. It is something that could not have been public at all; the private

---

[1] *Mental Acts*, pp. 3–4.
[1] Cf. Ryle's claim to show that 'exercises of qualities of mind do not, save *per accidens*, take place "in the head" ' (p. 28 above).

'happening' that is presumed to occur with, or even *be*, all remembering, concealed or otherwise. In fact his reason for distinguishing between remembering and the mental process is precisely to stress that remembering is not that kind of essentially private thing without which there would be no remembering as we understand it.

In order to give effect to Wittgenstein's disclaimer that he is denying mental processes, then, it seems that we must interpret him as giving some less stringent condition for the possibility of a term's having a public sense. The problem is how to do this without allowing once again for the possibility of essentially private emotions, rememberings, imaginings, and so on.

Now the alleged condition of intelligibility is that we must know that the experience we call by a particular name is the same as that which others call by that name. The conclusion drawn in the case of, say, emotions is that an emotion must be something that is not always concealed, that it must sometimes be manifested in behaviour. But it might be argued that the reason for drawing this conclusion in the case of emotions does not apply in the case of mental processes. One can point to an asymmetry between the two cases, in fact a twofold asymmetry.

First, a mental state of Cartesian anger is precluded on the grounds that it could not be a private species of a genus of which there were genuine public specimens. That is, according to the ('official') Cartesian conception, the notion of anger would be restricted to the private context, and any uses of the words 'anger' and 'angry' (etc.) to apply directly to phenomena outside that context could only be analogical. To describe a piece of behaviour as 'angry', for instance, would be as metaphorical as to describe the evening sky or a wound in this way. Consequently, there would be no public specimen of anger from which the literal use of the word 'anger' could be learnt; for the only anger in the world would be private feelings of anger. But this is not the case with putative mental processes. For by a mental process we mean a mental or private species of a genus of which there are genuine, even if remote, public specimens. Or we could say: in so far as there are such genuine public specimens, we understand what is meant by 'mental process'. We know what we mean by a *mental* (i.e. private) process, state, or act, because we know what we mean by a publicly observable process, state, or act. Consequently in this case, but not the former, the conditions of meaningfulness which Wittgenstein lays down can be met. The rules for understanding a language of mental processes can be understood as extensions of the rules of the language-game in which we speak of acts, states, and processes in the public world—in respect both of mental and physical phenomena.

Secondly, a 'mental-process' language-game would differ significantly from a 'mental activity' language-game. It would contain nothing corresponding to the behaviour-references that play a part in the language-game of, for example, emotions, or of overt mental activities and mental *conduct* in general. We do not *express* mental processes, nor is it clear that we can distinguish between different kinds of mental processes in the way that we distinguish between mental activities. So there would be nothing in the mental-process language-game of which it could be said that it served *only* as an indication or token of this or that process, but which, according to Wittgenstein's doctrine, we should have to say could count as an actual manifestation of a process. In fact the only sure indication of a mental process is engagement in some or other language-game, and it can be any language-game. Of course, just as we don't express mental processes, neither do we express what we do express by referring to mental processes. In the language-game of mental processes we would not be telling others about ourselves in the way that expressing emotion and stating intentions are ways of telling or signalling to others what we have 'in mind'. So it would be a very impoverished sort of game compared to the ones we play as exponents of the ordinary, but very rich, psychological vocabulary.

In the light of this asymmetry between mental activities and mental processes, therefore, we might attribute to Wittgenstein a version of the private-language argument that makes his insistence that a denial of mental processes is misleading intelligible. The version would be, roughly, one in which the general condition of a word having meaning is not that there be a public manifestation of its designatum—that would be so only in special cases—but rather that there be a publicly observable phenomenon that is the *kind* of thing we mean. The everyday psychological vocabulary is special because mental activities are *sui generis;* in their case the only possible instances of the kinds of thing we mean are instances of the things themselves. The general rule would be that descriptions must have public applications, not that their references can be only contingently private. The fact that the expression 'essentially inner process' can be used descriptively while 'essentially inner anger (remembering, imagining, expecting, intending, understanding, etc.)' cannot is that 'process' ranges over inner and outer while expressions of the latter kind are confined to the inner. In a way this conforms to the letter of the earlier rule, because one can still say that what gives 'process' a sense is the fact that only some of its references are private; but the point is that the more liberal condition would explain how a subclass of its private references can be *essentially* private.[1]

The more liberal condition also allows us to salvage the mental image. Like the term 'pain', 'mental image' can and does stand for something quite private. Assume its private reference requires a public sense. Then if to have a public sense it had to

[1] Of course this is much too imprecise. One would have to know how to decide whether a publicly observable phenomenon is to count as coming under the same genus as something in the putative domain of mental processes, objects, etc. It is also unsatisfactory. Suppose we could identify certain purely mental phenomena and single them out as processes, or as objects, or happenings. According to the proposed condition for introducing meaningful designating terms into our language it seems we would still be barred from introducing terms which referred to properties *peculiar* to mental processes, etc. The strictures about private languages would apply here too, and in fact one could never get further, in characterizing mental processes, etc. than saying that there are private instantiations of certain properties the terms for which we learn in contexts where they are publicly instantiated. Perhaps one could say quite a lot in this way, but one would at least be prevented in theory from expressing any characteristic of mental processes that did not have a publicly observable counterpart. This might seem fatal for any attempt to specify the *differentiae* of purely mental processes, and hence, ultimately, for any attempt to formulate the distinction between purely mental and other processes. But maybe as a last resort we could say that what cannot be said can at least be shown—though only in private.

have a reference that was only contingently private, we would have to deny the mental image. 'Image', however, like 'process' and 'object', is a term that ranges over inner and outer, and therefore the privacy of its reference when used to refer to the essentially private *mental* image *is* merely contingent. Weaken the requirement for public sense then by asking only that there be some public sample of the kind of thing referred to, and we can retain the mental image. The term 'image' does not get its sense for each of us in a private uncheckable ceremony. Consequently we have no need to call on an outward criterion for 'mental image' as we do with 'pain'.[1]

But Wittgenstein does say, does he not, that 'an "inner process" stands in need of an outward criterion'? If the mental image and the inner process are to be salvaged together, then, should we not expect the mental image to be as much in need of outward criteria as any inner process? There are two parts to a possible answer. The first part is simply to say No; in allowing 'mental image' private referential status we have not yet given it a place in the everyday vocabulary of mental activities, and it is only words referring to these that Wittgenstein says stand in need of outward criteria. It is as a supposed reference to mental activities that mental processes need outward criteria. But as for what we might legitimately call an inner process, that needs no criterion; it has no function in the vocabulary of activities. Secondly, as we have seen, we have in fact an outward criterion for 'mental picture', namely the picturer's description of what he imagines. But it is only in its representational function that the mental image needs an outward criterion. As a thing in its own right, an elusive, ephemeral object with ill-defined pictorial properties, it is of no moment at all, neither a criterion *of* anything nor itself in need of one.

Part of Wittgenstein's denial of inner references is concerned

---

[1] I am simply assuming for the sake of argument that something is wrong with the notion of the uncheckable ceremony. I am not sure exactly what thesis about language implies the ceremony, nor what the implications of the ceremony itself are. But I do think that Wittgenstein was intent on showing that mental content is essentially linguistic (in some sense), and that this is a reason for saying it is essentially public.

with processes and objects. It amounts to saying that they are no more than necessary preconditions of our having a psychological vocabulary at all, and not what that vocabulary is primarily about.[1] To accommodate this denial our *naïve* assumption about mental images would have to be qualified by saying that properties of the mental image itself do not count among the criteria we fix for saying things like '*A* imagined *X*' (or '*A* dreamt that *X*', 'expected that *X*', 'hoped for *X*', etc.); in other words there is more to imagining than the image, and even the image itself doesn't count. This is quite acceptable. On the other hand, the pictorial properties of the image do count indirectly, because if they were not the properties they are, *A* would not be giving the description he does give of what he imagines—which of course does not mean that what he imagines is something he finds out by recognizing the pictorial properties of his image; and if there were no pictorial properties he would simply not be describing anything imagined. So perhaps the Wittgensteinian position needs some qualification too.

Another part of Wittgenstein's denial is a direct appeal to experience. He is not saying there is nothing essentially private, only that what is essentially private doesn't count for very much, and in an important way doesn't count at all. But as far as what *is* essentially private is concerned, the available distinctions in experience do not lend themselves to description in terms of 'process' and 'object'. In so far as such terms have uses fixed for them in certain context, transferring them to mental phenomena is to impose upon these a picture to which they do not correspond. As for this, lacking any direct context of importance, it seems one may just as well take the point as leave it. A lot will depend on one's own experience, and on what better ways of describing it are available.

But Wittgenstein provides a context of the very greatest importance, and once the empirical denial is embedded in it the point and spirit of his claim becomes apparent. The context in question is the need to withhold from phenomenal distinctions descriptions which seem to give them a place in philosophical

[1] Cf. *Investigations*, Pt. I, §§ 304–6.

speculation. The reason it is misleading to refer to mental processes and objects is not simply that one refers to the wrong kind of thing, or that one uses inept phraseology, but that by transferring to the mental field the terminology of 'process' and 'object' one misrepresents the 'chemistry' of the phenomena in a peculiarly dangerous way. One attributes the wrong 'valences' to them, represents them as demanding certain kinds of explanation and as standing in problematic relationships to one another. In short, one generates confusion.

6. WITTGENSTEIN'S CONCERN WITH IMAGES

'What makes my image into an image of *him?*' asks Wittgenstein. 'Not its looking like him.' And the same applies, he says, to the expression, 'I see him now vividly before me' as to the image. What makes this utterance about *him* is 'nothing in it or simultaneous with it ("behind it")'. 'If you want to know who he meant, ask him.'[1] Wittgenstein's reference to images here is part of a more general denial that mental states, episodes, or processes explain such fundamental features of mental life as the understanding of languages generally, or what another person means in particular.[2] Negatively, he says that finding nothing in the 'unexplored medium' corresponding to what we mean by 'state', 'episode', or 'process', we should not persevere with the kind of explanation that says there must be such things nonetheless. Instead, and positively, we should regard such features of mental life in terms of the 'mastery of techniques', that is in terms of notions for which we have publicly available criteria for deciding whether a person understands another person's words, or what he is referring to. If we want to know whether a person means what we think he does, don't look *behind* what he does openly, but put further questions to him. His answers, in terms of the criteria *we* fix, will decide the matter.

---

[1] *Investigations*, p. 177.
[2] For a criticism of Wittgenstein here see K. W. Rankin, 'The Role of Imagination, Rule-Operations, and Atmosphere in Wittgenstein's Language-Games', *Inquiry*, Vol. 10 (1967), No. 3.

Wittgenstein pushes the denial of inner processes and objects to the limit because he sees the picture of the 'inner process' and the 'inner object' as diverting attention to the wrong quarter. But he is sensitive to his own excesses. He asks himself 'But you will surely admit that there is a difference between pain-behaviour accompanied by pain and pain-behaviour without any pain?' 'Admit it?' says Wittgenstein, 'what greater difference could there be?'[1] And again, to the question 'But you surely cannot deny that, for example, in remembering, an inner process takes place', he replies, 'What gives the impression that we want to deny anything?'[2] This impression, he says, 'arises from our setting our faces against the picture of the "inner process"'. But since the picture has been implanted in our minds we *must* set ourselves against it. For this picture does not give us the correct idea of the use of the expression 'to remember'. The picture 'with its ramifications' prevents us from 'seeing the use of the word as it is'. An inner process, so called, presents itself as a discrete item which can have no part in the language-game of reporting memories and expressing pain. It is about a process in this sense that Wittgenstein says that it 'is not a *something*, but not a nothing either', and that when it comes to explaining the use of words like 'pain' and so on 'a nothing would serve just as well as a something about which nothing could be said'.[3]

However, once the denial has served its purpose large questions remain. For even if we accept the view that language is a complex of learned conventions and implicit rules to which we are somehow bound, there is still a question about the status of theoretical discourse about minds, about how to understand the given fact of mental life, about its *nature*—as one still wants to say. The implications of Wittgenstein's view for such discourse seem to be, first and plausibly, that any theory of mind must assume the possibility of the situations in which the conventions can be learnt, and secondly, but very contentiously, that the question of what items we include in our explanations of mental life is no more than the question of whether we can find in experience a

---

[1] *Investigations*, Pt. I, § 304.   [2] Ibid., Pt. I, § 305.
[3] *Ibid.*, Pt. I, § 304.

use for the corresponding terms in the context of such learning situations. In short, we only refer to a certain type of entity if we find we have a use for a term designating it—an excellent beginning; and this is determined not by theoretical considerations, pictures of reality and the like, but by the range of possible developments in our ordinary language habits—a valuable precaution perhaps against empty metaphysics. But this in turn appears to be nothing but a matter of what distinctions we can invest with the ordinary non-theoretical kind of importance they can acquire in already established language-games. In other words it seems that for Wittgenstein the introduction of a designating expression can have no explanatory function at all. It is the grammar of everyday discourse that decides what significance their designations have. As he remarks: 'Grammar tells us what kind of object anything is.'[1]

[1] *Investigations*, Pt. I, § 373.

VII

GIVING 'IMAGINATION' A USE

I. INTRODUCTION

In the remainder of the essay I shall discuss imaging—and imagination—in the light of each of the two essential ingredients which I have said Wittgenstein requires of a grasp of mental terminology: distinctions in experience and contexts of importance. That they are essential I shall not dispute. What I find profoundly unsatisfactory in Wittgenstein's remarks on the nature of mind is his view, implicit in the comment that *grammar* tells us what kind of object anything is, as to what constitutes a context of importance. But we will come to that in the final chapter. Here I shall pursue a line of inquiry about imagination strictly in the spirit of at least the first ingredient, with its stress on the need of a phenomenological base for our concepts of experience.

An inquiry of this kind is certainly called for, given a dominant motif in recent discussion of imagination: namely that imaging is *not* involved in all of what we 'correctly' call imagining.[1] The point is well taken. But one is led to wonder about *its* context of importance. 'Conceptual clarity' would be widely canvassed these days. But if the point is that imaging is not a necessary part of *imagination*, how—as we asked earlier in connection with

[1] Cf. Ryle, *The Concept of Mind*, p. 257; Annis Flew, 'Images, Supposing and Imagining', *Philosophy*, Vol. XXVIII (July 1953), No. 106, who distinguishes between three senses of 'imagine': 'one in which (the context makes clear that) the word is used to report the occurrence of mental imagery; a second in which "imagined" is used as substantially equivalent to "thought"; and a third in which "imagine" is used as substantially equivalent to "suppose" ' (p. 246), and argues that 'in neither of the latter two senses does imagining necessarily involve imagery' (p. 246); E. J. Furlong, *Imagination* (Allen & Unwin, London, 1961), e.g. pp. 19–26; and John King-Farlow, ' "Mine" and the Family of Human Imaginings', *Inquiry*, Vol. 12 (1969), No. 2. References to what is 'correctly'

Ryle—is the assumption justified that what people correctly *call* imagining is also what they would correctly subsume under 'imagination'? Certainly there are uses of 'imagine', for example 'imagine' as 'falsely believe' and 'suppose', in which the presence of images seems not to be implied, but if this is to be an item of conceptual interest, and not just a 'find' for collectors of ordinary-language homonyms, the imaginings in question would have to be arranged in some sort of family group, one or two of them perhaps even disinherited, and the true kin provided with a suitable patriarch, such as Ryle's 'hypothetical frame of mind'. The conceptual importance Ryle himself attaches to the point of usage is to be found in his assault on the Faculty of Imagination, as betokening one special kind of mental process. Perhaps this negative theme also underlies much of what goes by the name of conceptual clarity. But whatever the motives, the result has been seriously to misrepresent the extent, and also the variety, of the phenomena—the distinctions in experience—which might provide a basis on which to establish, or 'fix', a concept, or a family of concepts, of imagination.

2. FIXING SOME CONCEPTS OF IMAGINATION

If fixing a concept is a thoroughly Wittgensteinian notion, it is less clear that this is true of fixing a concept of *imagination*. What we fix, in Wittgenstein's typical practice, are uses for expressions, for example 'I am now imagining *this* to myself',[1] and it is expressions with their uses in ordinary contexts that he generally

called imagining tend to be somewhat haphazard. Thus H. H. Price fastens on one ambiguity of the verb 'to imagine', when he says that although 'to imagine' sometimes means 'to have mental images . . . more usually it means "to entertain propositions without believing them"' ('Survival and the Idea of "Another World"', in J. R. Smythies [ed.], *Brain and Mind* [Routledge & Kegan Paul, London, 1965], p. 5), while J. O. Urmson fastens on another when he says that '["*X* imagined such and such"] may mean that someone freely and creatively invented, made up, such and such as a piece of imaginative fiction; or it may mean that someone falsely believed that the state of affairs actually obtained' ('Memory and Imagination', *Mind*, Vol. LXXVI [January 1967], No. 301, p. 85).

[1] *Investigations*, p. 213. Anscombe translates 'ich stelle mir jetzt *das* vor' as 'I am now having *this* image'.

gives as examples of concepts. If the criteria for 'I am now imagining *this* to myself' differ from those, say, for 'He is now imagining *that* to himself', then these two expressions form different concepts. Since it is not a precondition or part of the enterprise of fixing uses for these expressions that one also fix a concept of 'imagining' that is common to both, there would seem to be no call for such a unifying or shared concept. Indeed it is characteristic of Wittgenstein's highly 'contextual' approach that concepts, for him, do not so much collect as individuate uses of expressions and thus the phenomena they refer to. Of aspect-seeing, for example, he says: 'There are here hugely many interrelated phenomena and related concepts.'[1]

Whether Wittgenstein would be in principle opposed to the idea of fixing a concept of imagination that would apply to what are, for him, conceptually diverse contexts is at least unclear. What is clear is that in practice he makes use of such concepts. Thus he speaks of imagination as the capacity to form images (*Vorstellungskraft*) and also as the capacity to see similarity in difference (*Phantasie*), both of which are involved, he thinks, in the seeing of aspects of things. Since Wittgenstein himself has not fixed uses for the word 'imagination' in either of these senses it may be an illuminating exercise, as a preliminary foray into this neglected area, to fix some for him.

Wittgenstein is concerned with aspect-seeing in general. Our own interest is more specifically with pictorial aspects, and more specifically still with mental images. So we shall begin with imagination as *Vorstellungskraft*.

We begin by noting how Wittgenstein distinguishes the famous duck-rabbit example (a drawing visible alternately as a picture of a duck—facing in the one direction—and of a rabbit—facing in the other) from two other cases. One is where the aspect is simply a perceivable property of a figure, which can be 'reported simply by pointing' to the respective part of the figure in question.[2] Wittgenstein's example is of a regular octagon divided into eight alternately black and white segments and visible as a white Maltese cross on a black background or a black Maltese cross on

<hr/>

[1] *Investigations*, p. 199.   [2] Ibid., p. 207.

a white background.[1] Such aspects are analogous to shapes and colours, and belong, as it were, to the visual impression. Whereas in the case of the duck-rabbit you only see the relevant aspects 'if you are already conversant with the shapes of these two animals', in this case there is no analogous condition for seeing the aspects. The other case he distinguishes from the duck-rabbit, however, requires imagination (*Vorstellungskraft*).

'It is possible to take the duck-rabbit simply for a picture of a rabbit . . . but not to take [a] bare triangular figure for the picture of an object that has fallen over. To see this aspect of the triangle requires *imagination*.'[2]

But in what way does it require imagination. Two possibilities, which correspond to two distinct possible uses of 'imagination', can be discarded. The first is that to arrive at possible representational themes for a given drawn figure requires imagination in that it requires a capacity simply to *think* of, or bring to mind, themes that the figure itself is not sufficiently detailed to represent; in this sense, the more thematic possibilities one can think of the more *imaginative* one may be said to be, though perhaps the ability to think of just one possibility is itself an exercise of imagination in this sense, in so far as it involves the spontaneous calling up of an idea which is only metaphorically appropriate for the given visual stimulus, that is an idea for which the adequate visual stimulus is lacking.[3] Imaginativeness is not of course confined to modes of sensing; it can be witnessed in the activities of, say, the improvising pianist, the extemporizing raconteur, and the inventively playful child. Such active, or 'muscular', performances are called imaginative if they show originality, or originativeness, and 'wit', at least in the older and wider sense of that term; that is if they are neither stereotyped or imitative nor random or automatic.[4] However, this concept of imagination is

---

[1] It is possible to see both crosses simultaneously against their common background.

[2] *Investigations*, p. 207, Wittgenstein's emphasis.

[3] Cf. our example of a visual simile on p. 157 above.

[4] Cf. E. J. Furlong's tripartite distinction of 'imagination'. This corresponds with his use of 'with imagination' (Furlong, op. cit., e.g. pp. 83–94).

perhaps closer to what Wittgenstein calls *Phantasie*, and which he sees as required to sense similarity in difference, as in hearing something as a variation on a particular theme.[1] Moreover, to invoke imagination in this capacity alone would be to neglect something essential to Wittgenstein's preoccupation at this point, namely the phenomenon that the visual ideas are ones that appear *on* the figure as its aspects, and not ideas that are simply stimulated by the figure but can in principle be considered in visual separation from it.

The second possibility is that in the case of seeing the triangle as an object that has fallen over we must be imagining *that* the triangle is such an object, or, in an expression that has this same use, but is perhaps more appropriate because unlike the former it is confined to this use, imagining the object *as* such an object. These uses suggest a concept of imagination as supposal or supposition. If I imagine the triangle as a fallen object I am treating it, at least visually, as if it were a fallen object. Again, this 'exercise of imagination' too may not be confined to sensing: imagining things as fulfilling descriptions the imaginer knows them not to fulfil can also involve treating them in practice as if they fulfilled them, and if in practice perhaps not necessarily visually or in any other sense mode; it may be a question rather of 'expectations and preparednesses to act'.[2] Now certainly, to see more than one is given is in a sense to see something other than what is given; in the present case it is to see something fallen when there is nothing fallen before one's eyes. And it might be thought that this required either the incipient or the suppositional belief that what is given is a fallen object. But that is not required. In order to see the figure as a fallen object we do indeed have to add something to what we perceive; but not what we need to make the triangle appear *to be* a fallen object, only what we need to give it a fallen-object appearance. And if we give it that then that is what it has, not something it is imagined as having, in the supposal sense of 'imagine as'. In other words it is to bring the triangle into line with the duck-rabbit as something describable as a picture of *X* that we need imagination in the sense Wittgenstein

[1] *Investigations*, p. 213.   [2] Furlong, op. cit., p. 28.

means. It is to enable us to do in the absence of visual clues what, given the necessary 'conversancies', we do when the clues are provided. It is to enable us to *form an image*.

Now the paradigm for this expression is surely the case where no clues at all are provided; that is where ideas are framed, as Berkeley says, out of nothing. This latter concept is therefore closely related to Wittgenstein's. In both cases the image is mental. Supplementing the available visual clues is not doing anything materially to the thing we see. And Wittgenstein himself says, regarding the aspects in which one can see the triangular figure:[1] 'it is as if an image [*Vorstellung*] came into contact, and for a time remained in contact, with the visual impression'.[2] The effect is as if the visual clues had been supplied for us, so that we see the triangle in one of its 'roles', just as when we stand before a picture.

'. . . [a] triangle can really be standing up in one picture, be hanging in another, and can in a third be something that has fallen over.—That is, I who am looking at it say, not "It may also be something that has fallen over", but "That glass has fallen over and is lying there in fragments" . . .'[3]

In other words there is a pictorial appearance of a glass that has fallen over and is lying in pieces. This case differs significantly both from the Maltese crosses and also from seeing a real picture. In the former there is no picture—they just *are* Maltese crosses—and in the latter the picture is not mental, it is there for anyone properly conversant to see. The concept of imagination we might fix here then is one in which 'imagination' means the forming of a mental image, where an image is mental if it is *not* there for anyone to see, whatever their conversancies. A slightly different concept would be one in which it was required of the image that is not there for anyone to see, that it be formed out of nothing, as in 'imaging'.

---

[1] The triangle (a right-angled triangle lying on its hypotenuse) can be seen 'as a triangular hole, as a solid, as a geometrical drawing; as standing on its base, as hanging from its apex; as a mountain, as a wedge, as an arrow or pointer, as an overturned object which is meant to stand on the shorter side of the right angle, as a half parallelogram, and as various other things' (*Investigations*, p. 200).

[2] Ibid., p. 207.   [3] Ibid., p. 201.

It is important to note that in the former sense of 'imagination' it no more requires imagination to see a physical picture or representation (i.e. one that is not mental) as such than it does to see the Maltese crosses. All that one needs to see, say, a photograph as a picture of something is a certain visual knowledge, a capacity to see the illusion offered, and to see that, one must simply be conversant with the shapes, etc. of the object represented;[1] or, as one might just as well say, be conversant with how something looks, or can look. There is no extra *visual* capacity here that is not exercised also in the case of seeing the crosses. In fact one can revise the crosses example to introduce a conversancy there which is *not* required in seeing a picture. One might treat the term 'Maltese' intentionally, so that it does not follow from someone's seeing a cross of the kind called Maltese, and sees it in the way in which it would be normally said to be recognizable as a cross of that description, that he sees a Maltese cross. If it is so treated, for the person to see the cross as a Maltese cross he must be conversant not only with the shape, but also with the *name* for that shape. In fact what distinguishes seeing a real picture from seeing the crosses is not a visual knowledge requirement, but a situational knowledge requirement: to see a picture one must know that what one has been able to recognize and is seeing is not being seen in a 'material' sense of see, that the appearance it is putting in is *only* a pictorial one.

Now if we wanted to say that the very fact of there being the look of something that one knows is not before one, and so of something one sees only intentionally, does require or involve imagination, it would have to be in yet another sense of 'imagination'. It is in such a sense that Sartre would say it involved imagination to see a photograph or a portrait as a picture of something, since he holds that to see what one knows to be seen only intentionally is *in itself* to adopt the special attitude he calls 'imaging-consciousness'. For Sartre, then, the sentence, 'That glass has fallen over and is lying there in fragments', when used to describe what is seen in a picture, would be an expression of this attitude, simply in so far as the user is addressing himself to

[1] Some qualifications are noted below.

what he knows not to be perceived. The attitude itself is one in which, roughly, instead of seeing the world as it simply is, that is as it 'precedes' consciousness of it, we pre-empt its nature and see it in our own rather than its terms, in the present case imposing a fiction-reality on what we know is only a real likeness of a broken glass.[1] If we were to align seeing the Maltese crosses with *this* use of 'imagination' we would have to use the term 'Maltese' in a sense in which, e.g. no merely two-dimensional 'Maltese crosses' could be genuine samples of such crosses. We may think of the case, for example, where only certain medals and insignia would count as Maltese crosses, or even perhaps two-dimensional crosses of a certain very large size, or of a particular colour. But then seeing a drawn cross as Maltese would now require imagination in the sense we are trying to track down too, because that would be needed for the illusion of depth, size, or colour to appear; something would have to be 'added'.

The reason that 'to take the duck-rabbit simply for the picture of a rabbit' does not require imagination in our sense is that we add nothing to it in order to see it in that way. It is true that when

---

[1] It is crucial to take Sartre's usage literally when judging whether it is justified. We must recall that when Sartre claims that imagining is one of the two main irreducible and mutually exclusive *attitudes* of consciousness, it is indeed attitudes that he means. Thus Ishiguro finds that Sartre is led to the 'mistaken' and 'evidently wrong' view that 'when I see the actor as the person he is mimicking, I cannot be really perceiving the actor . . . [and similarly that] if I see a painting as a portrait of *X* . . . I am no longer perceiving the painting'. ('Imagination', in Williams and Montefiore, op. cit., p. 176; cf. Sartre, *L'Imaginaire*, p. 156.) But to do justice to Sartre here we would have to understand by 'perceiving' that other main *attitude* of consciousness, namely perceiving-consciousness, and if the replacement is made it is by no means so evident that he is wrong. Sartre does not claim that imaging-consciousness precludes perceiving in other senses (e.g. 'Yes, I saw Olivier as Macbeth'). The real test, it seems to me, is whether merely intentional seeing can be construed as essentially involving incipient entry into illusion, this latter being the most plausible candidate for the essential ingredient of an *attitude* of imagining. I have suggested elsewhere (see 'Wollheim and Seeing Black on White as a Picture', p. 114) that so long as the illusion entered into is not that one sees the intentional object *in place of* the materially seen picture, but that in seeing the former in a picture one is nevertheless seeing it materially, then entry into illusion can be regarded as typical of, and in that sense essential to, though not necessary for, merely intentional seeing. I regard this as partially vindicating Sartre's usage.

we exchange one aspect for the other we are not doing anything materially to the drawing (although doing that might help, e.g. turning the drawing round slightly) and that there is this much similarity with the triangle case. But the aspect or image that one then sees is still not seen by virtue of any supplement to the available visual clues; it is more like ignoring some of the clues, though the effort, if any, is only an initial one, and is not required to sustain the image. One may think, on the other hand, of rather sketchy duck-rabbit drawings where imagination in our sense would be required, at least for some people. And this shows why we should add, as Wittgenstein points out, that making good the deficiency of clues mentally and having them supplied for us are not always as different as they sound. For if one sees in a picture, for example, what one describes by saying, 'That glass has fallen over and is lying there in fragments', one cannot say 'what a picture must be like to produce this effect'. 'There are, for example, styles of painting which do not convey anything to me in this immediate way, but do to other people. . . .'[1] An aspect is not something we can make people perceive, even when it comes closer to seeing what belongs to the visual impression than to what requires imagination. It has, thinks Wittgenstein, something to do with 'custom and upbringing'.

Now one way of expressing the concept of imagination that we are trying to fix on the basis of Wittgenstein's observation here would be to say: It requires imagination to see something as a picture when no picture is visible on the basis of the visual impression together with whatever conversancies would be needed to ascribe a certain perceived pictorial value to the visual impression. However, a necessary qualification suggests that we have still not quite got to the heart of the concept, or exhausted its possible applications. Although in the case of the triangle seen as a fallen object we do have a picture; that is, there is something we see which has a representational theme, though one we have invested it with, it is not by virtue of its *having* this that it requires imagination to have it; for the duck-rabbit case is also one of there being a representational theme, and it does not require

[1] *Investigations*, p. 201.

imagination. So must it not be because the picture is produced, rather than that it occurs, that imagination is required? In invoking imagination Wittgenstein seems to be thinking of how we can *transform* a figure *into* a picture.

But then we might choose to regard the transforming by itself as the node of our concept, rather than that the transformation is specifically into a picture. That is, we might take the fact that the aspect gained is a pictorial one to be accidental to what the term 'imagination' covers here. Now Wittgenstein himself obscures this possibility by suggesting that in any case all aspect-seeing is potentially or indirectly pictorial. He proposes as a criterion: 'What I can see something as, is what it can be a picture of'; explaining further that 'the aspects in a change of aspects are those ones which the figure might sometimes have *permanently* in a picture'.[1] There are at least two main kinds of case where this criterion would be too stringent. Take an example of the first kind:

(1) On waking in an unfamiliar room and with my head turned to the wall, I take the slightly luminous quality of the wallpaper, something I have not noticed before, to be imparted to it by the sun shining through the window. On turning to catch a glimpse of the promising day, however, I discover that it is dull and raining as usual. The luminosity of the paper is a property imparted to it by its manufacturer, and not by the sun. What I do here is first see the wallpaper as reflecting sunlight, and then subsequently see it as luminescent paper.

Now, seeing the paper first in one way and then in the other seems a clear case of a change of aspects. Moreover, it seems to accord with the facts to say that the wallpaper itself acquires the aspects in question as *seen* qualities; that is to say, it is not simply a matter of *attendant* expectations, preparednesses, and beliefs, or of images 'in power', as Hume would say. But the difference in quality nevertheless depends upon differences *in* expectation and belief directed *at* the wallpaper, and not upon any inherent pictorial quality *of* the wallpaper. In that case, the difference corresponds neither to anything that could be depicted nor to

[1] *Investigations*, p. 201.

anything that could be used to portray it. The aspects here are not pictorial.

Wittgenstein's stricter criterion might be defended on grammatical grounds. 'Aspect' is closely related to 'property' in that to call something an aspect of a thing is to suggest that it is not out of the question to regard it as a genuine property of a thing, visible to anyone suitably placed and relevantly conversant. To talk of 'gaining' an aspect, as we have done, might be somewhat misleading therefore—and precisely so because it requires *imagination* to gain an aspect. Indeed the diversity of representational themes attributable to the triangle in our earlier example is not a function of its own pictorial richness. Rather the reverse; it is due to the triangle's failure by itself to be a picture of anything; to become pictorial it has to be incorporated *into* a picture. Similarly with the wallpaper case, only here it is a state of expectation and belief that is required to induce the seeing of the property in question, and not anything like an image which, as in the case of the triangle, 'comes into contact, and for a time remains in contact, with the visual impression'. So the non-pictorial counter-example is not properly speaking an example of aspect-seeing.

However, Wittgenstein himself makes no such move in defence of his proposed criterion; and we may suppose that the criterion is intended to cover all the 'hugely many interrelated phenomena' that he discusses under the heading of 'seeing as'. We shall follow him then in continuing to speak of aspects as if they were coextensive with the phenomenon of seeing-as.

But in any case there are non-pictorial counter-examples that come very close to the triangle case, in that there does seem to be an image that comes into contact with the visual impression in just the way Wittgenstein describes. Consider the following situation:

(2) I discover myself, bound, in what I take to be a basement. The curtains over what looks like the window are drawn, and in thinking of how to escape I envisage various possibilities consistent with the situation I believe I am in. But then it occurs to me that for all I know I might well be in an attic. Due not only to

my active interest in how to escape, but also to a strong tendency to acrophobia I literally see the room in the second way but manage by an effort to see it in the first, though I am not sure which, if either, is the correct way.

Expectations and beliefs are involved here too, but the reason for saying that these ways in which I see something do not fulfil Wittgenstein's criterion is not, as before, that the expectations and beliefs are necessary for the ways in question, but that the properties, though they could in other circumstances be perceived to be instantiated by the thing in question (e.g. if the walls of the room were transparent, or I was outside the room), cannot be so perceived in the envisaged situation. Where wallpaper can be directly perceived to be reflecting light or to have a built-in luminosity, once the appropriate expectations have been verified, in the present example the room acquires its seen qualities by its perceptible qualities being given, so to speak, paraperceptual values and extensions. The walls are *seen* as extending up and not down, or down and not up, the ceiling as (in a manner of speaking, but one literal enough to acrophobics) close to the sky, or as supporting the weight of the rest of the house, etc. So even if the room is seen as in fact it is, its being as it seems is not something that, in the envisaged situation, can be perceived.

It was suggested that Wittgenstein's concept of imagination could be expressed in terms of forming a picture when no picture is visible on the basis of what is perceived. But now that it seems we might well dispense with the requirement that what is formed be a picture, an alternative way of fixing the concept may be suggested. It is significant that the non-pictorial aspects still consist of properties that in other circumstances can be seen to belong to the objects in question. In fact they are all related to expectations and beliefs about what *might* be perceived. Now this is also true of what things can be *imagined as* being, in the sense we have roughly fixed for the use of the expression 'imagining as'. So as a first step to reformulating the concept we might propose an alternative to Wittgenstein's criterion of 'seeing as'. Instead of what I can *see* something *as* being what the thing might have permanently in a picture, it could be 'what I might imagine the thing in question as being'. The concept of imagination could then be fixed as coextensive with the phenomenon of seeing-as where seeing-as requires some mental supplement to the perceptible object.

Before examining this suggestion, it will be convenient to interpolate some remarks on the concept of 'imagining as' which will enable us to place it a little more precisely in relation to the concept we are mainly concerned with.

By simple modification, our two non-pictorial samples can be used to illustrate what we are referring to as 'imagining as' or 'imagining that'. We will keep to the former expression provisionally. Thus, in (1), having discovered that the sun is not shining I can once again look at the wall and imagine it as reflecting sunlight. It is just like seeing it as reflecting sunlight except that in this case I know it is not reflecting sunlight. I am supposing, but still directing my suppositions, as it were, towards the perceived environment, the space I am in. So also in (2). Sitting in my familiar basement I may test my nerve by imagining it as an attic, perhaps becoming a little giddy in doing so. However, in this example the modification is not really necessary; it already contains an element of supposition, in the form of conjectural envisagement *about* the facts rather than, as in the more normal case, active supposal in the face of them. But here this is not a difference with any 'point'. To the acrophobic the suggestion of the fact of elevation is as much to be resisted as the recognition of the fact itself, and his deliberate attempt to dispel the suggestion is no less an effort of imagination as 'imagining as' than the deliberate imagining of what is known not to be true. Not all imagining-as is a matter of play.[1]

---

[1] Cf. J. L. Austin's claim ('Pretending', *Proceedings of the Aristotelian Society*, Supp. Vol. XXXII [1958]) that pretending (that) differs from imagining (that) by being a preliminary to (or even accompanied by) behaviour where the latter is preliminary only to, say, asking questions like 'How should I feel if I was on top of a mountain?', and his illustration: 'I can "always" imagine, *e.g.*, that my prison walls are not there, but it may be "no good' pretending they aren't there, they're solid enough to stop me doing the things that follow on the pretending' (p. 278). But imagining the walls aren't there might be a 'way out' for the claustrophobic who is interested as much in the feeling as in the fact of freedom.

There are two important *caveats*, however. First, the fact that expectation and belief enter into imagining-as must not obscure the fact that imagining-as also involves imagination in the other capacity that we are trying to pinpoint, namely imagination as that which enables the imaginer-as to see something in the way that he imagines it as being. That is, it contains a qualitative modifying of visual experience of the kind noted by Wittgenstein in the case of the triangle being seen as a picture. In this sense it *involves* something essentially 'inner', even if supposal itself is not anything essentially inner. Secondly, not all imagining-as need be *active* supposal, whether deliberate or playful. We noted that Sartre uses a concept of imagining-as to cover all cases of seeing things which the person seeing knows he only sees intentionally, as in the case of seeing something depicted. But although this, in Sartre's view, is something we do 'spontaneously', he does not think we necessarily do it either deliberately or intentionally. On the contrary, he thinks we are more typically drawn, or seduced, than self-propelled into the attitude he calls 'imaging-consciousness'. We have no need to *try* to treat the unreal as real, we have a natural tendency to do so anyway. But then we should be able to try to resist the tendency by deliberately counteracting the spontaneous pull of the unreal towards being seen as if it were something real, in fact by trying to treat it as lying under its proper category, the 'unreal'—in rather the same way as a sufferer from acrophobia may try to resist the awful illusion of height by convincing himself of the fact he knows to be true, namely that he is safely at ground-level. The tension here between what we are drawn to and what we consciously or actively try to imagine reflects something of the diversity of the phenomena that concepts of imagination can be fixed to cover. A point we shall return to in the next chapter.

Here, however, is a useful point at which to locate a special use for 'imagining *that*'. So far we have dealt with imagination in cases where there is a visual transformation not accounted for by any material change in what is visible. We have fixed a concept of imagination for the transformation itself—at least provisionally. We have also fixed one for the deliberate subversion and replacement of genuine expectations and beliefs about the visible, and noted another (Sartre's) where a natural tendency to such subversion and replacement is itself something we might deliberately try to subvert and replace. In all these cases there has been something we *see* in a certain way which is not the way it can properly be said to be perceived. But there are also cases where *nothing* is, or is specifically pointed out as being, seen in a way corresponding to what is imagined, and in which, therefore, the 'imagining-as' terminology will not be applicable. There are two distinct uses here, corresponding to the two uses of imagination just mentioned. If I walk down a dark corridor some slight noise might lead me to feel that I am being followed. Visual imagery cannot account for this feeling, because even my mind's eye can only 'scan' the scene accessible to my ordinary eyes. And hearing the sound, a creaking floorboard for example, as a footfall cannot account for it either. Nor am I seeing *myself* as being followed; I am just being myself feeling that I am being followed. All I can say is that I am in a certain state which includes expectations (e.g. that something will catch up with me, would be glimpsed if I turned round quickly) and sometimes even quite clearly demarked bodily reactions, gooseflesh, tingling, cold shivers, and the like. The only sensory item to which to affix this complex perceptual orientation is the sound itself, which obviously cannot bear it, and is in any case dispensable; it is only a cue and I can acquire this orientation without that stimulus. Indeed it might be the (not, I think, genuinely paradoxical) fact that I hear the *silence* as ominous that first sets me off. I should say then that I *imagine that* I am being followed, even though I think it possible that I am not. One could reserve 'imagines-that', therefore, for cases where there is nothing to pinpoint as what is seen-as. And it is imagining because, just as in the cases of seeing-as which require imagination to gain the aspect, the content of the visual, or in general sensory, experience involves a supplement or addition to the available vista. This then is the first kind of case. The second is simply where I *deliberately* imagine that I am being followed; that is, imagining-that in the (active) supposal sense of imagining evolves naturally out of the same expectation and belief component that in cases of visual (or more generally sensory) transformation in general led us to identify aspect-seeing with 'imagining as'. Supposal is 'properly' confined to expectation and belief, to what one is prepared for as opposed to what one sees, and so demands the 'that' rather than the 'as' construction.

The reader must not suppose (in a sense that we have so far excluded from 'imagination') that the above is an attempt to reconstruct, even less describe, ordinary usage. What I am trying to do is show how uses of the term 'imagination' can be fixed for distinguishable features in visual experience. The expressions employed for these uses nonetheless correspond to *some* extent with ordinary usage, and in a way it might be helpful to think of these uses as a blueprint to which ordinary uses of these and similar terms more or less approximate. Helpful if, and to the extent that, it throws light on ordinary usage, but also, as I have noted, as a corrective to the Rylean influence in the philosophy of mind, with its scorn of the inner and consequently of the visual aspect of imagination. A blueprint that does justice to distinctions in experience shows how imagination, conceived as— one feels compelled for lack of another term to say—a *process* of visual supplementation, and of which imaging is a limiting case in which there is nothing to supplement, is at work in a number of operations, whether also processes or more properly 'activities', of imagination where these latter are directed at the sensibly present environment. It is involved, for example, where the supplementation achieves an imaginative—i.e. unstereotyped—pictorial theme; when it is constitutive of my undeliberate, and perhaps compulsive, expectations about my immediate environment; or when these expectations are deliberately invoked. The blueprint also shows why in these cases, although this process is not what we would have to call, in Ryle's terms, 'the collateral occurrence of another, cogitative act',[1] it nevertheless may be said to be a specific nuclear operation. When embedded in a piece of imaginativeness or supposal, for example, it does not occur as another *act*—although if it is something I can do it may be an act when it is not so embedded. It is simply a

[1] See p. 46 above.

capacity, a faculty even, on which imaginativeness and supposal—in the kinds of cases with which our blueprint is concerned—draw. A user of our blueprint might even go so far as to say that it is indeed the presence of this nuclear process that makes it proper to call the activities and exercises that depend on it 'exercises of imagination' as opposed to a user of Ryle's alternative blueprint who would need to justify the term here by appealing to a certain 'hypothetical' frame of mind.[1]

We can test the value of our own blueprint by applying it to two further uses of 'imagine that'. To both there corresponds an ordinary use, but one which at first sight might seem to reveal the blueprint's shortcomings, in the one case by not fitting into it, and in the other by falling outside its frame. The first use is of 'imagine that' in cases where there *is* something visible that is imagined as or to be something. 'Imagine that's the enemy and this is us.' That may be the chair over there and this may be the chair over here. Why then are we not asked to imagine the chair over there *as* the enemy position and the chair over here *as* ours? The answer is that we might, in another context, have been asked to do just that: to see the chairs *as* those things, and savour the supposition, or perhaps even to act upon it by initiating military manoeuvres in the direction of the 'enemy' chair. We would be being asked to play, visually or muscularly. But the expression 'imagine that', given as an enjoinder, is more typically a presage of earnest than of play. We are being asked to set the scene for some serious conjecture or appraisal, to think of what follows from the situation being as we imagine it. And we are not being asked to imagine the chairs *as* the respective positions, so much as imagine the respective positions as being *the same as* that in which the chairs stand. In short, the reason for using the 'imagining that' rather than the 'imagining as' form here is that it is not the supposition itself we are being asked to focus on or envisage, but rather the consequences and possibilities that the supposition is designed to make it *easier* for us to envisage.[2]

The second use is of 'imagine that' as 'falsely believe (or

---

[1] See p. 55 above.
[2] Cf. Furlong, op. cit., pp. 31 ff. on 'directed imagining'.

suppose) that'. I suggested that this usage falls outside the frame of our blueprint. It does so because if the expressions are used interchangeably there is no need to refer to anything inner, to a modification in visual or sensory experience not due to any material change in what is visible. Ryle exploits this to show that there need be nothing essentially inner about imagination: to wait for what you are not going to get is 'already to imagine', and for that you only need 'the proper niche'.[1] But this usage is clearly anomalous, and our blueprint shows why. The paradigm of imagining as false belief is where conscious expectation is not fulfilled. Thus, in our first example, the man who wakes up and believes he sees the sun reflected on the wallpaper but then finds that there is no sun shining, both imagined *and* falsely believed that the sun was shining. His eager expectations were dashed, but they had been there. Far from this paradigm we have our man running for his usual morning bus, tripping, and falling, and missing it for the first time in ten years. We can say that he *believed* he would catch the bus this time as always before, and hence that he believed this falsely, simply because 'belief' shades off into 'standing assumption', and our man would be indignant if we questioned his belief that he would, catch the bus—'After all these years, I ask you!' But we cannot, so far, reasonably say that he *imagined* that he would get the bus as usual. To do that—both on our blueprint *and* in ordinary usage—he would have to have envisaged the possibility, and I think also accepted it as a probability, though not a certainty. That is—as we question him at breakfast—although, now he came to think of it, he could not be quite sure that he would catch the bus as usual, he imagined that he would do so—that is, it seemed fair enough to say that he would. The basis for this use of 'imagine' could be this. If, on being asked whether I expect a certain outcome or eventuality, I say 'I imagine that will be the case', I am doing something like reporting an impression; I am saying how it looks to me, though 'it' here refers not to any perceptible object, or even to the envisaged occurrence, but to something we could call the apparent likelihood of, or perhaps my general state of expectancy

[1] See p. 51 above.

concerning, the outcome. It is a far-stretched, if not far-fetched, analogical extension of seeing-as. It is a kind of seeing-as in which not only is nothing literally *seen* as, but the thing that is seen-as is not what could be seen literally at all. The remote analogy may explain the sleight of hand whereby we shift from saying that a person falsely believed something because he *only* imagined it and did not *believe* that he was only imagining it, to saying that he only imagined something because he falsely believed it.

3. A NON-WITTGENSTEINIAN CONCEPT

We have exploited Wittgenstein's discussion of 'seeing as' to uncover a wide feature of visual experience that might be referred to by one use of 'imagination'. Wittgenstein himself says of this feature that it 'requires imagination' where it enables the perceiver to see something as a picture. But we have seen how the way in which expectation and belief are linked to the ways in which we can see things makes for a looser connection between the phenomenon or feature and the notion of a picture than the etymology of the term 'imagination' would suggest; loose enough in fact for us to reject Wittgenstein's suggested requirement that what imagination produces in this sense must be a picture.

But now I want to exploit the notion of seeing-as further, to see how the sense in which imagination produces not necessarily pictorial ways of seeing things is not necessarily a sense in which the imaginer himself produces them. Again it is contrary to the letter of Wittgenstein's view that seeing-as can be exploited in this way. In arguing for the kinship of the concept of an aspect to that of a mental image he says that 'the concept of "I am now seeing it as . . . " is akin to "I am now imagining *this* to myself"'.[1] The similarity between the two is that:

'Seeing an aspect and imagining are subject to the will. There is such an order as "Imagine this", and also: "Now see the figure like this"; but not: "Now see the leaf green".'

[1] *Investigations*, p. 213.

That is, one can picture something to oneself deliberately, hence also be enjoined to picture it; and this is not the case with shapes and colours. The grammar shared by aspects and images helps to show the mistake of postulating inner sense-organs. But once again it can be seen that the grammatical feature in question is not necessary to either concept,[1] and that some of the clarity Wittgenstein seems to see in the distinction between what requires a sense-organ and what does not may be illusory.

Consider the following pair of cases (the second batch of non-pictorial cases promised above:)

(3) I am a (university) man of settled, scholarly ways and limited interests, bound for the most part to my study, and perhaps to those of a circle of similarly narrow-minded acquaintances. But one day I happen to be brought, say by a rich and worldly friend, into quite different surroundings, seeing new and unfamiliar sights, and acquiring new visual and other information about my environment. On returning home, I find my study itself has an altogether new and unfamiliar 'feel'. It has acquired definite characteristics which it did not have before: it has become spartan (at best), less 'central', and (at worst) tawdry and insignificant. But it quickly loses these characteristics as the memory of the unfamiliar fades and restores to my study *its* old familiarity.

(4) A stranger to the ways of modern society is confronted for the first time with the activities of retail selling and buying. But coming from an ethnically distant society in which the distribution of commodities is regarded as the generous act of a God who must be suitably propitiated beforehand, he sees the supermarket cash-girls as receiving angels acting on behalf of the divinity, and money as payment in kind, rather than in currency (though the concept of 'payment in kind' would not be one that *he* had, in that it implies by negation the concept of money).

Now we noted that our earlier examples (1) and (2) could be

---

[1] Though if we accept the grammatical point made earlier—about 'aspect' being close to 'property'—this denial should be confined to 'seeing as' and 'image'.

modified to allow the seeing to be imagining-as, or imagining-that. But in (3) and (4) it is unclear that one can succeed in picturing or imagining the situation as having the kind of property or quality concerned. Example (3) is of seeing something familiar in a new, unfamiliar way. But it seems that one ascribes unfamiliarity to things on the basis of how they themselves appear, that is on the basis of an impression received. The way that something strikes one as unfamiliar combines the 'impressive' quality of shapes and colours with subjective variability of the kind Wittgenstein suggests may be due to 'custom and upbringing'. Thus it seems to be as impossible to picture one's familiar room as being unfamiliar as it would be to see it as a room that does not have the physical characteristics one perceives it to have, despite the fact that the unfamiliarity of something is not a property of the thing in its own right. Similarly with 'institutional' seeing-as, where custom and upbringing are more transparently relevant. For although one could plausibly argue that it was possible to imagine to oneself that the situation one knows to be correctly described in one set of institutional terms is correctly described in another, it is doubtful whether what one *sees* the situation *as* in this way can be what the ethnic stranger sees it as; just as it is doubtful that when he becomes conversant with the new institution he can ever, even in imagination, see again what he originally saw.

Consider now (3) and (4) individually. In the case of (3), it is difficult to say, indeed, whether the qualities in question are qualities of the room at all and not rather of the *perceiving* of the room; for there are no ways, as there are in (1) and (2), of testing whether the quality is or is not instantiated by the room; indeed the question whether the room is in fact insignificant, spartan, tawdry and so on, is surely inappropriate, for one would not say simply on the basis of seeing it as insignificant, for example, that one had been *wrong* to think of it as, say, the centre of the universe; it is unlikely that one had consciously ascribed that kind of significance to it at all. The ways in which the room is seen do not necessarily therefore correspond to properties consciously ascribed to, or thought to inhere in, the room itself. And even if they are, the subsequent ascription of another, incompatible property of this kind to the room would probably lead one not to say that one had been wrong about the room, but that what seemed to be a quality of it was in fact nothing but a quality of the awareness one had of it. But this assumes that the room itself is something neutral, that the qualities in question are in some way added to it. Not a difficult notion in practice perhaps, since we know what it is to give true and false descriptions of the room, and that implies that we have adequate criteria for finding out what *is* true of the room itself as opposed to the ways in which it appears to us. But not a simple notion either. The addition is not something we *experience*. So the idea of the neutral room is not an empirical one: *it* corresponds to no distinction in experience.

Case (4) differs again from (3) in respect of the nature of the criteria required to distinguish what is true of a situation from the way in which it is seen. For in this case it is not enough to identify perceptual properties of the situation, one must also refer to its institutional characteristics, to such facts as that the cash-girls are not acting for a divinity, and that what the customers give in return for the merchandise is in fact money.

Now our four examples of non-pictorial ways of seeing-as suggest a number of points. First, they indicate the extent and variety of seeing-as in ordinary perceptual situations. Things, people, places, and events can appear to us as having (though not necessarily *to* have, in so far as this implies recognition) qualities, whether or not we are aware that the qualities are true of them. The reason in each case for saying that what is seen *as* something is not that what we see can be used to picture something, or be what the thing can be pictured as being, but simply that, in general and whether the perceiver considers this or not, it is possible to see the thing in other ways—whether these ways can be ways of seeing it truly (as in [1], [2], and [4]), and if truly also perceptibly (as in [1]) or quasi-perceptibly (as in [2]), or only institutionally (as in [4]), or ways of seeing it that do not amount to ways of seeing it truly or falsely at all (as in [3]).

Secondly, the examples show how we may, as we sometimes do, come to talk of perceptual operations in terms of 'imagination'. The justification for this way of talking is provided in two parts, by revealing certain distinctions, and by showing how they might be honoured with the title 'imagination'. The first part can be summarized as follows. The very fact that the quality of a perceptual experience can be bestowed upon it by the perceiver's expectations and beliefs (as in cases [1] and [2]), by his immediate context (as in [3]), or by his more long-term cultural background (as in [4]), leads one to conceive of at least some of the character of perceptual experience in general as being the product of mental processes. The world does not present itself to us in perception as a complex of straightforwardly perceptible properties; however much a 'perceiving machine' may simply scan and record the outside world,[1] in our case something is added to that world, something that is determined by, and can therefore be said to reflect, our beliefs, expectations, and social environment. The justification for honouring these processes with the title 'imagination' is that in the sense in which Wittgenstein seems rightly to say we sometimes require imagination to see a pictorial aspect, there is a basis for fixing a use of 'imagination' in a much wider context of perceptual experience, and that this basis lies precisely in the notion of the 'mental' addition that is brought to the visual impression in these cases of seeing a pictorial aspect. The possibility of the wider application of the notion is uncovered by distinguishing the different kinds of visual experience susceptible to the model of seeing-as. As a term, 'imagination' has some advantages over 'seeing as'. It covers cases where there is nothing to pinpoint as what is seen as something, and cases where we cannot easily say that what is seen (in the sense of *how* we see what thing we see) is something about the thing we see and not about the way we see it. It also conveys better the notion of activity, or in view of the distinction we have made between 'activity' and 'process' we should perhaps prefer the latter term here: whereas imagining-as and imagining-that are activities, 'mental' adding is a process,

[1] See p. 170 above.

and one that is only to some extent, and in certain kinds of case, under our control. Also the term 'image', although obviously most at home in picturing and the seeing of pictorial aspects, is more faithful to the phenomena than 'aspect', even where the aspects are not pictorial. When we see what we call an aspect we do not really see such a thing in separation from that of which it is an aspect: we only talk of aspects because we know that we might see what we do see in some other way, and perhaps not a way in which we are even equipped to see it. What we see in the sense of how we see it is unitary, just like a picture. Besides, as we noted earlier, it is not always appropriate to say that what we see is an aspect *of a thing*; aspects are often better explained by the versatility of our seeing-as than of the thing seen. The basic notion of 'what we see' here is 'how we see what thing we see'. It is this inherently intentional notion that the word 'image' may not unmisleadingly capture. Whether Wittgenstein would go this far with us is hard to say. But at least the only way in which our four examples do not correspond to what he says requires imagination is that the changes in these cases are not into pictures. But this is not an essential difference, and in other respects the correspondence is complete. There is a transformation of what is perceived, and the visual experience is one that differs in a parallel way from that in which we see shapes and colours, in so far as the properties assigned in perception to the visually discernible situation are not properties that it can be *recognized* (or strictly speaking *perceived*) as having. In the absence of reasons to the contrary one might conclude, therefore, that Wittgenstein should have accepted these non-pictorial examples as due, if not to *Vorstellungskraft*, at least to a mental function that is a *Kraft* of essentially the same kind.

But there is a very un-Wittgensteinian direction in which these thoughts might lead. We might go on to think that because what we see when we see an aspect is unitary, perceptual experience in general must be in some respect essentially subjective and private; for if some properties of perceptual experience are admittedly subjective, because bestowed 'mentally', and yet it is impossible simply on the basis of the experience itself, in

isolation, to discriminate the subjective from the objective—
the supplement from the neutral basis—it seems that from the
point of view of experience, in abstraction, the contents are
all of a kind. It may be seen to follow from this that visual
experience is something essentially private. In which case it
might be thought to follow further that inasmuch as visual
experience must be taken, as it ordinarily and of course correctly
is, to disclose a world of common objects, this is but another
instance of the seeing of one thing as another. But now the thing
that is seen is a private *object*, the seeing of it a *process* (not an
activity anyway), and the world of public objects that we also
see just one of its aspects.

Many philosophers would certainly regard this view of
the matter of perception as quite mistaken. I shall not argue
whether it is or not, but it is relevant to note a common rationale
for objecting to it. Often what philosophers object to in a view
is some unacceptable consequence they think follows from it:
in this case, that we could never know anything beyond the
contents of our own experience. It seems clear to them, as to
all of us, that we do know more than this. They then point out
that the view, by its alleged implications, simply fails to make
the distinctions we do make—and which our language is primarily concerned with—between what we perceive and what we
cannot strictly speaking be said to perceive at all. This leads them
to say that the view is obscurantist, that it makes 'monolithic'
distinctions which ignore the obvious, as well as the subtle,
differences that we in fact acknowledge.

There is something of Wittgenstein in this, though I would
not like to say how much. But it would seem possible to object
in return to these philosophers that the view that visual experience
is in some important sense private only entails that we never
know anything beyond our own experiences if it is assumed
that we can only know what we 'directly' apprehend. However,
nothing in our line of thought supports this unwanted assumption:
we have been led to think of the privacy of perception by thinking
first of cases of what *is* perceived and then of cases where the
private element is unthinkable without reference to a common

world, continuing identities, cultural backgrounds, and so forth. We can accept all the distinctions we ordinarily make between how we see and what we see; it is only that we accept them on a basis other than that of visual experience itself, or rather of individual visual experiences. Given this I suggest that the privacy of visual experience is an epistemologically revealing notion, and the denial of its privacy in principle a piece of philosophical obscurantism on its own account.

To accuse Wittgenstein of this obscurantism would be absurd, considering the extent of his preoccupation with the phenomena in question. And yet there is the persistent warning against the notion of privacy, and of inner processes and objects, a warning that suggests we have pursued a path which the punctilious Wittgensteinian would have avoided. There are other indications of this also. The whole idea of fixing a concept of imagination in the way suggested runs counter to the drift of Wittgenstein's thought. Instead of looking to the diversity of the phenomena and multiplying our concepts in accordance with our ordinary, everyday interests in them, we have shed diversity and presumed to designate some general feature of mind that quite overrides the distinctions called for in everyday language-games. And although we may be said to have assumed a grammatical investigation—in the sense of an examination of language habits—we have certainly not been engaged in such an investigation. But, as I noted earlier, the unsatisfactoriness of Wittgenstein's treatment of the phenomena is precisely that it seems to preclude a theoretical interest in them. In a way he is too phenomenological, much more so than Sartre. For Wittgenstein no structure is *presumed* to connect the phenomena in this way rather than that. Where Sartre imposes a specific dualism we might say that Wittgenstein merely holds dualism up as a possibility in order to resist such a prejudice.

And yet this is not strictly true. Indirectly Wittgenstein does impose a kind of dualism, a linguistic dualism. In assimilating the image to the aspect, and vice versa, he is not testing the capacity of the notion of an image to explain the interesting phenomenon (or rather vastly many interrelated phenomena) of seeing things in different ways; he is bent rather on showing how neither images nor aspects constitute concepts of 'mental ——' where the blank is to be filled by a word designating in its ordinary sense an object in the physical world. To suppose that they did would be to lend the inner that specious air of autonomy that leads so easily to the kind of epistemological frustrations noted above. On the contrary, the concepts of an image and of an aspect are *fixed*[1] in terms of the *importance* the expressions referring to images and aspects acquire for us[2] (e.g. the fact that we can give different descriptions, etc.) in the ordinary contexts. And it is this that gives us the right to say things like 'I am now imagining *this* to myself' and 'I am now seeing it as...', not some inner happening. But in saying this Wittgenstein is in effect denying that such a word can ever designate something mental, because it is necessarily in the physical context that we *fix* its meaning. In other words, because of what is required of a word's having meaning, the mental itself eludes description. We can only speak about it indirectly, in connection with what people do with the physical.[3] It is as if, just as with Sartre it is the world-as-qualified, so with Wittgenstein it is the language-game-as-played that alone can properly denominate the mind active. However, if this is Wittgenstein's view it seems evidently mistaken. Why should we not assume that there are certain terms, including 'image', 'object', 'state', 'activity', and 'process', whose uses are not *finally* fixed by their physical applications, and for which a literal application may therefore still be found in the unexplored medium. That this condition cannot be fulfilled by at least some terms seems a denial of an obvious linguistic fact. Whether the non-linguistic world offers a foothold for such terms is a factual matter to be decided at least in part by experience. But not altogether or straightforwardly by experience. For the linguistic fact itself implies a certain indeterminacy in the conditions that are to count as, say, a mental state or a mental process. A rider might be suggested, therefore, to Wittgenstein's remark

---

[1] *Investigations*, p. 204.   [2] Ibid., pp. 202 and 205.
[3] The prototypical instance is the language-game with 'Slab!', 'Brick!', 'Beam!', etc.; cf. *The Blue and Brown Books*, pp. 77-8.

quoted earlier, about the first step being the one that altogether escapes notice. He says: 'We talk of processes and states and leave their nature undecided. Sometime perhaps we shall know more about them—we think.' We could add that the nature of a mental process and a mental state may indeed be undecided, but that to assume that their nature was decided by the uses of the terms 'process' and 'state' in the contexts in which we learn them would invoke the premature rejection of a possible analogy.

VIII

SPECULATIVE CONTEXTS

I. INTRODUCTION

In what seems an acceptance in principle of dualism, yet a denial of dualism based specifically on physical analogies, Wittgenstein warns against projecting the physical on to the mental. Disappointment at not finding what we expect makes us suppose either that better introspective vision would reveal the true state of mental affairs, or that these affairs are conducted without a mind. The former alternative leads to groundless perplexity, the latter is a misleading denial. But what should we do instead? Wittgenstein's negative answer is the unexceptionable one that we should not *expect* the mental to mirror the physical. His positive answer is that what the mind is can best be seen by a grammatical investigation, that is that we should look for its nature in what people do with words. Not just mental words: there are no such in 'That was a marvellous holiday!', but someone uttering it is *remembering*, and possibly also *imagining* or *visualizing*, and these words are mental. To find out what memory and imagination are, therefore, we are to take note of what someone said to be remembering or imagining says and does. And so with all mental activities.

But does this really give us the *nature* of these activities? Would a comprehensive account of this kind give us all that can be said of the mind? No, and I shall argue that the view implicit in Wittgenstein's positive answer is as misleading as the views he warns us against. If the nature of a mental phenomenon were to be decided by a grammatical investigation, the only topic of philosophy of mind would be the grammar of dualism itself, that is, the nature of the distinction between the physical and the mental that is embedded in our ordinary ways of speaking.

But whatever an examination of these ways may reveal to us of the content of 'mind', it cannot show us everything. The view is wrong in suggesting that what grammar cannot tell us we should not want to say.

It is important to do justice to Wittgenstein. One shouldn't attribute to him a criterion of sense about mind that plays too easily into the hands of those disturbed by the persistence of the belief in mental imagery. Philosophers who share Dennett's concern that 'these ghostly snapshots have not yet been completely exorcized from current thinking'[1] might of course welcome a grammatical criterion of meaningfulness about mind. By applying to the word 'where' the principle that the uses of words are finally fixed in their physical applications, they could achieve an instant exorcism; for on this principle they could conclude that because the 'where' in the question 'Where is my mental image?' doesn't ask 'How many inches from my nose?' then it is only to be expected that the answer is 'Nowhere'.

Such a crude criterion is certainly far from Wittgenstein's own intentions. One suspects that the authentic Wittgensteinian approach here would be truly preventive, to get rid of the nowhere along with the image by trying to remove the motivation for asking 'Where?' We ask it because we assume that because the fact that a chair or a table exists entails that it exists somewhere, the same must be true of mental images. To avoid this result, the safe step is to adopt a negative and precautionary dualism in which we simply do not expect a mind to be spatial, nor mental images to have any whereabouts.[2] It is not that the grammar of 'where' proves there are no mental images; rather the *experience* of imaging reveals nothing on to which we can latch any question of *where* imagery is. There is no reason, then, to be puzzled by their absence. As Wittgenstein says in another context,[3] a discrimination in visual experience must stand on its own as that which gives us a reason to use an expression. That I can 'see' my nursery gives me no reason to ask where my mental picture of it is. That is no part of what I must grasp to do this rather everyday thing.

---

[1] Dennett, op. cit., p. 132.   [2] See p. 182 n. above.   [3] Cf. p. 178 above.

And yet this discrimination *exists*, the image occurs, as do all the other 'hugely many interrelated phenomena and possible concepts' which Wittgenstein acknowledges,[1] and samples of which we examined in the previous chapter. Why then should we not do a somewhat uneveryday thing and ask questions about their existence? How the image, and not just our grasp of the concept 'image', is possible and how it is related to all those things concerning which we have no qualms or difficulties about asking 'Where?', 'What?', 'Why?', or 'How?'. I have already argued that certain of these discriminations offer a foothold for the use of the term 'image'; and I have suggested that it is not an argument against the term applying here that, in order to do so, it must shed some of its normal grammatical attachments. We saw that in any case some of the attachments it must shed play no part in its essential point; a good deal of that point remains. But part of the justification for bringing these cases together under that term was the assumption that we could talk in each case of a visual supplement, a contribution to the content of the visual experience that was due to the mind. We noted earlier Wittgenstein's warning against discussing these phenomena in terms of mental contributions to some neutral object, as if this way of talking *followed* from the facts noted.[2] I want to suggest in conclusion that an assumption of this kind about visual contributions can be given a type of context, or frame of distinctions, which lend it importance—in a way, moreover, that would satisfy Wittgenstein's principle that what we need in order to understand a mental phenomenon is a *conceptual* justification, not a causal one.[3]

2. DIFFERENCES ABOUT IMAGINATION

To have a concept of *imagination* one must view the varied and interrelated phenomena from some distance. One must step outside the ordinary contexts which first determine the importance of distinctions, no longer have one's eye-balls glued to the distinctions themselves—as Wittgenstein sometimes seems

[1] *Investigations*, p. 199.   [2] See p. 178 above.   [3] See p. 179 above.

to suggest we should to know the mind. The perspective must be one in which the distinctions can be grouped and sorted under a limited number of heads. But there are different ways of sorting, different groupings, for instance, for what one might choose to call 'imagination'.

A classic example of difference about imagination is in Berkeley and Hobbes. Berkeley, we recall, finds a paradigm of mental activity in the capacity to form mental images. Images, for Berkeley, are characteristically at our disposal: we make them, and 'by the same power' unmake them. With Hobbes it is quite different. Far from regarding imaging as a paradigm of voluntary activity, he finds it 'evident, that the imagination is the first internal *beginning* of all voluntary motion'.[1] So where Berkeley says the image is excited by the will, Hobbes says the will is excited by the image.

Plainly a difference. But how to understand it? Is it, for example, terminological? As presented above, it might well be. We could suppose that Berkeley was impressed by, and so duly noted, the way images seem to be at the imager's disposal, while Hobbes was equally and compatibly impressed by, and so too duly noted, what puts them *at* the imager's disposal. This interpretation may seem to be supported by the famous passage where Hobbes says:

'When a body is once in motion, it moveth, unless something else hinder it, eternally . . . so also it happeneth in that motion which is made in the internal parts of a man when he sees, dreams, etc. For after the object is removed or the eye shut, we still retain an image of the thing seen, though more obscure than when we see it. . . . IMAGINATION therefore is nothing but decaying sense . . . .'[2]

This looks very like an account of the origin of our image-repertoire, and there would be no inconsistency between saying, on the one hand, that one's imagining X, or that p, is an exercise

---

[1] *Leviathan* (Fontana edn [introd. and ed. by John Plamenatz], Collins, London, 1962), p. 86, my emphasis.
[2] Ibid., p. 63.

of freely willed activity, and, on the other, that the fact that 'X' or 'that p' are among the things one can freely will to imagine is to be explained by a theory of mental traces.

But of course we know quite well that Berkeley and Hobbes's descriptions are not compatible. It is not *simply* a matter of labels. Hobbes's view of images as mental traces is part of a general conception of mental or human activity at large, a view according to which mechanical explanations can be applied as much to the 'activity' of imagining as to the availability of that activity's topics. Thus where Berkeley speaks without qualification of the dependence of ideas of imagination on the will, and of their being 'excited at random',[1] Hobbes remarks: 'When a man thinketh on any thing whatsoever, his next thought after, is not altogether so casual as it seems to be', and claims: 'as we have no imagination, whereof we have not formerly had sense, in whole, or in parts; so we have no transition from one imagination to another, whereof we never had the like before in our senses.'[2] So where Berkeley identifies activity with willing, taking will to be a deeply significant and unanalysable fact of experience, for Hobbes, to the contrary, what we call 'will' adds nothing new to a human action, and is indeed only a special case of what he conceives as the mechanism of appetitive behaviour. For although he considers all human action to be voluntary,[3] and in some cases action to be preceded by deliberation, he represents the general pattern of action as one of an 'alternate succession of appetite and fear',[4] and what we call will as merely the final operative appetite.[5] According to Hobbes, therefore, the exercise of will in the operations of a mind upon its ideas is not a basic idea at all, it is to be explained ultimately in terms of the motive and attractive power that ideas themselves have to generate or excite action. Thus the *terminological* difference between these two philosophers reflects a fundamental difference of view about the kind of

[1] *Principles*, op. cit., p. 72.
[2] *Leviathan*, p. 68.
[3] *The English Works of Thomas Hobbes* (Molesworth edn, 1839, reprinted Oxford 1961), Vol. IV, p. 272.
[4] Ibid., IV, p. 68.
[5] Ibid., III, p. 49. 'Will therefore is the last appetite in deliberating.'

activity characteristic of mind. While Berkeley puts mind on the side of an agency that 'knows or perceives' ideas, and 'exercises divers operations ... about them',[1] and equates imagination, as we saw earlier, with a power exercised *on* ideas, Hobbes puts mind on the side of the ideas and equates imagination (and memory) with the power latent in ideas themselves.

The fact that the way philosophers allocate labels reflects differing views on mental activity poses a philosophical question to which there are two possible, alternative answers. If in arguing for certain descriptions philosophers are presupposing and therefore in effect defending particular conceptions of mind, their would-be critics must decide whether to reject such speculations as misguided and vacuous in general and superfluous to the main task of sorting out the available distinctions, or else to accept the possibility in principle and relevance, perhaps even inevitability, of diverse interpretations of the phenomena. In the first case the appropriate criticism will be that the available discriminations are all we can go on and the bias imposed by the conception must be winnowed off as a 'speculative tare' (in Ryle's graphic phrase). In the second case criticism is a more complex affair. In some instances a conception will be criticizable from this latter viewpoint simply for failing to cover the 'facts', in which case it differs in no essential way from the criticism that emanates from the former viewpoint; but in others the question of coverage will depend on whether or not the critic accepts, or at least does not reject, the conception's own interpretation—in other words, description—of the facts.

Berkeley and Hobbes provide examples of conspicuous lack of coverage—more conspicuous perhaps in Berkeley's case than in Hobbes's. Berkeley, it will be recalled, says it is *no more* than willing and 'straightway this or that idea arises in my fancy'. Willing to imagine something is therefore a sufficient condition of imagining it. But he also thinks it is a necessary condition. 'When we talk ... of exciting ideas exclusive of volition, we only

---

[1] *Principles*, op. cit., p. 61.

amuse ourselves with words.' The claim that willing is sufficient
need not detain us. Obviously it requires qualification. For
example, one may simply fail to imagine at all because of damage
to visual centres in the brain; or one may want and try to imagine
something specific (say, six hundred and forty-two billiard balls)
but without having appreciated that this lies beyond one's
discriminatory powers; or one may get something less distinct
than one wanted. (A blur instead of a face). The qualifications
here, however, are ones that Berkeley himself might easily have
admitted. The same cannot be said of the claim that willing is
necessary for imaging.[1]

We have seen how the model of an active agent exercising
divers operations 'about' ideas is over-simple, to say the least.
However, it isn't that Berkeley confines his account of imaging
selectively to its active modes—a partiality which might be
philosophically justifiable—but that 'power and agency' for him
are concepts whose content is too narrowly and rigidly determined; they apply properly only to the free, conscious activity
that he experiences in himself. By determining the concepts in
this way he has ensured that it is empirically false to apply them
to *ideas*. If this is what they must have in order to be potent in
themselves—even in a Hobbesian sense—then it is all too clearly
true that they are not 'active' things. Berkeley therefore effectively precludes the possibility of describing in terms of mental
power and activity whatever in imaging cannot count in the
ordinary sense as an action of the *imager's*. His 'ideas' can be
neither excitants nor the results of unconscious or uncontrolled
excitations. This might seem tantamount to depriving psychologists of their topic. If, as some of them have claimed, there are
cases of imaging in which even the description of what *thing*
it is we imagine has to be read off the image, and even cases (of

---

[1] The distinction between what counts as a failure of the first claim as opposed
to one of the second may itself be 'blurred'. If all I get is a blur, might I not say
that I nevertheless imagined a blur, and so not only failed to imagine what I
willed to, but imagined something I did not will to? To decide this one may ask
whether it is a picture we did not mean to get (e.g. black and white instead of
colour) or not a picture at all.

so-called imagination images)[1] where what appears corresponds[2] to nothing in our previous visual experience, Berkeley's bias in favour of willing will seem wholly obscurantist.

If Berkeley identifies activity too closely with willed activity, taking will to be a deeply significant and unanalysable fact of experience, Hobbes might seem to go too far in the other direction. It is true that by putting mind on the side of the ideas and equating imagination (and memory) with the power latent in ideas themselves, Hobbes's picture might be regarded as the more enlightened one, in that it grants what many would allow, namely that imagination can activate the will and determine (even apparently willed) action. But Hobbes has an equally obscurantist bias in favour of mechanisms. Activity, for him, is no more than the operating of a mechanical process; action being simply the outcome of mechanical forces, and thought a series of movements in the brain. According to this conception, the notion of agency, as an irreducible concept, is theoretically excluded. If mental activity is nothing but a mechanical process, it seems there can be nothing that *properly* denominates the mind active. By seeing conscious agency as the vanishing focus of complex motions and forces, Hobbes effectively obscures the distinctions we may wish

---

[1] McKellar defines these as images 'whose form and content differs markedly from what the subject has seen or otherwise perceived' (McKellar, op. cit., p. 202). This use of the expression differs from that of, e.g., G. T. Fechner, the results of whose observations of imaging are reported by James, op. cit., II, pp. 50 n. Fechner uses it to refer to images which 'feel subject to our spontaneity'. The difference in usage perhaps reflects a divergence in opinion as to whether the autonomous or the spontaneous features of what are loosely subsumed under 'imagination' are the important ones. See also Richardson, op. cit., pp. 93 ff.

[2] 'Corresponds' needs interpretation. Empiricists, in order to explain the possibility of fanciful creations ('winged horses, fiery dragons, and monstrous giants', etc. [Hume, *Treatise*, p. 537]), concede that the archetype ideas of sense may correspond to the image only in part. But carried too far this concession tends to trivialize the empiricist thesis that 'all ideas are derived from impressions' (Hume, ibid., p. 63). It may then amount merely to saying that sensory knowledge is acquired from sensory experience. Usually, however, it is understood as the claim that, however complex the description (of a particular) under which we imagine something, there must have been occasions on which we perceived *particulars* which are in some sense recognizable components of the complex particular imagined.

to stress between actions of *ours* and actions that are not ours (of course in a sense other than that in which to deny that an action is ours is to say that it is someone else's).

This then is one kind of criticism that can be made of a philosophical description by a critic who will not reject philosophical bias out of hand. The bias embodied in the description may be such as to exclude ways of describing the phenomena which seem too 'fixed', too natural and familiar, for us to see any point in accepting the proposed change. Thus when descriptions which incorporate words like 'activity' and 'power', though still using them to make the kind of contrast they ordinarily make, reallocate them so that only very little—or even none—of what we want to call activities and powers can count as such, then we reject the source of the bias, the view that imposes it. It is a criticism that can be made, as I have said, even by the critic who does reject philosophical bias out of hand. The critic here stands by the 'hugely many interrelated phenomena', tests the philosophical account against the blueprint of everyday usage, and finds it wanting.

I stress this, because I think that the view of philosophers who deny there are mental images can be found wanting at the same common philosophical court. To deny images is to give a distorted picture of reality. Good or bad, there is just no riddance to mental images. For whatever reasons of bias one philosopher may wish them gone, the ghostly snapshots—if he *will* have it that way—remain to haunt him. But equally, for whatever reasons of bias another philosopher may hail the mental image as proof of an unfashionably 'inner' medium, there is nothing there to *prove* his bias true. There are only the discriminations—though I think we may call them images, even mental *pictures*, provided we are conscious (and who ever really is not?) of the obvious disanalogies between physical and mental pictures; and the discriminations lend themselves to a number of possible descriptions.

Because there *is* a domain of mental images, then at least part of Ryle's picture of reality is wrong: the anti-immanentist part; there *is* a clandestine space to puzzle us. But it doesn't follow that his over-all picture is wrong; or if it is, that it can be shown to be so in just the same way. In discussing Ryle I raised the question of why he was not content with a simple 'post-perceptual' analysis of imaging, since this would preserve the ordinary belief in imagery but at the same time give it a suitably dependent place in the general scheme of things. I questioned whether it might not have been his special doctrine of sensation that prevented him from accounting for images, though it seemed more likely that the special doctrine was invented to get rid of them. Nevertheless one might put the post-perceptualist thesis alongside the anti-immanentist one as two limbs of Ryle's general outlook, and ask whether it too gives a distorted picture of the mental world.

We shall return to this question briefly in a moment. But first let us look at a topic on which it is not possible to criticize what philosophers say as 'distorting' the world by appealing to the blueprint of everyday usage or by testing their definitions for coverage, because here the critic himself must depart from that blueprint and embrace some special view of the phenomena. The topic is the authorship of the mental image.

3. PERSONAL ACTIVITY AND MENTAL PROCESS

How do we decide when or if a mental image is a product of a process or an act of the imager? The answer depends on what (not on who) the imager is. Berkeley again provides the cautionary example. We noted how he said that *he* could excite ideas in his mind at pleasure and that the ideas arose from his no more than willing, but also that it was the *mind's* activity that the phenomena 'properly denominate'. He assumes, therefore, that his own activity and ·that of his mind are one and the same. In the kind of case he was thinking of this may seem a safe assumption. If anything can be regarded as a mental activity, then what I do when I deliberately conjure up an image of my boyhood home is surely at least one kind of paradigm. One might say that here 'my doing X' and 'the mental activity of doing X' are just two expressions for the same state of affairs. But we would clearly be disinclined to say this of other kinds of imaging, for example dreams and hallucinations; here, or so it appears, I am not so much doing as being done to. So when do 'my' imagings cease to be mine in the sense that my conscious actions are said to be mine?

Consider an actual case of difference on this point. Miss Iris Murdoch has criticized Professor Hampshire for assigning, in *Freedom of the Individual*, a rationalist's role to imagination, treating it as a source of material upon which the rational faculty of the mind can work.[1] In criticizing this view she says that she, for her part,

'should like to use the word "imaginings" (in a sense more like its normal one) to describe something which we all *do* a great deal of the time. This activity, which may be characterised by a contrast with "strict" or "scientific" thinking, is (like so many totally familiar things) not easy to describe, but one might attempt a description as follows: a type of reflection on people, events, etc., which builds detail, adds colour, conjures up possibilities in ways which go beyond what could be said to be strictly factual. When this activity is thought to be bad it is sometimes called "fantasy" or "wishful thinking."'[2]

Now in saying that she would *describe* the phenomena in question as 'imagining', Murdoch suggests that she finds in them conditions answering to a concept of imagining. In particular she finds in them conditions answering to a notion inherent in the normal use of the term, namely activity. So she is cornering for the agent, the Self, an area of mental phenomena that might otherwise be assigned to 'process', 'happenings', 'occurrence' or

[1] Stuart Hampshire, *Freedom of the Individual* (Chatto & Windus, London and Dunedin, 1965), cf. p. 107. 'If one distinguishes between that which occurs in the mind, without the subject's conscious agency, and one's own directed thinking, aimed at appropriateness and with precautions against misguidedness, one is not thereby bound to underrate the imagination. . . . There may indeed be truths, and insights of many kinds, which typically are arrived at in some state of passivity of mind, and not as the conclusions of the kind of thought that conforms to a norm of logical order and directedness.'

[2] Iris Murdoch, 'The Darkness of Practical Reason', *Encounter*, XXVII (July 1966), No. I, p. 48. On the same page she says: 'Imagining is *doing*, it is a sort of personal exploring.'

'mind'. This 'grouping' (or *vis-à-vis* Hampshire, 're-grouping') is given its point, it has a context of importance. Not, however, the ordinary one—the framework of distinctions that are already important for us—for Murdoch is doing more than just making a straightforward empirical observation to the effect that here is a range of *doing* that can, according to the conventions of ordinary usage, be properly described as 'imagining'; what she is really saying is that 'activity' should be *extended* to cover doings of this not fully reality-oriented or directed, in a sense not fully conscious, kind and that activity of this kind plays an important role in mental activity at large. Important in two connections. First, and generally, in the context of understanding people's actions, Murdoch remarks that 'many of the beliefs which are relevant to action are unlike disciplined scientific or scholarly beliefs'. Thus she claims that 'to be a human being is to know more than one can prove, to conceive of a reality which goes "beyond the facts" in . . . familiar and natural ways'. Moreover, the activity of imagination is 'usually and often inevitably, an activity of evaluation. . . . When moments of decision arrive we see and are attracted by a world *we* have already (partly) made'.[1] Secondly, such activity of imagination and the self is important for her in the particular context of the philosophical discussion of freedom—as it is too for Berkeley and Hobbes. For 'the capacity for rational detachment in our decisions . . . would not . . . be a guarantee of freedom except in cases where efforts of imagination and will were not, as it happens, also required by the situation'.[2] That is, freedom is only contingently guaranteed by the capacity for rational detachment. It is an abstraction to consider freedom apart from efforts of will and imagination.

There are two distinct points here. On the one hand, the range of phenomena to which the word 'activity'—in terms of its primary point—may apply is wider than Hampshire assumes; and on the other, the features to which we should extend the term are necessary for our understanding of *free* action. Clearly the point is not that these activities (she also callst hem 'work-ings') of the imagination are free actions in just the same sense

[1] *Encounter*, XXVII (July 1966), No. 1, p. 49, my emphasis.   [2] Ibid., p. 50.

that rational decisions and choices are presumed to be free; that is, she is not obscuring a distinction between 'actions of ours' and other actions attributable to us as unfree organisms rather than as free agents. Rather, her view is that it is not essential to something being an action of *someone's* that it is a free action in that sense. The view that freedom is to be understood not as freedom *from* these workings, or as the ability to exploit them to the advantage of rational choice, but as arising within their context, is a corollary to this. Or perhaps rather the wider concepts of action and the self are corollaries to the richer concept of freedom. In any case, it is her willingness to extend the notion of the self's activity to something less conscious or deliberate than rational choice that encourages Murdoch to regard her use of the term 'imagining' as closer to its normal use than is Hampshire's. For Hampshire's narrower concepts of action and of the self automatically restrict the range of active imaginings, with the result that the part of the concept that is significant from his own point of view cannot but be described in terms of the self's passivity.

Now this difference about the denotation of 'self' is clearly one about the *nature* of imagination. If the self is conceived narrowly as a rational self detached from the workings of imagination —on a Berkeleyan paradigm—then because those workings are not *doings*, or activities, of the self, they must be processes, occurrences, happenings, effects. But if the self is conceived more broadly—on a quasi- (non-mechanistic) Hobbesian paradigm— as immersed in these workings, then at least some of these workings will count as activities, and so properly denominate the self active—and thus not be mere mental processes.

Of this kind of dispute and difference, then, I suggest we say the following. We have the concept of an active-passive dimension, and along this dimension we can set the range of mental phenomena that, by various stretches of ordinary grammar, can be called activities, exercises, workings, or processes of imagination. But whether imagination in any such sense is something in the face of which the self is passive or is itself a kind of activity *of* the self depends in the first instance on how we

247

determine the concept of 'self'. A narrow concept of self will imply an autonomous power of imagination independent of the self's own activity, while a broad concept of self will attribute this activity and the products of the power of imagination to the same general authorship. The indeterminacy of the concept of 'self' means that the location of the axis of the active-passive dimension is variable. In order, therefore, to be able to say of any given phenomenon whether it is something in the face of which the self is passive or is a kind of activity of the self, one must first specify the scope of the self's activity, that is determine the concept of 'self'. Passivity of the self occurs early in Hampshire's scheme because he identifies the self with the conscious agent that knows what he is doing.[1] For Murdoch, on the other hand, the axis is so placed as to allow the self to be the agent of doings of which he is not fully conscious.

I can think of no one, or simple, answer to the question of what gives 'point' to a statement of any one view of the criteria of 'self', that is for how to fix the grammar of 'I', 'You', 'He', etc. In some cases it may be a predictive empirical claim to the effect that a certain unity will be discovered within what seems at present a range of diverse and unintegrated phenomena, allowing a richer, i.e. wider but still unified, concept of the self. A closer look at the phenomena themselves might reveal this. Thus a detailed investigation might give us reason to see something of an activity of imagining in what James calls those 'coercive hauntings of the mind by echoes of unusual experiences for hours after the latter have taken place'.[2] We could not, of course, say of these hauntings, as of Murdoch's 'workings', that they formed the background of belief relevant for our actions, since typically these are imaginings that *divert* us temporarily from our current courses of action. But it is not clear that they cannot be regarded as activities of ours in some sense. Their possible significance may be lost in James's pale phrase 'unusual experiences', for perhaps it is less the novelty than the importance

[1] *Thought and Action* (Chatto & Windus, London, 1959), p. 75: 'consciousness simply consists in knowing what I am doing.'
[2] James, op. cit., II, p. 44.

of the original experience that causes it to obsess us. Indeed our hauntings may reveal something of the nature and direction of the apparently more active workings of imagination that Murdoch draws attention to; they may show, for instance, the *kind* of thing that disturbs us, and which our more active imaginings, in whatever sense *they* are truly actions of ours, may often serve (and be *used?*) to help us suppress or forget. Perhaps this means that there is no hard and fast distinction between activities and processes. But if so, this only makes it harder to justify any particular claim as to where, or how, to draw the line. It becomes harder still if we accept the word of Freudian, Jungian, and other writers on the psychoses, who say that the line between the personal and the 'transpersonal' is itself a variable of mental health; and furthermore that the narrower the domain of the self, the greater the autonomy—the seemingly independent *personality*—of the psyche, which then indeed becomes the major *source* of unusual experiences.[1]

However, claims about what 'self' designates are not simply claims about what would emerge upon a closer look at the phenomena. This makes it sound as if the natures of things had already been decided, and that all we needed to verify a claim of this kind was better vision, more accurate measurement, perhaps a wider range of cases, as though the concepts we use in making such claims were already finally fixed. But conceptions can be brought to bear upon the phenomena which require some loosening of the conventional correspondence between dis-

---

[1] Cf. Ehrenzweig, *The Hidden Order of Art,* pp. 137 and 191; and Adler, *The Living Symbol,* pp. 4, 50 n, and 299. Philosophers, evidently not psychotics themselves, have believed in an autonomous imagination. Augustine, for example, whom it is interesting to compare with both Berkeley and Hobbes in this respect, took the mind's *activity* to reside in the force of attention that directs the mind's gaze and is needed to immobilize the autonomously creative imagination which would otherwise interrupt, with its free play, the perceptual relation of the mind to the world. (See *De Genesi ad Litteram,* Bk. XII.) The difference with Hobbes is more basic. Where Augustine sees *attention* as an inner force directing the mind's gaze upon the world outside, Hobbes sees this result as being achieved by the sheer light of day: 'The decay of sense in men waking, is not the decay of the motion made in sense; but an obscuring of it, in such manner as the light of the sun obscureth the light of the stars' (*Leviathan,* p. 64).

tinctions conveyed by words and distinctions marked in experience. Such a conception underlies Murdoch's claim that when we arrive at a moment of decision 'we see and are attracted by a world *we* have already (partly) made'; and the claim itself incorporates a proposal to broaden the ordinary conception of 'what we make'. Similarly with Sartre's claim noted earlier, which enlarges the notion of *agency* so far as to make it coextensive with that of the subject of intentional acts.[1] Indeed for Sartre, who further equates agency with mind, there is a sense in which passivity never enters the mental scene at all, or only as the product of an *act* of consciousness.

Now I think it clear that an appeal to ordinary grammar will not help a critic here. Certainly not the grammar of 'I', 'You', 'He', etc.: the correctness of 'I hallucinated' or 'I dreamt' has no bearing on how we conceive the kind of doing, if doing, that is hallucinating or dreaming. The pure personal pronouns are indifferent to the active-passive dimension. A better differentiation is achieved, as King-Farlow demonstrates,[2] by examining the relationships expressed by the possessive pronoun 'mine'. For here we can at least note, by marking different senses in which something (a painting I have painted, or one I merely own, a wound unwittingly inflicted by another, or by myself, or deliberately self-inflicted) can be mine, how the activity-passivity dimension revealed in the differences is mirrored in the 'family [if a family] of human imaginings'.[3] But the differentiation achieved here is only that called for by the phenomena 'as they stand', that is, given only our uncritical understanding of where the axis of the active-passive dimension lies. And it seems in any case quite clear that the grammar of 'mine' gives no specification of the self as a *mental* agent. It marks only those differences between what we consciously do and suffer which have the most immediate bearing upon practical life.

I suggest, therefore, that a critic of one view of where human

[1] Cf. *L'Imagination*, p. 126, and *The Transcendence of the Ego*, pp. 93 ff. above.

[2] John King-Farlow, ' "Mine" and the Family of Human Imaginings', *Inquiry*, Vol. 12 (1969), No. 2.

[3] Ibid., pp. 225–6 and 235.

agency begins and ends must be a subscriber to some other view, and that neither view can be confirmed grammatically. So long as we are unable to forsee, or even conceive, a situation in which the concept of 'self' could be said to have been finally fixed, there will always be room for bias in an over-all description of mind, a bias provided by a conception of the self that overrides the grammar of 'I' and 'mine'. Whatever the conception, it will appear, not necessarily explicitly, as a kind of evaluation, as a way of looking at mind which stresses this rather than that distinction. Such differences in stress will often be dismissed as expressions of metaphysical, or even just professional, bias. But whatever justice there may be in such dismissals, it would be wrong to assume that partial views can be combined to form an impartial synthesis. A synthesis that culled its material only from contemporary sources would require some savage editing. In this section, for instance, we have in effect distinguished between two levels of conceptual difference and indeterminacy. At one level a concept like 'imagining' is fairly constant, even though its application varies with the determination of its component concepts. We have, for example, a fairly stable notion of imagining as an activity, and a not quite so stable one of it as an activity of representing. But at the level of the component concept of 'activity' we find far less stability—just as with 'self'. If we stretch our terms of reference beyond the local influence of rationalist and empiricist epistemology, we find a variability in 'imagining' just as great as that in 'activity' and 'self'.

4. POST-PERCEPTUAL AND PRE-PERCEPTUAL IMAGININGS

Now we return to the question raised earlier, as to whether Ryle's post-perceptual account of imagination could be criticized in the same way as his claim that there are no mental pictures. It is important here to distinguish between a post-perceptual account of, say, visualizing, and a post-perceptual account of imagination in general. A post-perceptual account of visualizing merely makes the point that what we visualize are, as Ryle says, 'common objects', i.e. objects of perception, and not special ones accessible only to the mind's eye. But a post-perceptual account of *imagination* says that all our imaginings are really no more than reproductions or reconstructions of perceptual experience. If we followed Murdoch, however, we could accept a productive as well as a reproductive sense of 'imagining'. For her, 'imagining' denotes 'a type of reflection on people, events, etc. which builds detail, adds colour, conjures up possibilities in ways which go beyond what could be said to be strictly factual', and the world in which we make our decisions is one '*we* have already partly made'. The concept of imagination that we fixed experimentally in the previous chapter, though tied to the notion of image-formation, also covered productive aspects of 'visual supplementation'.

This amount of productive power one could scarcely hesitate to attribute to the mind; and I would consider it quite proper to call that faculty, or process, of visual supplementation which enabled reflections of the kind Murdoch notes to be *visually* presented ('represented' would be out of place here in its 'picturing' sense, since what is visually presented here is not something that could be depicted) one 'power of imagination', and perhaps the *activity* of the reflections themselves an exercise of another power of imagination, which sometimes employs or is supported by the former.

As to the more drastic consequence we tentatively drew from our earlier case-descriptions, namely the suggestion of the 'privacy of perception',[1] this I think does involve a speculation about mind, and cannot be convincingly demonstrated to anyone unwilling to accept some of the assumptions underlying it. The test as to whether it is speculative is, I suggest, whether it is possible to avoid the consequence by giving a different interpretation of the relevant distinctions in experience. I don't wish to defend a theory of mind here, so I shall not test this possibility. It is enough to have pointed to the reasonableness of a 'pre-perceptual' alternative to post-perceptualism, and to note that the conception of mind in which 'imagining' denotes exclusively

[1] See p. 231 above.

post-perceptual phenomena is itself one that contains certain epistemological and ontological restrictions on its also denoting a capacity inherent in perception itself.

A useful last glimpse at this topic can be provided by Sartre's special version of the pre-perceptual function of imagination. In its main outline and detail Sartre's account of imagination in *L'Imaginaire* is post-perceptual. It is the real world we imagine. In imagining something we are conjuring before us some absent thing that we know not to be among the real things perceptibly before us. We 'set it up' as though *it* was what was before us, though aware all along that what is really before us is the background of perceptibly present things against which we set off this spurious presence—the imaginary object. But now Sartre sees this contrast to be inherent even in the case of seeing perceptibly present things as the things they are. For to see some object as, say, a person, one is implicitly contrasting it with things that are not persons—denying, one might say, that it is one of *them*. And he thinks imagination is involved here too. He writes: 'all apprehension of the real as a world implies a hidden reaching beyond towards the imaginary';[1] and: 'Imagination is not an empirical power added to the mind itself in so far as it is free; every concrete and real situation of the mind in the world is pregnant with the imaginary, in that it is always present as a way of going beyond the real.'[2]

Compare this with that other variation of the *creator spiritus* theme we noted at the outset. Berkeley saw the mere conjuring up of an image as evidence of a creative spirit. Sartre, more spectacularly, sees imagination as providing the very world itself as an object of consciousness, and—in a way that is again reminiscent of Berkeley[3]—as therefore also providing consciousness. Imagination is for Sartre 'a necessary and transcendental *condition* of consciousness'.[4]

---

[1] *L'Imaginaire*, p. 238; cf. pp. 235 and 237.　　　　　[2] Ibid., p. 236.

[3] In the *Commentaries*, for example, he writes: 'Mind is a congeries of Perceptions. Take away Perceptions and you take away the Mind put the Perceptions and you put the mind' (op. cit., p. 367, Entry 580, Berkeley's style). Here *percipere* seems to be the *esse* of the mind; the mind does not exist independently of its ideas.　　　　　[4] *L'Imaginaire*, p. 239.

Such speculations are by no means vacuous. If one can think of someone who lacks the visual conversancy needed to see, say, the duck-rabbit either as a duck or a rabbit, but can only see the outline as an outline without a pictorial theme, might one not go on to postulate a mental power to remove which would make the visual experience that person has of the outline no longer an experience of it *as an outline?* I think one might. But why call this power 'imagination'? It might seem more reasonable, as Mary Warnock suggests, to say that it is a linguistic power, and that in so far as imaging is, like perceiving, a way of identifying something, they *both* involve 'going beyond' what is thought about in this particular way.[1] It is just that imaging also involves going-beyond in another way too—i.e. ignoring the perceptible environment in favour of an image. The discriminations that Sartre notes don't *seem* to bear out his claim that identifying something as real is to exercise, even only incipiently, the capacity to see things in their perceptual absence. But it is not to be excluded that a suitably discriminating analysis of the perceptual situation would show something in favour of Sartre's claim.

5. THE POINT OF DUALISM

A speculative context is provided by an idea, a model, or a conception, anything that can provide a minimal framework of distinctions in which existing distinctions can be fitted without undue strain. Such a context gives a point to a certain description of a phenomenon even if the description departs to some extent, perhaps even radically, from the one ordinarily given it. The context itself has descriptive point whenever the nature of something cannot be decided, finally and forever, whether by a grammatical investigation or by logical demonstration. The non-demonstrability of a view, however, is no reason to reject it as unworthy. Nor can it be essential to the truth of one view that no other alternative should be possible. The fact that a philosopher often speaks as if the truth of his own views was justified

[1] Cf. Mary Warnock, 'Imagination in Sartre', *British Journal of Aesthetics*, Vol. 10 (1970), No. 4, p. 326.

by the manifest 'vacuousness' of the alternatives is not necessarily a sign of rationalist hubris. After all, if *he* is to convince then it is the acceptability of his descriptions of the phenomena that must do this for him. It is they that are his conception at work, and from inside his conception it may well be that the alternatives *are* vacuous.

Thus Sartre states that it is a *contradiction* to suppose that the mental is in some way reducible to the physical, or subject to the same kind of explanation. But if we accept his assumption that mind goes together with meaning and physical world together with causation, then it may reasonably be thought to follow that the two domains are irreducible and mutually exclusive. The point to remember is, as we mentioned earlier, that terms like 'consciousness' and 'object' in Sartre's account must be given the meanings he intends them to have—even if in doing so we obscure distinctions that the words are ordinarily used to mark. Take 'conscious' for example. It might be thought that the phenomenon known as 'association of ideas' (for Hobbes a matter of imagination) revealed something of the nature of processes that are not conscious, not at least in the sense that actions are conscious. For the link of or train of association that joins two thoughts together cannot be something we are conscious of in the same way that we are conscious of the thoughts that it links.[1] And yet we are not *surprised* by our own associations, as we can be by what just 'happens' to us, so there is perhaps still some point in insisting that they are conscious, active processes.

Some of the descriptions Sartre's model forces him to give, however, might seem to leave one little option but to reject the account out of hand—given even fairly extraordinary or unconventional interpretations of the words used. For example, one plausible explanation of the futility and helplessness often experienced in dreams might be that the dream state is a reflection of, or is caused by, the sleeping state of the body. But because Sartre's interpretation of the suggested correlation between physical

[1] Cf. Iris Murdoch's review of Sartre's *Emotions*, in *Mind*, Vol. LIX (1950), No. 234, p. 270.

state and dream event must preclude any causal relation between physical states of affairs and the contents of (even dream) consciousness, the only way a state of the dreamer's body can enter into a relation with consciousness is by consciousness taking it as its intentional object; so the dreamer must be apprehending his unresponsive or immobile sleeping body as a sluggish, weighed down, dream body. But since, too, in Sartre's view, consciousness must be aware of whatever is said to 'operate' on it, and in this case it cannot be aware of it as a sleeping body, for that would imply waking consciousness, the dreaming consciousness must somehow apprehend the immobile, sleeping body as an image of a sluggish dream body.[1]

It would certainly be hard to specify criteria that would enable one to decide whether to stretch the notion of consciousness to include in its intentional aspects physical things of which it is not aware (which it does not intend) as the things they are or seem to be, or to allow that the things of which it is not aware can causally determine properties of dream images. And yet it could still be said on Sartre's behalf that it is not all that clear that we should adopt the latter alternative just because a causal explanation allows us to preserve our present concept of consciousness. There are factors that might lead us to prefer the other alternative, or perhaps—despite Sartre's assumption—to cease to regard them as excluding one another.[2] And in any case the simple dualist framework of act and object, however it may depend for its meaning on physical analogies, provides a context, a speculative context—not a precautionary barrier, as in Wittgenstein—in which proposals to modify the descriptive apparatus do acquire some point and importance. On the whole it would

---

[1] Cf. *L'Imaginaire*, p. 211. 'How can we admit that the red light *provokes* the mental images of blood? We would then have to say it remained unconscious, which is absurd—or that it was grasped as red light, which would imply the waking state. In fact, it is the red light which is grasped *as* blood.'

[2] See, e.g. Gay Gaer Luce and Julius Segal, *Sleep* (Heinemann, London, 1967), p. 199: '. . . neurophysiologists have shown us that the dreaming brain, while in some ways as responsive as the waking brain, tends to censor external distractions, as it does when a person is focusing his attention upon a difficult problem.'

seem to be more enlightening to project the model of conscious activity as far as the available distinctions will permit than to withhold it altogether just because it is a model. More light can be thrown on mental phenomena by testing a picture—though not being held captive by it—than by letting the distinctions stand on their own in their original contexts of importance.

Mary Warnock has recently pointed to a feature of Sartre's literary and philosophical work that has some affinity with his conception of the role of imagination. Parts of these writings, she says, 'manifest to a marked degree [the] freedom to treat things in the world as "going beyond themselves" . . . ' and she notes: 'Sartre's way of thinking seems to be very properly characterized as "going beyond the real".'[1] Recall Iris Murdoch's suggestion that 'to be a human being is to know more than one can prove, to conceive of a reality which goes "beyond the facts" in . . . familiar and natural ways',[2] and make it stand as a specification for a philosopher human being too, then Sartre fills the bill better than most, though—true to the profession—his style befits one who knows he has found the facts better than one who thinks he has gone beyond them.

In pointing out the susceptibility of mental concepts to diverse interpretations, Hampshire remarks: 'The prevailing conception of the human mind, or soul, has greatly changed within historical memory.'[3] Even a prevailing conception affords room for dispute, as evidenced in differences of concept-determination, and of stress. As Hampshire also says: 'The distinctions [the philosopher] chooses to stress will be in part a matter of his own interests. . . .'[4] But it isn't just an accident of perspective that determines a philosophical interest in a given range of mental phenomena, it is the philosopher's own conception of mind.

Failure to make a philosophical interest in a certain description clear tends to conceal the precise content and nature of the con-

[1] Mary Warnock, 'Imagination in Sartre', *British Journal of Aesthetics*, Vol. 10 (1970, No. 4, p. 329.
[2] See p. 246, above.
[3] Stuart Hampshire (ed.), *Philosophy of Mind* (Harper & Row, New York and London, 1966). Editor's introduction, p. 3.
[4] Ibid., p. 4.

clusions embodied in the description. This I take to be the crucial gloss on Ryle's claim that 'philosophising essentially incorporates argumentation'. The philosopher of mind's descriptions do indeed have the form of arguments, but the function of these arguments is to convince us of a conclusion that can never be reached by way of the premisses alone. He tends to work from within his system, and there his demonstrations are premissed on his conclusion. Disentangling the conclusion from its premisses reveals the nature of the argumentation, and also gives the phenomena a chance to breathe more freely and speak for themselves. I have tried to do this for at least some philosophers' arguments about imagination, a topic that has received more than its fair share of vested philosophical interest, or for that matter of vested philosophical disregard and neglect.

REFERENCES

Adler, Gerhard, *The Living Symbol*, Routledge & Kegan Paul, London, 1961.
Adler, Gerhard, *Studies in Analytical Psychology*, Routledge & Kegan Paul, London, 1948.
Albritton, Rogers, 'On Wittgenstein's Use of the Term "Criterion" ', *Journal of Philosophy*, LVI (1959), No. 22.
Anscombe, G. E. M., 'The Intentionality of Sensation: a Grammatical Feature', in R. J. Butler (ed.), *Analytical Philosophy*, Second Series, Basil Blackwell, Oxford, 1968.
Anscombe, G. E. M., 'Pretending', *Proceedings of the Aristotelian Society*, Supp. Vol. XXXII (1958), reprinted in S. Hampshire, *Philosophy of Mind*.
Armstrong, David M. (ed.), *Berkeley's Philosophical Writings*, Collier-Macmillan, London, 1965.
Augustine, St, *De Genesi ad Litteram*, Bk. XII.
Austin, J. L., 'Pretending', *Proceedings of the Aristotelian Society*, Supp. Vol. XXXII (1958).
Ayer, A. J., *The Problem of Knowledge*, Penguin Books, Harmondsworth, 1956.
Brentano, Franz, *Psychologie vom empirischen Standpunkt*, Vol. I, Bk. 2, Ch. 1, Engl. trans. by D. B. Terrell in Roderick M. Chisholm (ed.), *Realism and the Background of Phenomenology*, Free Press, Glencoe, Ill., 1960.
Cowley, Fraser, *A Critique of British Empiricism*, Macmillan, London, 1968.
Dennett, D. C., *Content and Consciousness*, International Library of Philosophy and Scientific Method, Routledge & Kegan Paul, London, 1969.
Ehrenzweig, Anton, *The Hidden Order of Art*, Weidenfeld & Nicolson, London, 1967.
Ehrenzweig, Anton, *The Psycho-analysis of Artistic Vision and Hearing*, 2nd edn, Geo. Braziller, New York, 1965.
Flew, A. G. N., 'Facts and "Imagination" ', *Mind*, LXV (1956), No. 259.
Flew, Annis, 'Images, Supposing and Imagining', *Philosophy*, XXVIII (1953), No. 106.
Føllesdal, Dagfinn, 'Husserl's Notion of Noema', *Journal of Philosophy*, LXVI (1969), No. 20.
Furlong, E. J., *Imagination*, Muirhead Library of Philosophy, George Allen & Unwin, London, 1961.
Galton, Francis, *Inquiries into Human Faculty and its Development*, London, 1883.
Geach, Peter, *Mental Acts*, Studies in Philosophical Psychology, Routledge & Kegan Paul, London, 1958.
Hampshire, Stuart, *Freedom of the Individual*, Chatto & Windus, London, 1965.
Hampshire, Stuart, *Thought and Action*, Chatto & Windus, London, 1959.
Hampshire, Stuart (ed.), *Philosophy of Mind*, Sources in Contemporary Philosophy, Harper & Row, New York, 1966.
Hampshire, Stuart, Critical Notice: *The Concept of Mind* by Gilbert Ryle, *Mind*, LIX (1950), No. 234, reprinted in Wood, O. P. and Pitcher, G. (eds), *Ryle*.

259

Hannay, Alastair, 'To See a Mental Image', *Mind* forthcoming.
Hannay, Alastair, 'Wollheim and Seeing Black on White as a Picture', *British Journal of Aesthetics*, Vol. 10 (1970), No. 2.
Hobbes, Thomas, *Leviathan*, ed. and abridged with introd. by John Plamenatz, Fontana Library, Collins, London, 1962.
Hobbes, Thomas, *The English Works of Thomas Hobbes*, Molesworth Edn, London, 1839–45, reprinted Oxford, 1961.
Houlgate, Laurence D., 'The Paradigm-Case Argument and Possible Doubt', *Inquiry*, Vol. 5 (1962), No. 4.
Hume, David, *A Treatise of Human Nature*, Bk. I, ed. and introd. by D. G. C. MacNabb, Meridian Edn, World Publishing Co., New York, 1962.
Husserl, Edmund, *Ideen zu einer reinen Phänomenologie und phänomenologische Philosophie*, Martinus Nijhoff, The Hague, 1950. Engl. trans. by W. R. Boyce Gibson, *Ideas—General Introduction to Pure Phenomenology*, Muirhead Library of Philosophy, George Allen & Unwin, London, 1931.
Ishiguro, Hidé, 'Imagination', in Bernard Williams and Alan Montefiore (eds), *British Analytical Philosophy*, International Library of Philosophy and Scientific Method, Routledge & Kegan Paul, London, 1966.
Ishiguro, Hidé, 'Imagination', *Proceedings of the Aristotelian Society*, Supp. Vol. XLI (1967).
Jaensch, E. R., *Eidetic Imagery*, International Library of Psychology, Philosophy, and Scientific Method, Routledge & Kegan Paul, London, 1930.
James, William, *The Principles of Psychology*, II, Dover Publications, New York, 1950.
King-Farlow, John, ' "Mine" and the Family of Human Imaginings', *Inquiry*, Vol. 12 (1969), No. 2.
Lawrie, Reynold, 'The Existence of Mental Images', *Philosophical Quarterly*, Vol. 20 (1970), No. 80.
Luce, Gay Gaer, and Segal, Julius, *Sleep*, Heinemann, London, 1967.
Malcolm, Norman, 'Wittgenstein's *Philosophical Investigations*', *Philosophical Review*, LXIII (1954), No. 368.
McKellar, Peter, *Imagination and Thinking: a Psychological Analysis*, Cohen & West, London, 1957.
Mohanty, J. N., *Edmund Husserl's Theory of Meaning*, in *Phaenomenologica*, Vol. 14, Martinus Nijhoff, The Hague, 1964.
Murdoch, Iris, 'The Darkness of Practical Reason', *Encounter*, XXVII (July 1966), No. 1.
Murdoch, Iris, Review of Sartre's *Emotions: Outline of a Theory*, *Mind*, LIX (1950), No. 234.
Myers, C. M., 'The Determinate and Determinable Modes of Appearing', *Mind*, LXVII (1958), No. 265.
Odegard, Douglas, 'Images', *Mind*, LXXX (1971), No. 318.
Price, H. H., 'Survival and the Idea of "Another World" ', in Smythies, J. R. (ed.), *Brain and Mind*.
Rankin, K. W., 'The Role of Imagination, Rule-Operations, and Atmosphere in Wittgenstein's Language-Games', *Inquiry*, Vol. 10 (1967), No. 3.
Richardson, Alan, *Mental Imagery*, Routledge & Kegan Paul, London, 1969.
Ryle, Gilbert, 'Autobiographical', in Wood, O. P. and Pitcher, G. (eds.), *Ryle*.

REFERENCES

Ryle, Gilbert, *The Concept of Mind*, Hutchinson's University Library, London, 1955.

Ryle, Gilbert, 'Ludwig Wittgenstein', *Analysis*, XII (1951), reprinted in Copi, Irving, M. and Beard, Robert W. (eds), *Essays on Wittgenstein's Tractatus*, Routledge & Kegan Paul, London, and the Macmillan Co., New York, 1966.

Sartre, Jean-Paul, *L'Être et le néant: essai d'ontologie phénoménologique*, Gallimard, Paris, 1943.

Sartre, Jean-Paul, *L'Imagination*, Presses Universitaires de France, 4th edn, Paris, 1956.

Sartre, Jean-Paul, *The Transcendence of the Ego: An Existentialist Theory of Consciousness*, trans., annot., and introd. by Forrest Williams and Robert Kirkpatrick, Noonday Press, New York, 1957, from 'La Transcendance de l'Ego: Esquisse d'une description phénoménologique', *Recherches Philosophiques*, IV (1936–7).

Sartre, Jean-Paul, *L'Imaginaire: Psychologie phénoménologique de l'imagination*, Gallimard, 29th edn, Paris, 1948.

Scruton, Roger, 'Intensional and Intentional Objects', *Proceedings of the Aristotelian Society*, 1970–1.

Shorter, J. M., 'Imagination', *Mind*, LXI (1952), No. 244.

Smythies, J. R. (ed.), *Brain and Mind*, International Library of Philosophy and Scientific Method, Routledge & Kegan Paul, London, 1965.

Squires, J. E. R., 'Visualising', *Mind*, LXXVII (1968), No. 305.

Urmson, J. O., 'Memory and Imagination', *Mind*, LXXVI (1967), No. 301.

Warnock, Mary, 'Imagination in Sartre', *British Journal of Aesthetics*, Vol. 10 (1970), No. 4.

Weinberg, Julius R., *Abstraction, Relation and Induction: Three Essays in the Honor of Thought*, University of Wisconsin Press, Madison and Milwaukee, 1965.

White, Alan R., 'Seeing What is Not There', *Proceedings of the Aristotelian Society*, 1969–70.

Wittgenstein, Ludwig, *Philosophical Investigations (Philosophische Untersuchungen)*, trans. by G. E. M. Anscombe, Basil Blackwell, Oxford, 1958.

Wittgenstein, Ludwig, *The Blue and Brown Books*, Basil Blackwell, Oxford, 1958.

Wittgenstein, Ludwig, *Zettel*, ed. by G. E. M. Anscombe and G. H. von Wright, trans. by G. E. M. Anscombe, Basil Blackwell, Oxford, 1967.

Wolgast, Elizabeth, 'Wittgenstein and Criteria', *Inquiry*, Vol. 7 (1964), No. 4.

Wollheim, Richard, *On Drawing an Object*, Inaugural Lecture, University College, London, 1964, H. K. Lewis, London, 1965.

Wood, Oscar P. and Pitcher, George (eds), *Ryle*, Modern Studies in Philosophy, Macmillan, London, 1970.

Woolhouse, Roger, 'Berkeley, the Sun that I See by Day, and That Which I Imagine by Night', *Philosophy*, XLII (1968), No. 164.

INDEX